Authority and Asceticism from Augustine to Gregory the Great

CONRAD LEYSER

CLARENDON PRESS · OXFORD

OXFORD
UNIVERSITY PRESS

Great Clarendon Street, Oxford, OX2 6DP
Oxford University Press is a department of the University of Oxford.
It furthers the University's objective of excellence in research, scholarship,
and education by publishing worldwide in

Oxford New York

Athens Auckland Bangkok Bogotá Buenos Aires Calcutta
Cape Town Chennai Dar es Salaam Delhi Florence Hong Kong Istanbul
Karachi Kuala Lumpur Madrid Melbourne Mexico City Mumbai
Nairobi Paris São Paulo Singapore Taipei Tokyo Toronto Warsaw

and associated companies in Berlin Ibadan

Oxford is a registered trade mark of Oxford University Press
in the UK and certain other countries

Published in the United States
by Oxford University Press Inc., New York

British Library Cataloguing in Publication Data

Data available

Library of Congress Cataloging in Publication Data

Leyser, Conrad.
Authority and asceticism from Augustine to Gregory the Great / Conrad Leyser.
p. cm. — (Oxford historical monographs)
Includes bibliographical references and index.
1. Asceticism—History—Early church, ca. 30–600. 2. Authority—Religious
aspects—Christianity—History of doctrines—Early church, ca. 30–600. 3. Monasticism
and religious orders—History—Early church, ca. 30–600. I. Title. II. Series.
BV5023 .L49 2000   274'.02—dc21   00-044074

ISBN 0–19–820868–5

1 3 5 7 9 10 8 6 4 2

Typeset by Regent Typesetting, London
Printed in Great Britain
on acid-free paper by
Biddles Ltd, Guildford and King's Lynn

For Kate

PREFACE

My grandmother, who grew up a century ago in an austere reformed Jewish household in Cologne, told the following story from her childhood. One day, her mother entrusted her with the task of watching the soup. And watch she did, with fierce and increasingly anxious attention, until it had all boiled away. On returning to the kitchen, her mother naturally concluded that her trust had been betrayed. The story carries a universal message—about the powerlessness of good intentions and the vulnerability to error of those in authority—that the figures discussed in this book would have had no trouble in recognizing. But the story also speaks to me in particular, with all the terrifying force of an archetype. I started work on the doctoral thesis that forms the basis for this book in 1985: for fifteen years now I have been watching the soup, as it were, during which time almost everything else in my life has changed. Readers may well decide I have misinterpreted my task, and that the pot has long since cracked and charred.

The field is now, also, much changed. When I began research, the writings of ascetics in the late Roman West were comparatively understudied, at least in the English-speaking world. Although this is, happily, no longer the case, my focus has obstinately remained the language of moral authority used by western ascetics in the uncertain political context associated with the barbarian invasions. A traditional approach to these 'later Latin Fathers' might seek to define them through their perceived contribution to the development of the medieval monastery or episcopacy. By contrast, I have sought to interpret their work in terms of the prolongation and adaptation of a very ancient discussion about how a man should hold power, a discussion focused self-consciously on rhetorical performance. An analysis of the ethical relation between speaker and listener, rather than a concern with the institutional authority of bishops or abbots, seems to me to characterize ascetic thought and practice in this period.

My debts are legion. I thank for generous support of my research the British Academy and the Arts and Humanities Research Board, the Arnold, Bryce and Read Funds at Oxford University, the British School at Rome, Dumbarton Oaks, the Andrew Mellon Foundation at

Columbia University, the University of Manchester Research and Graduate Support Fund, and for hospitality the Forschungstelle für Geschichte des Mittelalters of the Austrian Academy of Sciences, under the directorship of Walter Pohl. I am no less beholden to libraries and librarians in Oxford, Rome, Washington DC, Sheffield, New York, Wellesley, Manchester, and Vienna. Without the shepherding of the series editor, the late Colin Matthew, and of Anne Gelling at Oxford University Press, together with the acumen of my copy-editor, and the last-minute redemptive work on the proofs by Gerard Hill, the book would have been still tardier.

At different times, and in different ways, I have drawn on the wisdom and encouragement of the following: Francesco Scorza Barcellona, Peter Brown, Caroline Bynum, Elizabeth Clark, Maximilian Diesenberger, Joel Kaye, William Klingshirn, Simon Loseby, John Matthews, Paul Meyvaert, Bob Moore, William North, Frederick Paxton, Salvatore Pricoco, Helmut Reimitz, Philip Rousseau, Carole Straw, Anita Tien, James Vernon, Mark Vessey, Wes Williams, and Klaus and Michaela Zelzer. To reading groups in New England and Manchester, and to those here who read the draft in its final stages, I can only offer my own bewilderment at my failure to follow counsels I knew to be good and true.

It remains for me to thank those whose patience has endured the longest: Robert Markus, who guided me towards and across the subject, Henry Mayr-Harting, my supervisor and sub-editor, whose *doctrina* and *discretio* have sustained me throughout, and my family in its various dimensions. Henrietta and Karl, my parents, have wished for me my own voice: 'Mach's gut', my father would say to me as I was leaving, and I only hope I have. My siblings Ottoline, Crispin, and Matilda, have remained gracious in the face of so much medieval history. My dear daughters, Hester and Hildelith, have been delightfully less indulgent. This book is dedicated to their mother, my beloved, who has given of her mind and heart in ways I can but strive to return.

Conrad Leyser

Manchester
20 June 2000

CONTENTS

ABBREVIATIONS

Periodical titles are abbreviated according to the conventions given in *L'Année Philologique*

SERIES TITLES AND WORKS OF REFERENCE

ACW	Ancient Christian Writers (Westminster, Md.)
CCSL	Corpus Christianorum, Series Latina (Turnhout)
CSEL	Corpus Scriptorum Ecclesiasticorum Latinorum (Vienna)
DACL	*Dictionnaire d'archéologie chrétienne et de liturgie* (Paris)
DSp	*Dictionnaire de spiritualité* (Paris)
DTC	*Dictionnaire de théologie catholique* (Paris)
FC	The Fathers of the Church (Washington)
MGH	Monumenta Germaniae Historica (Berlin)
AA	Auctores Antiquissimi
Epp	Epistulae
SRM	Scriptores rerum merovingicarum
NPNF	Nicene and Post-Nicene Fathers
PG	Patrologia Graeca
PL	Patrologia Latina
PLS	Patrologia Latina, Supplementum
SC	Sources Chrétiennes (Paris)
TTH	Translated Texts for Historians (Liverpool)
TU	Texte und Untersuchungen

PRIMARY TEXTS

Full details are given in the Bibliography

Aug.Serm.	Augustine, *Sermones*
Civ.Dei	*Civitas Dei*
Conf.	*Confessions*
De corr. et grat.	*De correptione et gratia*
Enarr. Ps.	*Enarrationes in Psalmos*
Praec.	*Praeceptum*
Règ.Aug.	*La Règle de s. Augustin*, ed. L. Verheijen, 2 vols. (Paris, 1967)

VAug.	Possidius, *Vita Augustini*, ed. M. Pellegrino (Alba, 1955)
Conl.	Cassian, *Conlationes*
Inst.	*Institutiones*
Dial.	Gregory the Great, *Dialogi*
HEv.	*Homiliae in Evangelia*
HEz.	*Homiliae in Hiezechihelem Prophetam*
Lib.Resp.	*Libellus Responsionum*, in Bede, *Historia ecclesiastica gentis anglorum*, ed. C. Plummer (Oxford, 1896)
Mor.	*Moralia in Iob*
Ep.	*Registrum Epistularum*
RP	*Liber Regulae Pastoralis*
RB	*Regula Benedicti*
REug	*Regula Eugippi*
RM	*Regula Magistri*
RV	Caesarius of Arles, *Regula virginum*
Caes. Serm.	*Sermones*
VCaes.	*Vita Caesarii*
De vita cont.	Pomerius, *De vita contemplativa*

PART I

Fifth-Century Authorities

I

Augustine and the Problem of Authority

To a modern audience, Augustine of Hippo appears almost invariably as a forbidding and patriarchal figure.[1] This was an authority that some of Augustine's contemporaries were eager to confer on him—but there were others who had no pressing reason to include the bishop of a provincial North African town in their calculations of rank and power in the Roman Mediterranean. In 421, for example, Augustine, then in his sixties, wrote to Atticus, the bishop of Constantinople.[2] The letter represents a definitive formulation of Augustine's views on human sexuality, a topic on which he had meditated for over two decades— and with which, in the modern era, his name is indelibly associated.[3] The bishop of Hippo's contemporary reputation, however, no less than his posthumous renown, seems to have been beyond the ken of Atticus. We learn from Augustine that he had been waiting in vain to hear from the patriarch. At last, losing patience, he had written himself, with a face-saving explanation for Atticus's silence: there was a rumour abroad in Constantinople that he—Augustine—was dead.[4] Augustine was under few illusions then about the indifference towards him of his more distinguished colleagues. He knew the slightness of his own authority, in ways which invite his twenty-first-century readers to reconsider their assumptions about him.

To the late Roman and early medieval ascetics who are the subject of this book, the authority of Augustine was a source of fascination and no small bewilderment.[5] The vast corpus of his works commanded

[1] See e.g. J. Gaarder, *Vita Brevis: A Letter to St Augustine*, tr. A. Born (London, 1997), which uses the imagined voice of Augustine's common-law wife to chide him for his ascetic coldness in repudiating her after fifteen years of living together (although, in fact, it was the heat of his worldly ambition that led him to do so). See *Conf.* VI. 12. 25, ed. J. J. O'Donnell, 3 vols. (Oxford, 1992) i. 71, and for comment and further bibliography, ii. 383–5; and G. Wills, *Saint Augustine* (London, 1999), esp. 17–18, 41–3.

[2] *Ep.* 6*, CSEL 88, 32–8. The date of the letter is disputed: see R. Eno, *Saint Augustine, Letters VI (1*–29*)*, FC 81 (1989), 52–3 and the references there given.

[3] For a discussion of the letter in these terms, see P. R. L. Brown, 'Sexuality and Society in the Fifth Century A. D.: Augustine of Hippo and Julian of Eclanum', in E. Gabba (ed.), *Tria corda: Scritti in onore di Arnoldo Momigliano* (Como, 1983), 49–70.

[4] *Ep* 6*. 1. 1, CSEL 88, 32.

[5] A very traditional topic that has begun to receive renewed attention, partly in response to the discovery by Johannes Divjak of nearly 30 previously unknown letters of Augustine

their respect, but left those who sought augustinian guidance for their own exercise of power and responsibility in a state of confusion. Augustine bequeathed a compelling vision of human destiny: what society was like in the here-and-now—broken, fragile—and how it would be transformed in the heavenly city at the end of time. This view of human community, present and future, did not depend on the presumed continuation of the Roman Empire, but on a perception of the authority of God, at once overwhelming and inscrutable. In the Latin West across the fifth and sixth centuries, as the Empire disintegrated, Augustine's crystalline imagination of the eschatological order was increasingly relevant and attractive to Christian ascetics in these parts. What held their attention above all, perhaps, was Augustine's proposal of the monastery as the one place in the here-and-now where it was possible to glimpse the future glory of the heavenly city. The monastic community as emblem of the society of the blessed: this was a touchstone for later monastic patrons such as Caesarius of Arles or Benedict of Nursia who sought to articulate—often in the face of hostile opposition—why their use of scarce resources to found new, seemingly élite, communities was, after all, a ministry to the whole body of the faithful.

The augustinian conception of the monastery as a window onto the City of God brought problems even as it offered inspiration. In setting all his store by divine majesty, Augustine self-consciously minimized the role human authority could play. Without denying that political structures were necessary, Augustine refused to participate in the confident ideology of self-legitimation to which those in power in the later Roman Empire were accustomed. Flying in the face of the assumptions of his peer group, Augustine insisted that there was no certifiable claim to moral superiority with which to underwrite the unequal distribution of power in human society. A tension arose between Augustine's exalted ideal of monastic and human community and his reduced terms for the exercise of authority in and over the

(below n. 61). See the classic studies of H.-X. Arquillière, *L'Augustinisme politique: Essai sur la formation des théories politiques du moyen âge* (Paris, 1934); and H.-I. Marrou, *Saint Augustin et l'Augustinianisme* (Paris, 1959); and now J. J. O'Donnell, 'The Authority of Augustine', *Augustinian Studies* 22 (1991), 7–35; C. Quillen, 'Consentius as a Reader of Augustine's *Confessions*', *REAug* 37 (1991), 87–109; R. W. Mathisen, 'For Specialists Only: The Reception of Augustine and his Teachings in Fifth-Century Gaul' in J. T. Lienhard, E. C. Miller, R. J. Teske (eds.), *Collectanea Augustiniana, Augustine: Presbyter factus sum* (New York, 1993), 29–41; J. M. Vessey, '*Opus imperfectum*: Augustine and his Readers, 426–435 AD', *Vigiliae Christianae* 52 (1998), 264–85.

same communities—and this was not a tension he managed to resolve. Western ascetics in positions of public power found themselves drawing much of their political lexicon from Augustine, while confronting the fact that Augustine himself did not set any great store by what figures in authority, however well-intentioned, might achieve. The bishop of Hippo was, in the eyes of his most articulate and most prominent early Latin readers, insufficiently authoritarian: much of their writing is driven by an attempt, subtle and persuasive, to render his legacy otherwise.

In the nineteen-sixties, scholars in the English-speaking world came to a new view of the complexity of Augustine. Discussion of this changed paradigm continues to preoccupy Anglo-American scholarship (while the attention of continental scholars has remained focused, with extraordinary results, on tracing the manuscript transmission of Augustine's works).[6] Fundamental to this view is the conviction that Augustine was a man and a thinker who changed, and who was himself avid to observe his own transformations.[7] The pivotal decade in Augustine's development is seen to be the 390s, which witnessed his assumption of episcopal office in Hippo (395/6), and the writing of the *Confessions* (397–401).[8] Of course, Augustine's own story in the *Confessions* locates the decisive moment in his life some ten years

[6] Guided, above all, by the following: P. R. L. Brown, *Augustine of Hippo: A Biography* (London, 1967); a second edition, with a new epilogue, is forthcoming; R. A. Markus, *Saeculum: History and Society in the Theology of St Augustine* (Cambridge, 1970, 2nd edn., 1988). For historiographical context and critique, see A.-M. la Bonnardière, 'La "Cité terrestre" d'après H.-I. Marrou', in id. (ed.), *Saint Augustin et la Bible* (Paris, 1986), 387–98; J. M. Vessey, 'The Demise of the Christian Writer and the Remaking of "Late Antiquity": From H.-I. Marrou's St Augustine (1938) to Peter Brown's Holy Man (1983)', *JECS* 6 (1998), 377–411; J. J. O'Donnell, 'The Next Life of Augustine', in W. Klingshirn, M. Vessey (eds.), *The Limits of Ancient Christianity: Essays in Late Antique Thought and Culture* (Ann Arbor, 1999), 215–31; see also Vessey's observations, 209–11. For a survey of the discoveries by continental scholars, see Brown, *Augustine*, Epilogue. See below, n. 61, on the new letters of Augustine traced by Johanne Divjak; and on the new sermons discovered by Francois Dolbeau, see G. Madec (ed.), *Augustin prédicateur (395–411), Actes du colloque international de Chantilly (5–7 septembre 1996)* (Paris, 1998).

[7] See e.g. Brown, *Augustine*, 110, 114, 171; Markus, *Saeculum*, 40–1. Both acknowledge an important debt to F. E. Cranz, 'The Development of Augustine's Ideas of Society before the Donatist Controversy', *Harvard Theological Review* 47 (1954), 225–361 (cited Brown, *Augustine* 146 n. 1; Markus, *Saeculum*, 80 n. 4). On images of Augustine through the ages, see e.g. P. Courcelle, *Les Confessions d'Augustin dans la tradition littéraire: antécédents et postériorité* (Paris, 1963).

[8] Brown, *Augustine*, 146 n. 1, notes how little attention had been paid, at that time, to the 390s: all attention had been focused on the 380s and the conversion. At ibid. 146–57, he proposes a shift of emphasis, in tandem with Markus, *Saeculum*, 82–4. See also Markus, *End of Ancient Christianity*, 46–51.

previously—his final acceptance, after years of false trails and indecision, of the catholic Christianity of his mother Monica. The scene of conversion is set, famously, in a garden in Milan, but there are good grounds for supposing that Augustine is here recasting his Italian past in the light of his present situation in North Africa.[9] As his own writings from the late 380s betray, at that time Augustine regarded what had happened in Milan as a philosophical awakening, not a conversion to his mother's faith.[10] It seems that, in the summer of 386, Augustine announced his retirement, on grounds of ill-health, from his position as imperial rhetor, and retreated to a country estate outside Milan with family and friends to discuss philosophy.[11] This Augustine was a relatively conventional élite Christian of the late fourth century. He was confident of his abilities to make moral progress and to inspire it in others, and trusting in the dispensation of divine providence for the Christian Roman Empire. Most of his friends, at this period, and indeed for years to come, were more 'augustinian' than he was.[12]

In the early 390s, Augustine returned to North Africa to his home town of Thagaste, and it is at this point, it is widely, if not universally accepted, that the real break in his life occurs.[13] In the course of the next decade, as Augustine read and reread Paul's Letter to the Romans, and as he prepared himself (seemingly from 395) for undertaking episcopal office in Hippo, his earlier certainties evaporated. Paul convinced him that his confidence in the powers of human reason to fathom the rationality of God's grace was unfounded.[14] Augustine realized that he did not, after all, know why his life had taken the course that it had: it is this process of moral 'disillusion' that underpins the narrative of the *Confessions*. These are not the testimony of a

---

[9] *Conf.* VIII. 12. 28–9, O'Donnell, i. 101–2, and the commentary at ii. 55–71. On Augustine's revision of his narrative in the 390s, see also P. Frederiksen, 'Paul and Augustine: Conversion Narratives, Orthodox Traditions, and the Retrospective Self', *JTS* NS 37 (1986), 3–34.

[10] See *Contra Academicos* II. 2. 5–6, CCSL 29, 21. Compare *Conf.* VIII. 11. 27, O'Donnell, i. 100.

[11] See *De beata vita* I. 4, CCSL 29, 67, on the chest malady that forced Augustine to retire. For a characterization of Augustine at Cassiciacum, see Brown, *Augustine*, 110–27; also J. M. Matthews, *Western Aristocracies and Imperial Court, AD 364–425* (Oxford, 1975), 220–21.

[12] Brown, *Augustine*, 152.

[13] For an important dissenting voice, see G. Madec, 'Tempora Christiana: Expression du triomphalisme chrétien ou récrimination païenne?', in id., *Petites Études Augustiniennes* (Paris, 1994), 233–59.

[14] See P. Frederiksen, *Augustine on Romans*, Texts and Translations 23, Early Christian Literature Series 6 (Chico, Calif., 1982).

'born-again' fundamentalist. They are, in Peter Brown's phrase, a work of a professional 'convalescent', a man who is axiomatically uncertain of his powers of self-control or his ability to resist temptation: any strength that he has comes from divine grace, and the giving and witholding of that grace is inscrutable.[15]

The enduring achievement of Robert Markus's *Saeculum* is to have demonstrated how and why Augustine converted this personal history into a view of human history as a whole. In the *City of God* Augustine argued that, after the Incarnation, unambiguous divine revelation was to cease: at the Second Coming, the shape and number of the citizens of heaven would be revealed, but in the mean time, no one could know with any certainty of their eschatological standing. No person, group, or institution, therefore, could assert a reliable insight into the workings of God's grace in human affairs. As Markus has emphasized, Augustine's 'radical agnosticism' divided him from most of his peers.[16] Most in Christian intellectual circles were convinced that the Roman Empire was the privileged vessel of God's grace on earth: since the conversion of Constantine, ideologues such as Eusebius had been working to establish a triumphalist interpretation of imperial history, turning on the happy coincidence of the birth of Christ under the Emperor Augustus. Under the house of Theodosius in the early fifth century, the poet Prudentius assumed the Eusebian mantle as spokesman for an increasingly aggressive imperial Christianity. It was this triumphalism that Augustine undercut.[17] All those in authority, including bishops and abbots, should eschew illusory certainties about the moral effect of their conduct of power: no one, however powerful, could know whether their actions were in accord with the inscrutable agency of God's grace.

The underlying pastoral purpose of Augustine's point of view was not to induce passivity, but to combat the divisive effects of spiritual élitism. As a bishop, Augustine became increasingly sensitive to the ways in which claims to moral superiority could damage a Christian community. This was the theme underlying his two great polemic struggles against Donatist and Pelagian heresy, and his uncompromising pronouncements on salvation towards the end of his life in the 'semi-Pelagian controversy'. These last teachings on predestination,

---

[15] Brown, *Augustine*, 177 (cf. 167).

[16] Markus, *Saeculum*, 159, 168.

[17] For an attempt to argue, *pace* Markus, for a Eusebian reading of Augustine, see P. T. Kaufmann, *Redeeming Politics* (Princeton, 1990).

the psychological implications of which continue to baffle and dismay his modern readers, had a specific pastoral goal in the early fifth century: to establish the absolute equality of all the faithful in the sight of God, and the impossibility of staking any certain claim to greater virtue than one's neighbour.

Augustine from his mid-forties, as we now know him, was a man who believed in community, but whose ideas isolated him from many of his peers. Suspicious of the moral claims of authority, he found himself constantly in a position where he could not avoid assuming it—indeed actively chose to do so.[18] These were tensions inherent in Augustine's rethinking of human history and divine grace across the *Confessions* and the *City of God*: they were played out specifically in the arena of his monastic life at Hippo, right into the final decade of his life.

THE MONASTIC JERUSALEM

In the *Confessions*, Augustine's conversion is precipitated by the story of the monk Antony, the young Egyptian landlord who had given up all his possessions and retreated to the wilderness to lead an ascetic life—all in unhesitating response to Christ's advice to the rich man in the Gospel (Matt. 19: 21).[19] Augustine was not alone in being mesmerized by Antony. His contemporaries in Christian intellectual circles—men like Jerome, or Antony's biographer, Athanasius of Alexandria—hailed the blossoming of monastic asceticism in the deserts of Egypt and Syria as a much needed renewal of authentic Christianity, at a moment when violent sponsorship of the faith by the imperial regime was bringing in thousands of new 'converts'. The

[18] See Possidius, *Vita sancti Augustini* 19, ed. M. Pellegrino (Alba, 1955), 110–14, for the unremitting grind of Augustine's duties as a judge in his episcopal court. On this, see W. Selb, 'Episcopalis audientia von der Zeit Konstantins bis zur Novelle XXXV Valentinians III', *Zeitschrift der Savigny-Stiftung für Rechtsgeschichte*, Romanistische Abteilung, 84 (1967), 162–217; W. Waldstein, 'Zur Stellung der *episcopalis audientia* im spätrömischen Prozess', in D. Medicus, H. H. Seiler (eds.), *Festschrift für Max Kaser zum 70. Geburtstag* (Munich, 1976), 533–56; and K. K. Raikas, '*Episcopalis audientia*: Problematik zwischen Staat und Kirche bei Augustin', *Augustinianum* 37 (1997), 459–81. J. Lamoureaux, 'Episcopal Courts in Late Antiquity', *JECS* 3: 2 (1995), 143–67, is conceived independently of the main scholarly tradition on this subject.
[19] *Conf.* VIII. 7. 19 ff, O'Donnell i. 95 ff. Augustine's friend Ponticianus had himself encountered the *Vita Antonii* at Trier: *Conf.* VIII. 6. 14, O'Donnell i. 94. For further commentary, see here B. Stock, *Augustine the Reader: Meditation, Self-Knowledge, and the Ethics of Interpretation* (Cambridge, Mass., 1996), 74–111.

particular appeal of Antony and his peers in the desert lay not only in the otherworldly rigour of their mode of life—asceticism was not new to Christianity in the fourth century. It was the withdrawal itself into the desert that distinguished these ascetics from their forebears, and that seemed to offer a way of maintaining the moral drama of the Christian life in the post-persecution era. Their decision to leave the places of human habitation earned Antony and his followers the name 'monks', usually taken to mean 'solitary ones'.[20] In learned circles around the Mediterranean, there was much celebration of their moral achievement in so demonstrably forsaking 'the world'.[21]

Even as he invoked the figure of Antony, however, Augustine seems to have become increasingly aware that, whatever the intentions of the desert fathers and their advocates, the monastic movement threatened to introduce a double standard: a pure Christianity for the few, and a cheapened version for the remainder. His reservations were widely shared: many had observed how, in the hands of a polemicist like Jerome, the claims to moral superiority of the 'monks' could be positively dangerous.[22] Reacting against the zealous tone of many of his peers' enthusiasm for ascetic style, Augustine sought to remove the opportunities for spiritual élitism presented by the monastic life.[23] The monastery for Augustine was a site in which to practise and to perfect

---

[20] See F.-E. Morard, 'Monachos, moine: histoire du terme grec jusqu'au 4e siècle', *Freiburger Zeitschrift für Philosophie und Theologie* 20 (1973), 329–425; E. A. Judge, 'The Earliest Use of the Word "monachos" for Monk (P. Coll. Youtie 77)', *Jahrbuch für Antike und Christentum* 20 (1977), 72–89. *Monachus* for 'monk' in Latin first appears in the anonymous translation of Athanasius' *Life of Antony* (which was followed by the better-known translation of Evagrius of Antioch), *Vita Antonii* 14, PL 73, 134D. For a survey of recent literature on asceticism and monasticism, see now E. A. Clark, *Reading Renunciation: Asceticism and Scripture in Early Christianity* (Princeton, 1999), 14–42.

[21] On 'the world' and the desert, see Brown, *Body and Society*, 216–18; Markus, *The End of Ancient Christianity*, 66–9, drawing on K. Heussi, *Der Ursprung des Mönchtums* (Tübingen, 1936), 53.

[22] See the studies of D. Hunter, 'Resistance to the Virginal Ideal in Late Fourth Century Rome: The Case of Jovinian', *Theological Studies* 48 (1987), 45–64; 'On the Sin of Adam and Eve: A Little-Known Defense of Marriage and Childbearing by Ambrosiaster', *Harvard Theological Review* 82 (1989), 283–99; 'Helvidius, Jovinian, and the Virginity of Mary in Late Fourth-Century Rome', *JECS* 1 (1993), 47–71; and K. Cooper, *The Virgin and the Bride: Idealized Womanhood in Late Antiquity* (Cambridge, Mass., 1996), 92–108.

[23] On Augustine's distinctiveness as a monastic thinker, see R. Lorenz, 'Die Anfänge des abendländische Mönchtums im 4. Jahrhundert', *ZKG* 77 (1966), 1–61; R. A. Markus, 'Vie monastique et ascéticisme chez saint Augustin', *Atti del Congresso Internazionale su s. Agostino, Roma, 15–20 settembre 1986*, 2 vols. (Rome, 1987), i. 119–25. The classic studies remain A. Zumkeller, *Das Mönchtums des heiligen Augustinus* (Wurzburg, 1950; 2nd edn., 1968); A. Mandouze, *Saint Augustin: L'aventure de la raison et la grace* (Paris, 1968), 165–242, and the work of Luc Verheijen (see n. 28).

charity: this was far more important, in his view, than the performance of feats of asceticism, or in physically separating from 'the world'.

In this debate over the opportunities and risks of the monastic movement, a central place was occupied by the memory of the first Christian community at Jerusalem, as described in the Acts of the Apostles, 4: 32–5:

And the multitude of them that believed were of one heart and one soul in God: neither said any of them that ought of the things which he possessed was his own; but they had all things in common. [. . .] Neither was there any among them that lacked: for as many as were possessors of lands or houses sold them, and brought the prices of the things that were sold. And laid them down at the apostles' feet: and distribution was made unto every man according as he had need.[24]

The image of the apostolic community, its members materially and spiritually transparent to each other, dominated the ascetic imagination in the fourth and fifth centuries. From the outset, commentators on the monastic movement were keen to propose a direct historical continuity between the Jerusalem Christians and the desert fathers. The apparent implausibility of this claim—how could the multifarious communities and individuals on the outskirts of villages in Egypt and Syria possibly be related to an urban commune in first-century Palestine?—only lent rhetorical energy to the accounts of those, such as Eusebius, who advanced it. The upshot was a form of 'apostolic succession' tying the eastern ascetics and their western imitators, in all their variety, to the one point of origin in the Jerusalem community.[25] In the 420s, arguably the leading expert on desert asceticism in the Latin West, John Cassian, used this narrative of continuity between apostolic Jerusalem and monastic Egypt in order to remind his Latin readers of the tradition they must follow if they wished to live as 'monks'.[26]

Augustine's understanding of the Jerusalem community was differently disposed. Transfixed as he was by the possibility that community of property could actually establish the seamless communion of hearts, the genealogical claims of the monastic movement interested

---

[24] Authorized Version.

[25] Philo of Alexandria, *De vita contemplativa* 13, 18–25 ed. Daumas, 86, 90–4, adapted by Eusebius of Caesarea, *Historia ecclesiastica* II. 16–17. 2, SC 31, 71–3, and by Cassian, *Inst.* 2. 5. 1–3, and *Conl.* 18. 5. See below, Ch. 2, for further references and discussion; and for a survey of Christian discussion before 400 of the apostolic Jerusalem, P. Bori, *Chiesa primitiva: L'immagine della comunità delle origini—Atti, 2, 42–47; 4, 32–37—nella storia della chiesa antica* (Brescia, 1974).

[26] See below, Ch. 2.

him far less than the immediate opportunity presented by the
monastery as a place in which to seek again the *communitas* of the first
Christians, in anticipation of the state of the blessed in the heavenly
Jerusalem.[27] Of course, in practice, such anticipation could only be
fleeting: Augustine never forsook the position (once arrived at) that
full peace would only come to the human community in the city of
God at the end of time.[28] The rigour of his eschatology, however, did
not deter him—in fact it drove him to invest in the monastery as a
venue for the enactment of apostolic charity. Augustine's vision of
the past and future Jerusalem led him to redefine the meaning of
'monasticism' as an apostolic life. Flying in the face of the traditional
definition of 'monks' as 'solitaries', Augustine offered an alternative
etymology, a sense of what 'one' meant conditioned by his reading of
the text of Acts:

'Monos' means 'one', but not 'one' in any fashion. You can be 'one in a crowd':
one person with many people can be called one, but they cannot be called 'monos',
that is, 'one alone'. 'Monos' means 'one alone'. They live together as one who
make up one person, so that they really are as it is written, 'one heart and one soul'.
Many bodies, but not many hearts are rightly called 'monos', that is 'one alone'.[29]

It was not, then, the monks' seclusion from 'the world' that defined
their identity, but rather the transparency of their bond with their
fellows.

With a vigour that remains, perhaps, under-appreciated, Augustine
broke with the desert tradition represented by Antony. As he saw it,
the impulse of withdrawal from the world, however honestly offered,
could not represent the authentic Christian life, because it left unresolved the question of the social relations between ascetics and the

---

[27] See *De op. mon.* 25. 32, CSEL 41, 577–9 (echoed at *Civ.Dei* V. 15, CCSL 47, 149)
expounded by Markus, 'Vie monastique et ascétisme chez saint Augustin'. See also
L. Verheijen, 'Saint Augustin', in *Théologie de la vie monastique: Études sur la tradition patris-
tique* (Paris, 1961), 201–12; and 'Spiritualité et vie monastique chez S. Augustin:
L'utilisation monastique des Actes des Apôtres 4: 31–35', in id., *Nouvelle approche de la
Règle de St Augustin* (Bellefontaine, 1980), 76–105. Verheijen's work is made accessible to an
Anglophone audience in id., *Saint Augustine's Monasticism in the Light of Acts 4: 32–35*,
(Villanova, 1979); and G. Lawless, *Augustine of Hippo and his Monastic Rule* (Oxford, 1987).
[28] See *EnarrPs.* 147. 20, CCSL 40, 2156; on the theme of transparency and opacity, see
also *De Genesi contra Manicheos* II. 4. 5, PL 34, 198–9; *Civ.Dei* XXII. 29, CCSL 48, 856–62.
[29] *Enarr. Ps.* 132. 6, CCSL 40, 1931. Cf. Jerome, *Tractatus super Ps. 132*, CCSL 78, 276,
an exegesis that also associates Ps. 132 with the monastic life, but in order to contrast this
with the lives led by the rest of the faithful: 'Utique alius ad domum ire festinat, alius ad
circum, alius in ecclesia de usuris cogitat. In monasterio autem sicut unum propositum, unus
et animus est.'

communities they had literally or figuratively abandoned. If the monastic movement was to avoid the appearance—whatever the reality—of spiritual élitism, then it must articulate its place within the wider community of the faithful. Shunning the rhetorical allure of the great antithesis between Desert and City, Augustine initiated a necessarily more intricate discussion of the relation between Monastery and Church.[30]

In a sermon of the early fifth century, for example, Augustine sought to devise an ecclesiology that would allow monastic communities to be separate, but not divisive of the whole body of the faithful. The community of believers, Augustine proposed, could be divided into three orders: married householders, inmates of monasteries, and the episcopal rulers of the Church.[31] This three-tiered vision of the Church, which seems to have been Augustine's own, became an immediate and enduring standard in the lexicon of Latin ecclesiology;[32] we shall see that in the hands of Gregory the Great this scheme provided a language in which to discuss the moral authority of the third order, the rulers of the Church. Augustine's interest, however, was in the second group, those who dwelt together 'as one' in monasteries: how could their apostolic charity 'descend to the rest'? Augustine envisaged monastics at the 'leading edge', as we might say, of the Christian community. Figuring the whole body of the faithful as a garment, he imagined monks at the neck: when Christ anointed his Church with the oil of charity, it would run down first to those who dwelt together as one, and from there to all others. With such imagery, Augustine confronted the marginality of monasticism, which threatened to divide the body of the faithful, and transformed it into the means by which that body is made complete.[33] This was not to

---

[30] *Ep.* 48. 2, CSEL 34. ii, 138 puts it bluntly: 'nec vestrum otium necessitatibus ecclesiae praeponatis.' For the contrast between Augustine's overall scheme and that of his peers in the ascetic movement, see Markus, *End of Ancient Christianity*, 157–77.

[31] These three types of the faithful had been described by Ezekiel as the three men saved at the end of time, Noah, Daniel, and Job (Ez. 14: 14). See G. Folliet, 'Les Trois catégories de chrétiens à partir de Luc (17: 34–36), Matthieu (24: 40–41) et Ezéchiel (14: 14), *Augustinus magister* (Paris, 1954), 631–44.

[32] See G. Folliet, 'Les Trois catégories des chrétiens, survie d'un thème augustinien', *L'Année théologique augustinienne* 14 (1954), 81–96.

[33] This was a case he made through an exegesis of Ps 132: 2: 'Like the ointment on the head, which descends to the beard, the beard of Aaron, which descends to the end of his garment'. The ointment, for Augustine, represented the balm of charity and unity, running down from Christ the head, to the Apostles, represented by the beard, and from them to the Church, figured by the sacerdotal garment. In its descent to the garment, it would come first to the collar, which for Augustine, stood for 'those who live together as one', i. e. monks.

confer upon monastics an illusory ethical status. All Christians were equally vulnerable to moral collapse, Augustine insisted, and all stood in equal need of peace and charity. There were false monks, and, equally, there were married people who could live in charity on the model of the first Christian community at Jerusalem. What distinguished the monastery as a site of apostolic charity was that the full apostolic community of property could be imagined and, indeed, enforced there.[34]

Augustine came to this view of monasticism, as to so much else, in the 390s.[35] In correspondence with his friends and colleagues around the Mediterranean, he realized that his changed views did not always find a ready hearing. With Jerome, in particular, Augustine found himself in awkwardly tactful confrontation on questions such as the moral value of virginity,[36] and the qualification for the understanding of Scripture.[37] His logic, as it emerged with increasing conviction, was to argue against a virtuoso understanding of ascetic achievement or exegetical prowess. The 'holy arrogance' in the pursuit of other-worldliness proposed by Jerome seemed to Augustine to come dangerously close to the damnable sin of pride, encouraging individual perfectionism at the expense of the peace of the community as a whole. By the time he began the *City of God* in 410, he was convinced that the whole ascetic project as conceived of by Jerome was, at best, misguided.

Augustine's critique of the monastic movement is persistently misunderstood in two key respects. The first of them is his thinking on

When Christ puts on the garment, his head comes into contact first with the monks. 'Sed a barba descendere unguentum ad oram potuit, quae in capite est, ubi aperitur capitium. Tales isti sunt qui habitant in unum; ut quomodo per oras istas intrat caput hominis, ut vestiat se; sic per concordiam fraternam Christus intrat, qui est caput nostrum, ut vestiatur, ut ecclesia illi haereat.' *Enarr. Ps.* 132. 9, CCSL 40, 1933.

[34] See e.g. *Ep.* 243, CSEL 57, 568–79, for an attempt to prise a reluctant monk away from the sphere of his household (represented by his mother).

[35] See D. Sanchis, 'Pauvreté monastique et charité fraternelle chez saint Augustin: Le commentaire augustinien des Actes 4: 32–35 entre 393 et 403', *StMon* 4 (1962), 7–33. The Augustine of the early 390s had a more contemplative, less communitarian interpretation of Acts 4: 32: see e.g. *Enarr. Ps.* 4, CCSL 38, 19: 'Singulares ergo et simplices, id est, secreti a multitudine ac turba nascentium rerum ac morientium, amatores aeternitatis et unitatis debemus, si uni Deo et Domino nostro cupimus inhaerere.' ('We must be one and simple, that is, removed from the thronging multitude of mortal things which are born and die. We must be lovers of eternity and unity, if we desire to be joined to the one God our Lord.')

[36] Markus, *End of Ancient Christianity*, 45–6.

[37] See J. N. D. Kelly, *Jerome: His Life, Writings, and Controversies* (London, 1975), 217–18, 263–72; J. M. Vessey, 'Conference and Confession: Literary Pragmatics in Augustine's *Apologia Contra Hieronymum*', *JECS* 1: 2 (1993), 175–213.

human sexuality, the area in which modern hostility towards him masses most powerfully. Augustine has served, indeed, as a lightning rod for the tirades against the sexually repressed and repressive elements of the 'western tradition'—the irony being that the attitudes condemned are more characteristic of those against whom Augustine was arguing.[38] The patent inferiority of the body in relation to the spirit, the inherently dangerous and sinful nature of sexual desire, the liability of men to be tempted from the path of righteousness by unstable women: these were assumptions shared by many of Augustine's contemporaries, both pagan and Christian, impelling them into the lively market-place of competing medical and ascetic panaceas for the unruliness of the body. It was precisely in order to expose the frailty of these assumptions that Augustine offered, in the *City of God* (Book XIV), his own analysis of the human condition, based on a long-considered reading of the opening chapters of Genesis. Augustine's account of the Fall turned on the weakness, not of the body, but of the soul. Human history, as we know it, happened because Adam and Eve succumbed to pride, self-love, rather than love of the creator. This was a failure of will, a turning of the will away from the creator. It was not the eating of the fruit, but the disobedience to God which was the first and original sin.[39] If the Fall was not the result of any bad desire, to declare war on desire as an ascetic was, in its wilful misunderstanding of the human condition, to risk compounding pride with pride.

Augustine's analysis could not have been clearer—but it carried with it the seeds of its own, almost immediate, reversal (and it is on this reversed reading of Augustine that modern condemnation of him depends). The very eloquence with which he depicted the post-lapsarian condition left his ascetically-inclined readers all the more likely to turn to the palliatives Augustine urged them to reject. As Augustine saw it, God had made the punishment fit the crime of pride.

[38] For correctives, see Brown, *Body and Society*, 387–427; Markus, *End of Ancient Christianity*, 58–62; D. Hunter, 'Augustine's Pessimism? A New Look at Augustine's Teachings on Sex, Marriage, and Celibacy', *AugStud* 25 (1994), 153–77.

[39] *Civ.Dei* XIV. 13–15, CCSL 48, 434–8. A view both supported and denied by Scripture: Eccl. 10. 15 has pride as the root of all evil, while 1 Tim 6: 10 has desire as the root of all evil. These proof texts are reconciled by Augustine at e.g. *De genesi ad litteram* 11. 15, CSEL 28, 347, by drawing a distinction between the specific love of money, and the generalized desire to have more than one's due, which Augustine regarded as tantamount to pride. For discussion, see D. J. Macqueen, 'St Augustine's Concept of Property Ownership', *Recherches Augustiniennes* 8 (1972), 187–229 at 199–203, and 'Contemptus Dei: St Augustine on the Disorder of Pride in Society and its Remedies', *Recherches Augustiniennes* (1973), 227–93 at 238–9. Sixth-century readers of Augustine were to effect the same synthesis of these Scriptural texts for different purposes: see below, Ch. 3.

He had given Adam and Eve their independence, but 'not in such a way that they were completely in their own power'.[40] No longer immortal, they entered the dominion of the grave, ruled by the tempter; and even in life they now lost the autonomy to which they had aspired. God turned body and soul into sites of disobedience, confronting humans with a mirror image of their primal dissension from the divine will. Expelled from paradise, the body was now hopelessly vulnerable to desire in excess of all need, and the fractured will could do nothing about it. Only contortionists could exert their powers of volition over their limbs: most other men—and Augustine was thinking specifically of men—had to suffer the deep shame of being unable to control their sexual organ.[41] Again and again, Augustine stressed that this was a punishment for sin, not the reason for it. Trying to drive out from the body or the mind the spirit of fornication, for example, was to deal with the symptom, not the cause of the postlapsarian condition. But symptomatic relief was not in itself unattractive. Having so graphically rendered the ache of desire, Augustine left his early medieval readers open to the advances of ascetic technology, with its promises of physical self-control and of release from the torment of craving. And as we shall see, sixth-century readers of the *City of God* were not slow to claim the authority of Augustine to endorse their ascetic reappropriation of his work.

In a less fraught historiographical context, Augustine's emphasis on the communal aspect of monastic life has led many early medieval readers (in particular, St Benedict) and modern commentators to hail him as a founding father for cenobitism in the Latin West.[42] While this is in some respects a truism (the *coenobium* being the community) it misrepresents Augustine's immediate intentions. In the late fourth and early fifth century the term 'cenobitism' gained its meaning from its opposite 'eremitism', the ascetic life lived alone. These terms were put into circulation in the western Mediterranean by Jerome in an attempt to impose some taxonomic order upon the variety of ascetic experiments in the deserts of Egypt and Syria.[43] As Augustine saw it,

[40] *Civ.Dei* XIV. 15, CCSL 48, 436–8. Quotation at 437, ll. 12–13.

[41] *Civ.Dei* XIV. 16–20, CCSL 48, 438–43.

[42] So e.g. H. Leclercq, art. 'Cénobitisme', *DACL* II. 2, 3224–31; Lorenz, 'Die Anfänge des abendländische Mönchtums'.

[43] Jerome, *Ep.* 22. 34–6. On the cenobitic tradition in general, see Leclercq, 'Cénobitisme'; on Jerome in this context, see Rousseau, *Ascetics, Authority and the Church*, 100–13, 123–4; and now S. Driver, 'The Development of Jerome's Views on the Ascetic Life', *RTAM* 62 (1995), 44–70.

however, the monastic desert in the hands of its intellectual publicists had become a symbol of division, and he seems deliberately to have eschewed their vocabulary. In this sense, his ideal of the monastic community was expressly not 'cenobitic'.

Neither of these cautions should be taken to mean that Augustine had no interest in organizing monastic communities of celibate men and women. To the contrary, Augustine's critique of the monastic movement led him to develop and to implement a blueprint for the monastery as an institution patterned on the first society of Christians at Jerusalem. We know of at least three communities for which Augustine was responsible in Hippo: a monastery in a garden donated by his predecessor Bishop Valerius at his ordination to the priesthood, his own episcopal household, sternly organized around the community of property, as we shall see below, and a nunnery of which his sister had charge.[44] Circumstantial details about these communities are hard to come by until the 420s. In the text known to his early medieval readers as the *Rule of St Augustine*, the precise date of which remains uncertain,[45] Augustine specifies exactly how, in theory, apostolic charity will follow from sharing of material goods in the organization of the monastery. In the course of his prescriptions for a community of one heart and one soul we can begin to see Augustine confronting the challenges of social stratification and of political authority.

The *Rule* interleaves the language of the Psalms and the description of the first community of Christians at Jerusalem to describe a

[44] These conclusions have not been unanimously accepted: see e.g. A. P. Orbans, 'Augustinus und das Mönchtum', *Kairos* 18 (1976), 100–18, rebutted by A. Zumkeller, 'War Augustins Monasterium in Hippo wirklich ein Kloster? Antwort auf eine neue Hypothese A. P. Orbans', *Augustinianum* 31 (1981), 391–7; see also L. Verheijen, 'Les lettres nouvelles et la vie monastique autour de saint Augustin', in *Les Lettres de saint Augustin découvertes par Johannes Divjak: Communications présentées au colloque des 20 et 21 septembre* (Paris, 1983), 124–7 at 126–7.

[45] A full discussion of the questions of dating and priority attending the *Rule of St Augustine* is not needed here. I rely on the findings and nomenclature of Luc Verheijen, now widely although not universally accepted, which may be summarized as follows. The dossier of texts for male and female monastic communities transmitted in Augustine's name can be traced back to two distinct works: one the *Praeceptum*, composed *c*.400 for the 'garden' community of monks Augustine founded at Hippo in the mid-390s, before his ordination as bishop; and secondly the *Ordo monasterii*, written at about the same time, also for a male community, but not by Augustine himself. In the earliest manuscript witness (Par.Lat. 12634, discussed below, Ch. 5), these two texts are copied together and referred to as the *Regula s. Augustini*. I have adopted this 6th-cent. terminology, but in view of Verheijen's doubts about the authenticity of the *Ordo monasterii*, my discussion here focuses on the *Praeceptum*. See *Règ.Aug.* and L. Verheijen 'La Règle de saint Augustin: L'état actuel des questions (début 1975)', *Augustiniana* 35 (1985), 193–263. Lawless, *Augustine of Hippo and his Monastic Rule*, 121–54, 165–71.

community in the present: 'The chief motivation for your sharing life together is to live harmoniously in the house and to have one heart and one soul seeking God'.[46] Augustine then insists upon the common ownership of property. The monks' attention to the text of Acts—the example of the apostles—should prevent them from saying 'This belongs to me'. They hold all things in common.[47] Having proposed Acts 4 as the model for monastic living, Augustine considers the likely obstacles. Immediately following the opening section, he raises the issue of class division, and how it might rub against the injunction to live together as one. (The *Rule* is an under-used source for the social history of the city in Late Roman North Africa.[48]) No snobbery from the rich: they are to glory in the holy society of the poor, but without priding themselves in their ability to support the community with their wealth. Conversely, the poor are not to congratulate themselves on the exalted company they now keep.[49] Augustine saw that the maintenance of the humility of the poor was, perhaps, the hardest challenge for the community.

The community of hearts does not require a levelling of all standards. No one is to be refused those things which, in their weakness, they might need. Those who have come 'from somewhat delicate environments' should not be made to follow the full regime of those who were used to harder conditions;[50] while the poor were not to be denied those needful things which they have not been able to afford before.[51] Augustine elaborated a theory of needs, and insisted upon its acceptance within the community. There was to be no resentment from any quarter at concessions to the weakness of particular brethren. This would have been a parodic subversion of the whole basis of the community.[52] Augustine was not totally abandoning physical ascesis, but he feared that the monastery might become a place of ascetic competition. Competition bred *murmur*: the point of the community was that the strong should live with the weak 'without murmuring'.[53]

Augustine recognized that the community could not function with-

---

[46] *Praec.* 1. 2, *Règ.Aug.* 417–18; Lawless, 81. For commentary on this opening passage, see S. Pricoco, 'La Bibbia nel *Praeceptum* di s. Agostino', *Augustinianum* 36 (1996), 495–523, esp. 514 ff.   [47] *Praec.* 1. 3, *Règ.Aug.* 418.
[48] See C. Lepelley, *Les Cités de l'Afrique romain au Bas-Empire*, 2 vols. (Paris, 1979); also Brown, *Augustine*, pp. 19–27, 296–7.   [49] *Praec.* 1. 6–7, *Rég. Aug.* 419–20.
[50] Ibid. 2. 4, 422.
[51] Ibid. 1. 5, 418–19.
[52] Ibid. 2. 4, 422.
[53] A theme of great importance in the *Rule of St Benedict*: see R. W. Southern, *Western Society and the Church in the Middle Ages* (Harmondsworth, 1970), 219–20, and below, Ch. 5.

out some central authority: at the centre of distribution according to need is the superior. It is he who sees to the sharing out of the common stock of food and clothing, and who ministers to the monks' differing spiritual needs. The superior should 'correct the restless, console the fainthearted, support the weak, be patient for all'.[54] Augustine knew the power and insight demanded of the superior to be problematic. While the superior bears others' burdens, he has no one to bear his own: his is a lonely responsibility to God for the souls in his charge. Augustine attempted to find a solution by insisting that this perspective on authority became the shared knowledge of the community, in the same way that the community shared the apostolic language of distribution according to need.[55] The superior is to be obeyed but also pitied.[56] And when he is excessive in his correction of brothers below him, he should not be made to ask for pardon.

Requirements of discipline may compel you to speak harsh words to correct young people. Even if you feel your criticism has been immoderate, you are not obliged to ask their pardon, lest, as you deal with those who are, of necessity, subject, you should cleave too much to humility, to the point where you break your power to rule.[57]

The superior must instead seek forgiveness from God.

Augustine's own authority in the early medieval West has not a little to do with the reception of his *Rule*. Its lucid definition of monastic community, based directly in scripture, was a touchstone for generations of western ascetics who, perforce of geographical circumstance, could not directly imitate their forebears in the deserts of the East. No less compelling was the *Rule*'s sharp insight into the vulnerability of those who hold power. The acute exposure of the moral ruler was a theme to which Augustine's Latin readers would return over and over again in the next two centuries. We shall see the *Rule* invoked, then, in subsequent discussions both of community and of authority in western asceticism.

[54] *Praec.* 7. 3, *Règ.Aug.* 436.

[55] In this sense what holds the community together is not in the end shared property, but shared discourse: cf. the emphasis on reading and speaking at *Praec.* 1. 1–3 cited above, n. 47.

[56] *Praec.* 7. 4, *Règ.Aug.* 436.

[57] Ibid. 6. 3, 434; Lawless, 100–1. 'Quando autem necessitas disciplinae, minoribus coercendis, dicere vos verba dura conpellit, si etiam ipsis modum vos excessisse sentitis, non a vobis exigitur, ut ab eis veniam postuletis, ne apud eos quos oportet esse subiectos, dum nimia servatur humilitas, regendi frangatur auctoritas.' A passage of immense interest to Gregory the Great: see *RP* II. 8, and the discussion below, Ch. 6. Cf. *Ep.* 210, CSEL 57, 353–6, addressed to an abbess, encouraging her to use her powers of rebuke. See below, n. 86.

As Augustine well knew and his readers discovered, however, there was a tension between these themes. The immediate reception of his monastic teachings reveals that, while in the limpid clauses of the *Rule*, the exercise of power could be balanced against the needs of the community, such an equilibrium was less easy to maintain in the actual communities for which he was responsible. This was a lesson he learned in the final decade of his life, and it is to Augustine as the sixty-year-old bishop of Hippo that we now turn. The man in his forties who wrote the *Confessions* is well-known to us, so much so that we are sometimes in danger of making the older Augustine merely ancillary to his younger self.[58] Where his careers as a monk and a monastic patron are concerned, however, the older Augustine is often our sole informant.[59] The context for his testimony is a poignant one: Augustine could see his hopes for the monastic Jerusalem all but evaporating. In the 420s in other words, no less than in the 390s, Augustine 'lost a future',[60] and was forced to take command in an attempt to retrieve it.

MONASTIC SCANDAL

Probably in late 422, Augustine wrote to the Roman matron Fabiola. She was offering hospitality to a young man named Antoninus, 'my beloved son and fellow bishop', who had come to Rome to plead his case before Pope Celestine. Augustine had already informed the Pope of his view of the matter; in his letter to Fabiola, he unfolded at greater length 'who I am to Antoninus, and who Antoninus is to me, and what I am going to ask of you'.[61] It was a painful story of scandal and

[58] An especial problem where *De doctrina christiana* is concerned: Vessey, 'Conference and Confession', 195–6 cautions strongly against the tendency to assimilate the first three books of the treatise (all but completed 397) with the material Augustine added in 426/7. See also C. Kannengiesser, 'The Interrupted *De doctrina christiana*' in Arnold and Bright (eds.), *De doctrina Christiana: A Classic of Western Culture* (Notre Dame, 1995), 3–13; Brown, *Augustine*, Epilogue (forthcoming), shows how the discovery of the new letters gives new weight to the 420s.

[59] In sermons delivered in 425–6, Augustine describes his monastic career from the early 390s (*Aug.Serm* 355–6, discussed below), as does Possidius, writing in 431 (see esp. *VAug.* 5. 1, ed. Pellegrino, 52). These texts are used by Verheijen and others in reconstructing Augustine's monastic thought and practice in the 390s: without attempting to revisit the questions of the *Rule of St Augustine*, the discussion here focuses on Augustine's final decade in itself, not for the light that texts produced in that period may shed on his activities thirty years previously.

[60] A reference to Brown, *Augustine*, ch. 15 'The Lost Future', describing the sea-change of the 390s.

[61] *Ep.* 20*. 2, CSEL 88, 94, FC 49, 134; cf. *Ep.* 209 to Pope Celestine, CSEL 57, 347–53.

betrayal, involving an error of judgement on Augustine's part, and exposing the frailty of catholic pastoral pretensions in North Africa, especially in the wake of their triumph over the rival Donatist Church. Above all, however, the case of Antoninus raised questions about the value of the monastic life, as promoted by the bishop of Hippo for over a generation. Antoninus' behaviour confronted Augustine with the possibility that even exposure to monastic charity could sow division and reinforce patterns of exploitation in the Church.

Antoninus had arrived in Hippo as a small boy, with his mother and step-father. The family was, apparently, destitute. Augustine took them in, placing the boy in one of the monasteries supported by the Church of Hippo; Antoninus' mother was placed on the rolls of the poor, also maintained by the Church.[62] In the letter to Fabiola, Augustine invoked his personal stake in the affair, conscious, perhaps, of the hidden kinship between his own career and that of Antoninus, both of them bright prospects desperate to rise above their humble origins.[63] At the time, however, Augustine's interest in the boy was at a benign, routine distance; he relied on the prior of the monastery for reports on Antoninus' progress.

The bishop's lack of precise information was the immediate cause of the problem: Augustine was too busy, and his resources were over-stretched. His very success as a leader in the African church worked to diminish his pastoral energies. Having definitively crushed the Donatists in 411, Augustine had to take responsibilty for the influx of new converts from the old rivals. The Catholic hierarchy was short-staffed, especially in rural areas. One such place was the village of Fussala, far to the south-west of Hippo. The villagers needed a bishop. Augustine's first candidate ran out on him—but by then the elderly primate of Numidia was on his way to the consecration. Fearing the 'jeers of our enemies', Augustine pushed forward Antoninus from the

---

The discovery of the letter to Fabiola has made Antoninus' case—hitherto known only from the letter to Celestine—of compelling interest in the past fifteen years. See e.g. W. Frend, 'Fussala: Augustine's Crisis of Credibility (Ep. 20*), Verheijen, 'Les lettres nouvelles et la vie monastique', both in *Les Lettres de saint Augustin découvertes par Johannes Divjak*, 261–5, 123–7; J. E. Merdinger, *Rome and the African Church in the Time of Augustine* (New Haven, 1997), 154–82; and Brown, *Augustine*, afterword to second edition (forthcoming).

[62] *Ep.* 20*. 2. 1–4, CSEL 88, 94–5.

[63] See *Conf.* II. 3. 5, O'Donnell i. 17 for Augustine's description of his father as *municipis admodum tenuis*, and for the resulting break in his studies because his parents could not support him; cf. *Aug.Serm.* 356. 13, PL 39, 1580A (discussed below, pp. 23–5). B. Shaw, 'The Family in Late Antiquity: The Experience of Augustine', *Past and Present* 115 (1987), 3–51 at 5–10, explains the senses in which Augustine was and was not 'poor'.

monastery. The young man knew Punic at least, the language of the countryside.[64]

Initially overawed by his promotion, Bishop Antoninus soon overcame his inhibitions. Summoning two associates from the monastery at Hippo, he embarked on the full-scale exploitation and depredation of his flock. 'Anyone who fell into their clutches lost money, furnishings, clothing, farm animals, fruits, wood, finally even stones.' The episcopal court records at Hippo carried the doleful list of grievances of 'poor men and women, and worse still, widows'.[65] Taking advantage of his elevation, Antoninus had rounded on his own kind, as though to erase the memory of his lowly origins. And with bitter determination he refused to be unseated by the onslaught of complaints and legal procedures against him.[66] Hence the appeal to Rome, and Augustine's letters to Pope Celestine and the matron Fabiola. Concluding to Fabiola, Augustine wrote:

I simply wanted to make known to you my unhappiness that a young man trained by us in the monastery who, when we took him in, left nothing of his own behind, gave nothing to the poor, brought nothing to the community, the very same now glories as it were in his estates and homes, and wishes to make his own not only these things but also the very flock of Christ.[67]

Augustine had chosen the most unsuitable candidate for a most delicate appointment—a professional embarrassment for him and for the catholic hierarchy as a whole.

Moreover, the episode could not fully be explained in terms of an unfortunate oversight under duress. Antoninus' 'pastoral' operation held a ghastly mirror to Augustine's own stewardship of his Church. The bishop of Fussala had been able to summon monastic brethren to assist him in his business. In other words, the limited resources of the Church at Hippo had been used by its bishop to fund a monastery some of whose members were immature opportunists at best, at worst simply con-artists. Too preoccupied to notice what was happening in his own city, Augustine none the less repeatedly advertised the monastery as the site where the life of the apostolic community at Jerusalem could be recreated, and in particular where the social divisions created by wealth could be dissolved.[68]

[64] *Ep.* 20*. 3, CSEL 88, 96.
[65] *Ep.* 20*. 6. 1, CSEL 88, 97.
[66] *Ep.* 20*. 4–31, CSEL 88, 95–111.
[67] *Ep.* 20*. 32. 1, CSEL 88, 111; FC 49, 148–9.
[68] For such advertisement, all the more embarrassing because aimed at Donatists, see e.g. *EnarrPs.* 132. 6, CCSL 40, 1931: Augustine contrasts the unity created by monks with the

As he may himself have sensed, Augustine was a victim of his own success as a now elderly monastic patron. When he first moved to Hippo, he was still in the company of his friends—Alypius, Evodius, Severus—with whose lives Augustine's had been intertwined for the past decade. With the move to Hippo, however, this small group undertook to receive new members, such as Antoninus, or Possidius, who did not share their experience. For these younger men, coming in from the countryside, entry to Augustine's monastery represented their 'chance'. Monks trained in Hippo were much in demand in the North African Church. As Possidius—who himself became bishop of Calama in Numidia—reported: 'No fewer than ten men, known to us as holy and venerable, chaste and learned, were supplied by the most blessed Augustine to various churches in response to requests.'[69] For such men, monastic life in Hippo, patterned as far as its bishop was concerned on the Jerusalem community, had come to fill the role that municipal schooling had played for Augustine himself. Where the young Augustine had looked to the school at Madauros as his point of entry for a public career, now Possidius, Antoninus, and their peers turned to the ecclesiastical corporation at Hippo.

Augustine, of course, intended something quite different, having come to see his earlier ambitions as empty careerism. In the *Confessions*, he had taken pains to expose his rise to the top of his profession as a rhetor as nothing more than a child's game.[70] Rereading the *Confessions* in the 420s, Augustine found himself still moved by his own account—but to a hungry young man like Antoninus the story of his patron's spiritual odyssey was of little consequence. Antoninus confronted Augustine with the gap between his own, radically altered, expectations and those, unregenerate, of the next generation. While he could wear the news of the Constantinopolitan rumour of his death with a graceful irony, the indifference towards his life's work of one of those whom he had nurtured must have been more difficult to accept with equanimity.

chaos and violence spread by Donatist Circumcellions. Cf. *Ep.* 211/*obiurgatio* 4, *Règ.Aug.* I, 106: Augustine exhorts a community of nuns in Hippo to cease their quarrelling, all the more shameful in view of the unity achieved with the Donatists.

[69] Possidius, *VAug.* 11. 3, Pellegrino, 74. For a recent survey of modern discussion of Possidius' *vita*, see E. Elm, 'Die *Vita Augustini* des Possidius: *The Work of a Plain Man and an Untrained Writer*? Wandlungen in der Beurteilung eines hagiographischen Textes', *Augustinianum* 37 (1997), 229–40. See also W. Eck, 'Der Episkopat im spätantiken Africa: organisatorische Entwicklung, soziale Herkunft und öffentliche Funktionen', *HZ* 236 (1983), 265–95.

[70] See e.g. *Conf.* III. 3. 6–4. 7, IV. 2. 2, IV. 16. 30–1; O'Donnell, i. 27–8, 33, 44–5.

The scandal of Antoninus was not an isolated instance. Over the next five years the fabric of thirty years of monastic practice in the Church at Hippo and beyond seemed to unravel before the eyes of its ageing bishop. In the nunnery that Augustine and his sister had founded it seems that in the early 420s, after his sister's death, the nuns quarrelled over the appointment of a successor. Augustine denounced their strife, which threatened the very basis of their coming together to live in apostolic charity.[71] His disenchantment with all forms of the ascetic life is palpable. An 85-year-old man lived in continent marriage for twenty-five years, Augustine wearily reported, and then bought a 'music-girl'.[72] When Augustine heard that a Roman general stationed in Numidia was considering becoming a monk, he travelled far across the province to dissuade him.[73]

Most serious of all, however, was a breach of trust in Augustine's episcopal household.[74] Since his consecration, Augustine had insisted that the clergy in Hippo surrender their property and live together with their bishop in imitation of the Jerusalem community. In late 425, however, one of the priests, a man named Januarius, died leaving a son, also in Augustine's care, and a daughter in a nunnery. It came to light that Januarius had made a will, disinheriting his children in favour of the Church at Hippo.[75] Augustine was appalled; so fundamental was the requirement of apostolic poverty that he had never thought to monitor its observance. Summoning the whole congregation, he announced his intention to refuse the legacy, and to carry out

[71] The letter is included by the Maurists in Augustine's letters as *Ep.* 211, and traditionally dated to 423 (PL 33, 958). It was long thought to have led into the female version of the *Praeceptum*. Verheijen, however, showed that the first part of the letter (which he re-edited as the *obiurgatio*, *Règ.Aug.* I, 105–107), was distinct from the female *Praeceptum*, and argued that the *obiurgatio* could have been written at any point from 411 to 430 (*Règ.Aug.* II, 203). The *terminus ante quem non* of 411 is established by the reference in the letter to the unity of the Donatists achieved at the council of Carthage of that year.

[72] *Contra Julianum* III. 11. 22, PL 44, 713; Brown, *Augustine*, 405.

[73] *Ep.* 220. 3, CSEL 57, 433; Brown, *Augustine*, 422.

[74] Antoninus may have been a member of Augustine's household—or of the 'garden community'. See Verheijen, 'Les Lettres nouvelles et la vie monastique'.

[75] *Aug.Serm.* 355, 356, PL 39, 1569–81; see now G. Madec, *La vie communautaire: traduction annotée des sermons 355–356*, Nouvelle bibliothèque augustinienne 6 (Paris, 1996). For a detailed commentary, see F. Van der Meer, *Augustine the Bishop* (London, 1961), 199–206. The medieval future of Augustine's ruling in the Januarius case is considered by S. MacCormack, 'Sin, Citizenship, and the Salvation of Souls: The Impact of Christian Priorities on Late-Roman and Post-Roman Society', *Comparative Studies in Society and History* 39 (1997), 644–73 at 660–1. Cf. the parallel case of the matron Ecdicia, whose pious disposal of her family's property Augustine also condemned: see *Ep.* 262, and the discussion in K. Cooper, 'Insinuations of Womanly Influence: An Aspect of the Christianization of the Roman Aristocracy', *JRS* 82 (1992), 150–64, esp. 158–62.

a detailed examination of all the clergy. A month or so later, at Epiphany (426), Augustine reported that no other infraction had come to light. Within the year, however, he effectively abdicated as bishop, passing episcopal business onto the priest Eraclius. He was, as he stressed to the congregation, an old man.

It would be unwise to take Augustine's protestations of exhaustion entirely at face value. The Januarius affair and its aftermath did not represent the total defeat of the 'Jerusalem dream'. Rather, what Augustine had to concede was that his household would only function as an apostolic community if he directly exerted his authority. This he was, perhaps, reluctant to do: he preferred to think of the community in utopian terms, as self-regulating. But he was well able to provide the moral leadership required. In asserting his authority, Augustine turned to the method knew best: he told his own story.[76] In the two sermons before the congregation at Hippo, Augustine reinvented himself yet again, beginning with his arrival in the town in 391. None of this material appears in the *Confessions*, where the narrative stops at Ostia, just as Augustine and his friends are about to return to Africa. The new story carried a new message: Augustine wished now to present himself as a monk, and to ground his authority as a bishop in his lifelong commitment to the monastic life.

Clerical office had never been his goal, Augustine averred. He insisted that he had come to Hippo in order to found a monastery; and specifically to encourage his friend Evodius to 'spurn all the desires and allurements of this world'.[77] To his astonishment, the people of Hippo had set upon him, and had compelled him to accept ordination as a priest;[78] but he had not let ordination deflect him from his original intent. In a garden provided by Bishop Valerius within the precincts of the Church, he had founded his community, 'in accordance with the method and rule established under the holy apostles'.[79]

Augustine's account of himself in the sermons arising from the scandal of Januarius renders abruptly personal the insights and requirements of his theoretical or prescriptive monastic writings.[80] In

[76] The rhetorical strategy of the letters to Fabiola (and to Pope Celestine) had been essentially to involve his reader in his version of events. See Frederiksen, 'Paul and Augustine: Conversion Narratives, Orthodox Traditions and the Retrospective Self'.

[77] *VAug.* 3, ed. Pellegrino, 48. Cf. *Aug.Serm.* 355. 2, PL 39, 1569.

[78] *Aug.Serm.* 355. 2, PL 39, 1569; cf. *VAug.* 4, ed. Pellegrino 50–1, a classic scene of reluctance to power.

[79] *Aug.Serm.* 355. 2, PL 39, 1570; cf. *VAug.* 5, ed. Pellegrino, 52.

[80] For this reason—the similarity of language in the *Rule* and the *Sermons*—some scholars have dated the *Rule* to this period. See above, nn. 46, 60.

the *Rule* he considered the moral dangers that a poor man faced in gaining access to the resources of a monastery—dangers that Antoninus of Fussala had so spectacularly illustrated. Augustine is 'a poor man, born from poor stock', he now proclaims. The resources of the church at Hippo are twenty times the size of his own family income, he suggestively observes, daring his hearers to draw the conclusion that he had taken advantage of clerical office to elevate his social status. They knew, however, and he reminded them, that as bishop he had spurned the opportunities to wear silk robes. How much the more strictly, then, could the late Januarius and his peers be called to account.[81]

The specific goal of Augustine's public self-auditing was to justify a minute inquiry into the financial affairs of each and every member of the clergy at Hippo. What the bishop had voluntarily undergone, he could fairly require of the members of his household. The intimidating choice Augustine offered them was participation in his version of life in the community at Hippo, or complete withdrawal. In refusing Januarius' legacy, he argued explicitly that Januarius, in retaining his property, had never been a true member of the community. His peers in the clergy could write themselves in or out of their bishop's narrative. Unsurprisingly perhaps, the clergy were all found to be clean of private ownership, and Augustine could retire to his library with a clear conscience.

The anxiety of authority remained. In dealing with Januarius, Augustine became as concerned to disavow the power of his narrative charisma as he had been initially to disclaim financial ambition in seeking clerical office. On Epiphany of 426, as he was about to report back to the congregation on the results of his inquiry into his clergy, the bishop sought to conjure away his rhetorical authority. The scribe recording the sermon reported that at the appointed time Augustine began the service by ordering the reader Lazarus to read from Acts, 'so that you may see the form of life that we are trying to live out'. Lazarus read through from Acts 4: 31–5. He gave the codex back to Augustine, who said: 'I want to read too; I would rather read these words, than

---

[81] *Aug.Serm.* 356. 13, PL 39, 1580A: 'forte decet episcopum, quamvis non deceat Augustinum, id est, hominem pauperem, de pauperibus natum. Modo dicturi sunt homines quia inveni pretiosas vestes, quas non potuisses habere vel in domo patris mei, vel in illa saeculari professione mea.' Cf. *Praec.* 1. 5–6, *Règ. Aug.* i. 418–19: 'Qui autem non habebant, non ea quaerant in monasterio quae nec foris habere potuerunt. . . . Tantum non ideo se putent esse felices, quia invenerunt victum et tegumentum, quale foris invenire non poterant.'

plead my own case'. And he read out the verses again. His own intervention, he hoped, would appear transparent in the light of apostolic
Jerusalem.[82] Across the Januarius affair, Augustine compelled his
audience and his clergy to participate in the intimacy of his version of
events—while at the same time clinging to the dream that the
Jerusalem community could be self-regulating. Evidently persuasive
in the moment, this was a performance that depended entirely on
Augustine's own rhetorical bravura and his capacity to use his own
story for pastoral purposes. It was not to resolve the broader question
of a monastic bishop's charismatic as against his institutional power.

RELUCTANCE AND POWER

There are signs that Augustine, in his semi-retirement, was drawn
to reflect on the questions of community and authority and their
maintenance. In so doing, however, he confirmed rather than altered
his basic premises. Disillusion with the monastic community in the
saeculum seems to have made still more sharply focused his vision of
the eschatological community of the elect—and still more attenuated
his estimation of what those in power in the *saeculum* could knowingly
achieve. Abbots and bishops could not shirk their responsibilities—
they had been posted, like the prophets, as watchmen of the house of
Israel—but they could never be certain that the message they carried
to their flocks would have its intended effect.

In 427 the monks of Hadrumetum asked Augustine for clarification
of his letter of 418 to Pope Sextus, in which he condemned Pelagius
and his followers. Was Augustine really saying that ascetic effort had
no bearing on a person's eschatological destiny? They received a
notoriously unremitting statement of Augustine's position in the two
treatises, *On grace and free will* and *On correction and grace*. The monks
were friends, not polemic enemies like Pelagius and his followers,
but Augustine could offer them no security as to the value of their
earthly effort in the cause of their ultimate salvation. The saved
were a closed number, a complete community known to the mind of
God in eternity. There would be no defaulters from their ranks—
no Antoninus or Januarius—and no need for any protracted judicial
proceedings.

---

[82] *Aug.Serm.* 356. 1, PL 39, 1574D-1575A.

The number of the saints by God's grace predestined to God's kingdom with the gift of perseverance bestowed on them shall be guided thither in its completeness, and there shall be at length without end in its fullest completeness, most blessed, the mercy of the Saviour still cleaving to them, whether in their conversion, in their conflict, or in their crown.[83]

Human knowledge is as imperfect as human community. The corollary of this closed narrative of the elect is that we cannot know who is in the number. 'For who of the multitude of believers [cf. Acts] can presume, so long as he is living in this mortal state, that he is in the number of the predestinate?'[84]

The function of Augustine's teachings was not to discourage, but to strike fear into and to drive presumption out from the hearts of all. No one, not even monks, should for one moment assume that they are inside—or outside—the number. Augustine's message to the monks of Hadrumetum was that they should be neither encouraged to the point of presumption nor discouraged to the point of despair—their abbot should continue to dispense, and they should continue to accept correction for their sins. Whether or not the rebuke was ultimately effective—as part of the gift of perseverance to one of the elect— rested with God.[85]

To wield the knife of correction was, effectively, to stab in the dark.[86] Speaking for those in authority, Augustine insists:

in our ignorance of who shall be saved, God commands us to will that all to whom we preach this peace may be saved. . . . If he whom we rebuke is a son of peace, our peace shall rest upon him; but if not, it shall return to us again.[87]

[83] *De corr. et grat.* 40, PL 34, 941, NPNF 5, 488.

[84] *De corr. et grat.* 40, PL 43, 940, NPNF 5, 488.

[85] For Augustine's 'medicinal' view of correction, see L. Verheijen, 'Saint Augustin et les médicins', *L'Année théologique augustinienne* 13 (1953), 327–46, and *Règ.Aug.* I, 35–47; see also below, *Aug.Serm.* 339. V. Grossi, 'Correptio–Correctio–Emendatio in Agostina d'Ippona: Terminologia penitenziale e monastica', *Augustinianum* 38 (1998), 215–22, argues that Augustine's concept of *correctio* was ecclesiastical and disciplinary (as Verheijen's 'medicinal'), in contrast to the Stoic idea of fraternal correction that was to be developed subsequently in the monastic tradition—a point not incompatible with that advanced here. See now F. H. Russell, 'Persuading the Donatists: Augustine's Coercion by Words', in Klingshirn and Vessey (eds.), *Limits of Ancient Christianity*, 115–30, 125 ff.

[86] This is not to say that Augustine had no language of pedagogic inquiry or exhortation— only that he retained a sense of the arbitrary movement of divine grace. He told the narrative of his conversion as a repeated demonstration that divine rhetoric is beyond human control and understanding. At the climax in the garden of Milan, he is released from his agony by a series of textual coincidences: the child's voice, the memory of St Antony's own accidental conversion. He then opened the Bible at random himself. See *Conf.* VIII. 12. 29, O'Donnell, 101; cf. Monica's cure from alcoholism, ibid. IX. . 8. 18, 110–11.

[87] *De corr. et grat.* XV. 47, PL 34, 944, NPNF 5, 488.

Augustine insisted that those in power were still responsible for the sins of those in their charge, and unless they announced those sins, they would be held complicit. The Lord had appointed the prophet Ezekiel as the watchman of the house of Israel, with the duty to warn the people of the danger they posed to themselves:

For it is true that no one perishes except the son of perdition, but God says by the mouth of Ezekiel. 'He shall surely die in his sin, but his blood will I require at the hand of the watchman.'[88]

The existential condition of those in power was that they had to remain constantly vigilant to announce to the people their sins—all the while staring into the opacity of their mutual eschatological future.

All of this was not, perhaps, the answer for which the monks at Hadrumetum and their abbot had been hoping. The consternation apparently caused by the arrival of the treatises at the monastery and in North Africa and across the Mediterranean in southern Gaul would seem to give some historical warrant to the instinctive distaste for these late treatises experienced by Augustine's modern readers. In tracing the reception of these texts, however, we ought not to assume that Augustine's own mood was one of unremitting disappointment. The very absence of moral expectation on those in power could in fact represent a source of liberation. Taking advantage of his retirement, Augustine went back to complete his treatise *On Christian teaching*, which had lain unfinished for thirty years. In the new fourth book of the work, on how a teacher might best address his audience, he develops a breezy sense of exhilaration in the capacity of language to move the human heart.[89] Of course, a successful speaker should know that it was divine grace rather than his own powers of persuasion that brought an audience to tears, but this very realization allowed the Christian rhetor to free himself from the constraining canons of Ciceronian style. Confident in the power of God to render effective (or otherwise) all communication, and without illusion about the importance of his own intervention, a speaker could flout the conventions whereby a particular topic required the use of particular linguistic

---

[88] *De corr. et grat.* XVI. 48, PL 34, 945, NPNF 5, 488. Referring to Ez. 3: 17 and following, 'Son of man, I have made thee a watchman for the house of Israel', where the Lord entrusts the prophet with the duty of announcing to the people their sins.

[89] See e.g. *De doctr. chr.* IV. 24. 53, Green, 268–9: Augustine recalls moving the Christians of Mauretania to tears, and so bringing an end to their internecine feuds. See G. Bonner, 'Augustine's Visit to Caesarea in 418', in C. W. Dugmore and C. Duggan (eds.), *Studies in Church History* (London, 1964), 104–13.

register, and use whatever rhetorical art seemed to serve the purpose of peace and charity.[90] Such was Augustine's understanding of the operation of 'humble speech'.

Augustine's final reflections on power and persuasion are manifest in a sermon given towards the end of his life, on the anniversary of his consecration. Here he considered before his congregation the weight and nature of the burden of his office, the *sarcina episcopalis*.[91] The reading on this occasion, taken from Ezekiel, describes the Lord's commission of the prophet as the watchman of the house of Israel (Ezek. 3: 17–19), the image Augustine refers to in his treatise *On correction* to evoke the exposed position of those in power. It is tempting to link this sermon also with the events of 425–6, or at least with Augustine's growing realization that he had to exert his authority in Hippo if he wanted his flock to live in charity.

In invoking the figure of the watchman of the house of Israel, Augustine drew upon a long established tradition among Christian communities of thinking about authority and responsibility, a discussion embedded into the very terminology for 'bishops'. The Greek 'episkopos', used by Christians before the end of the first century to distinguish their resident leaders from wandering apostles, literally meant 'a watchman'. According to Christine Mohrmann, the 'episkopos' may already have been associated with the watchman of Ezekiel.[92] Mohrmann showed that the Latin use of the Greek term produced a new vocabulary, perhaps because the transliteration 'episcopus' did not convey the sense of 'watching' carried in the original. Thus while a bishop could be called a *sacerdos* to designate his role as a liturgical specialist, as a pastor with a legal responsibility for his flock on the Day of Judgement he was known as the *speculator* of Ezekiel.[93] By the early fifth century at the latest this tradition was encoded in some liturgies for the anniversary of episcopal consecrations; our witness to this liturgical tradition is none other than Augustine of Hippo in the sermon here under discussion.

[90] See *De doctr. chr.* IV. 3. 4 ff., Green, 198 ff. The classic treatment is Auerbach, *Literary Language*, ch. 2, discussed below, pp. 59–61. See also A. Primmer, 'The Function of the *de genera dicendi* in *De doctrina christiana* IV', in Arnold and Bright (eds.), *De doctrina christiana*, 68–86; D. Foster, '"Eloquentia nostra" (DDC IV. IV. 10): A Study of the Place of Classical Rhetoric in Augustine's *De doctrina christiana* Book Four', *Augustinianum* 36 (1996), 459–94.

[91] *Aug.Serm.* 339, *De proprio natale*, in G. Morin (ed.), *Miscellanea Agostiniana*, 2 vols. (Rome, 1930), i. 190–200.

[92] C. Mohrmann, 'Episkopos–Speculator', in id., *Études sur le latin des chrétiens*, iv (Rome, 1977), 232–52.　　　　　　　　　[93] Mohrmann, 'Episkopos–Speculator', 252.

The Lord's commission to Ezekiel, read out, compelled Augustine to consider the burden of responsibility. The Lord had charged the prophet to announce to the people their sins—otherwise he would require the prophet's blood for the people's disobedience. 'No obscurity in the reading permits us to excuse our negligence.'[94] What Augustine feared in particular was his susceptibility to blandishments from his congregation, which would reduce his vigilance as a watchman.[95] In reckoning the account he had to render at the Day of Judgement, Augustine articulated the rhetorical 'hard place' into which the verses drove him. 'What shall I do? [. . .] Can I keep silent? I am afraid to keep silent. I am compelled to preach; being terrified, I instil terror myself.'[96] He knew he must resist the offer of easy acquiescence with the desire of his hearers for a quiet life.

Augustine, however, refused to accept the isolation of power. He attempted to turn his discussion of his authority back again towards a meditation on community. That he in terror struck terror into his congregation prompted him to reason: 'Be afraid with me, and rejoice with me.'[97] The Lord had given Ezekiel amnesty if he announced to the people their sins and they ignored him. Augustine protested against this separation of the watchman from the people. He was not content to let his exhortations simply fall on deaf ears, to watch his people perish while he lived. He demanded complicity between himself and his hearers over their shared condition. A son instructed to keep his elderly father awake, lest he die, will not let him sleep, even if the father wishes to sleep.[98] So Augustine will insist that all remain vigilant, in defiance of those who wish to sleep, and without the certainty that he would succeed, or even that the vigilance of all would be equally rewarded. But at least he could not be accused of lording it over his flock.

The figure of the watchman, and Augustine's meditation on it, compelled the attention of his Latin readers, especially those who had themselves undertaken the episcopal burden. Augustine's sermon on Ezekiel circulated as an available part of the liturgy for episcopal consecration anniversaries. In early sixth-century Gaul, as we shall see, Bishop Caesarius of Arles was instructed by his tutor in rhetoric

---

[94] *Aug.Serm* 339. 2, Morin, 190–1.

[95] Ibid. 339. 1, 190.

[96] Ibid. 339. 8, 199.

[97] Ibid. 339. 8, 199.

[98] Ibid. 339. 8, 199; cf. *Aug.serm.* 9. 4, PL 38, 79, on doctors ignoring their patients' wishes.

in the duties of the watchman, and he in turn addressed a group of assembled prelates on the watchman theme. At the end of the century, in his *Homilies on Ezekiel*, Gregory the Great, whose very name means 'vigilant', described his entire approach to the papacy under the sign of the *speculator*.[99]

The moral drawn by Augustine's early medieval readers—very different from the lesson he himself had attempted to expound—was this. The dream of reconstructing the first community of Christians at Jerusalem could only be sustained through an extraordinary display of episcopal authority. Acts 4 proferred the hope of a community that was self-regulating. But if that was the promise of the Acts verses, it was not one they could deliver—not without the intervention of a rhetorical expert. Augustine of Hippo's contemporaries and his later readers, for all that they may have respected and even required augustinian authority, decided repeatedly that a systematic approach to the moral exercise of authority of the sort that Augustine had refused to give was the only way to preserve the hope of establishing a moral community.

This was a process drawn out until the age of Gregory the Great (and beyond);[100] but it was also an immediate preoccupation of Augustine's final years. In 428, he received a letter from two of his disciples in southern Gaul concerning the reception there of the treatise *On correction and grace*. The letter identified 'servants of Christ living in Marseilles' as so hostile to Augustine's teachings that they veered dangerously close to the error of Pelagius. While we can see the logic of this accusation to have been unfounded—doubts concerning Augustine's position did not necessarily mean any kind of affiliation to that of Pelagius—it is the case that the most prominent ascetic teacher in Marseilles had been working for over a decade on the question of moral authority, and had formulated his own approach. This was John Cassian, to whose teachings we now turn. The extent of his contact with Augustine remains tantalizingly vague, although it is clear enough that he was anxious to avoid a confrontation on the issue of grace and free will of the sort that Augustine's zealous followers were attempting to engineer.[101] Whether in open dialogue or not, Cassian had meditated

[99] Mohrmann, 'Episkopos–Speculator', 243–51.

[100] See D. Ganz, 'The Ideology of Sharing: Apostolic Community and Ecclesiastical Property in the Early Middle Ages', in W. Davies and P. Fouracre (eds.), *Property and Power in the Early Middle Ages* (Cambridge, 1995), 17–29, on Carolingian uses of the patristic discussion of Acts 4.

[101] The traditional view, that Cassian wrote *Conference* 13 in order to refute Augustine's

on the same problems and texts as had Augustine, and his solutions appeared quite as coherent to his hearers as did those of the bishop of Hippo.[102]

teachings on predestination, thus starting the 'semi-Pelagian controversy', no longer carries as much credence as it used to: see below, Ch. 2, for further discussion. Conversely, U. Duchrow, 'Zum Prolog von Augustins *De Doctrina christiana*', *Vigiliae Christianae* 17 (1963), 165–72, suggests that Augustine wrote in hostile response to Cassian's discussion of scripture in the *Conferences* (although Green, *De doctrina christiana*, pp. xiii–xiv, is unpersuaded). Intriguing as evidence for complicity between Marseilles and Hippo is the case of the monk Leporius, sent by Bishop Proculus to Augustine for correction of his way-ward Christological views, and discussed by Cassian in his *De Incarnatione Domini contra Nestorium*. See Leporius, *Libellus emendationis*, CCSL 63, 111–23 (bibliography at 97–8); E. Amann, art. 'Leporius', DTC, 9: 434–40.

[102] Cf. Brown, *Body and Society*, 423; Markus, *End of Ancient Christianity*, 167; E. Rebillard, '*Quasi funambuli*: Cassien et la controverse pélagienne sur la perfection', *REAug* 40 (1994), 197–210.

2

The Moral Science of John Cassian

In July of 428, Pope Celestine addressed a letter to the bishops of southern Gaul. He wanted, in particular, to express his concern about recent trends in the acquisition and conduct of episcopal office. It had come to his attention that unqualified candidates were being presented for ordination as bishops; mostly these were laymen without any experience of ecclesiastical office. In some cases, however, virtual strangers, and even known criminals, had been foisted on unwilling congregations. These maverick bishops seem to have been ascetics, or at least to have had ascetic connections. Celestine referred to the case of one Daniel, patron of a nunnery in the East, who had fled to Gaul seeking the amnesty of ordination, accused as he was of sexual relations with the sacred virgins in his charge.[1] It no more pleased the pope to learn of (unnamed) bishops dressed like recluses, 'with their loins girded up': this was an ostentatious, and overly literal, understanding of the spiritual purity demanded of the priesthood.[2] Far from regarding asceticism as a qualification for episcopal office, the pope seems to have been more impressed with the risks entailed in these ascetics' exercise of episcopal power, and with good reason: but four years previously, Celestine had heard the case of the charlatan Antoninus of Fussala.

The behaviour observed by Celestine was not mere boisterousness—nor was he alone in expressing concern on this score. Ascetics in southern Gaul were possessed of an ideological basis for their claims to moral superiority, which, they argued (to the alarm of their critics), obviated their lack of official qualifications for clerical office. Their most voluble spokesmen came from the island monastery of Lérins (offshore from modern-day Cannes), many of whom sallied forth onto the mainland to take up episcopal office in the cities of Provence. The Lérinians have left us with a clear sense, if not of the details of their monastic observance, then of its political style.[3] They were

---

[1] Celestine, *Ep.* 4, *Cuperemus quidem*, II. 4–5, PL 50, 433A/B.
[2] Ibid. I. 2, PL 50, 430–1. Cf. Cassian, *Inst.* I. 2, SC 109, 38–42, on ascetic dress.
[3] S. Pricoco, *L'isola dei santi: Il cenobio di Lerino e le origini del monachesimo gallico* (Rome, 1978) remains the best guide to Lérins. See also in this context, R. Nürnberg, *Askese als*

Theodosian Christians, who envisaged well-born ascetics like themselves at the vanguard of the new Christian imperial order.[4] Monastic
renunciation was no more or less than a more stringent and exacting
rendition of the *otium* in which the governing élite expected to indulge
between their exertions—*negotium*—on behalf of the state.[5] This was
a triumphalist asceticism, confident both of the divinely appointed
destiny of the Christian Empire, and of achieving spiritual perfection
on Lérins: the moral goals of the Lérinians were coterminous with
their political ambitions. They were, in other words, exactly the kind
of Christian Augustine had come profoundly to distrust, and it need
not surprise us to find loyal augustinians in southern Gaul writing to
their master in the late 420s, and also to the papal court, hoping to
bring down sanction upon these overweening ascetics.[6]

The Lérinians, however, were not the only face of the Gallic
monastic movement. Closely associated with them, and well known to
Pope Celestine, was John Cassian, an ascetic teacher who had gone
to great lengths to ensure that he could not be accused, like the
philanderer Daniel, of traducing the moral authority of his position.[7]
In his capacity as mentor to ascetics in southern Gaul, Cassian was as
fierce as any critic of the ascetic movement in his determination to
curb its tendency towards scandal. His response, however, was not to
distrust the ascetic project itself, but to make all the more exacting and
precise the means of assessing a person's integrity. Where Augustine
had come to doubt the possibility or value of achieving such a moral

---

*sozialer Impuls: Monastisch-asketische Spiritualität als Wurzel und Triebfeder sozialer Ideen und
Aktivitäten der Kirche in Sudgallien im 5. Jahrhundert* (Bonn, 1988); R. Mathisen,
Ecclesiastical Factionalism in Fifth-Century Gaul (Washington, DC, 1989); C. Leyser, '"This
Sainted Isle": Panegyric, Nostalgia, and the Invention of "Lérinian Monasticism"', in
Klingshirn and Vessey (eds.), *The Limits of Ancient Christianity*, 188–206.

[4] Pricoco, *Isola dei santi*, 223–44; id., 'Barbari, senso della fine e teologia politica: Su un
passo del De contemptu mundi di Eucherio di Lione', *Romano Barbarica* 2 (1977), 209–29.

[5] On *otium*, see J. M. André, *L'otium dans la vie morale et intellectuelle romaine* (Paris,
1966); Matthews, *Western Aristocracies*, 1–12; and on its possible Christian adaptation,
J. Fontaine, 'Valeurs antiques et valeurs chrétiennes dans la spiritualité des grands propriétaires terriens à la fin du IVe siècle occidental', in J. Fontaine and C. Kannengiesser (eds.),
Epektasis: mélanges J. Daniélou (Paris, 1972), 571–95. As J. Leclercq has shown, *otium*
acquires a pejorative sense in Cassian and thereafter: see his, '*Otia monastica: Études sur le
vocabulaire monastique du moyen-âge*, StAns 51 (1963).

[6] See PL 50, 528–30 for Celestine's response in 431 to the petition of Prosper and Hilary
against the 'new Pelagians' of southern Gaul. The Pope was reluctant to enter a discussion
of the technicalities of divine grace and predestination: as in 428 (above, n. 1), it was to the
proper exercise of episcopal authority that he directed attention.

[7] C. Stewart, *Cassian the Monk* (New York, 1998) is now the fundamental starting-point;
see also O. Chadwick, *John Cassian* (Cambridge, 1950; 2nd edn., 1968).

science, Cassian strove to establish secure grounds for the expert use of authority in the Church. His intervention was crucial in restoring public credibility to the ascetic movement.

Of Cassian's life and immediate circumstances, however, we know very little.[8] A contemporary of Augustine's, he was a priest who moved back and forth across the Mediterranean in the late fourth and early fifth centuries before taking up residence in Marseilles *c.*415.[9] Over the next decade or so, he composed for a broad and varied audience two works of ascetic instruction, the *Institutes* and the *Conferences*.[10] Here he depicts his former life as that of a wanderer (with an elder companion, Germanus[11]) among the desert communities of Egypt and Syria, petitioning the holy fathers to share with him the hard-earned fruits of their ascetic labours. As at least some of his readers would have known, however, Cassian's most important mentors were not the rustics of the desert. They were instead two of the key protagonists in the ecclesiastical feuds of the early fifth century: Evagrius of Pontus, the chief exponent of Origen in the East,[12] and John Chrysostom, the

[8] The only systematic 5th-cent. witness is Gennadius, *De vir. illust.* 52, ed. Richardson, TU 14, 82. For a summary of Cassian's career, based on a thorough marshalling of the primary evidence and secondary literature, see Stewart, *Cassian*, 3–19 and nn. 1–169. For debate, especially on the question of Cassian's origins, there is a whole literature from H. Marrou, 'La patrie de Jean Cassien', *Orientalia Christiana Periodica* 13 (1947), 588–96, to K. S. Frank, 'John Cassian on John Cassian', *Studia Patristica* 30 (1996), 418–33.

[9] Cassian seems to have been ordained a deacon at Constantinople by John Chrysostom, but the circumstances of his subsequent ordination to the priesthood (of which we know from Gennadius) are unclear; see Stewart, *Cassian*, 14 and n. 119. H. Marrou, 'Jean Cassien à Marseille', *RMAL* 1 (1945), 5–26, suggests that he was invited to Gaul by Lazarus of Aix, a disciple of Martin of Tours, after the council of Diospolis in 416, but Stewart, *Cassian*, 16 and n. 133, sounds a cautionary note.

[10] The twelve books of the *Institutes* are dedicated to Bishop Castor of Apt; the twenty-four *Conferences* are in three parts: the first ten are dedicated to Leontius, bishop of Fréjus (Castor's brother), and Helladius, a monk, soon to become a bishop (see *Conl.* 11. *Pref.*); the second set (*Conl.* 11–17) are dedicated to Honoratus and Eucherius, respectively abbot of the 'huge' monastery of Lérins, and Eucherius, an ascetic living with his wife and children on the island of Lero (both of these men were to become bishops, Honoratus in Cassian's lifetime). The third set (*Conl.* 18–24) are dedicated to a group of four monks living on the Iles d'Hyères and its neighbours—but see e.g. *Conl.* 18. 14, SC 64, 26–8, for consideration of the laity. For a survey of Cassian's contacts in Gaul, see P. Rousseau, 'Cassian: Monastery and World', in M. Fairburn and W. H. Oliver (eds.), *The Certainty of Doubt: Tributes to Peter Munz* (Wellington, New Zealand, 1995), 68–89.

[11] Germanus is attested as Cassian's companion by Palladius, *Dialogus de vita Iohannis Chrysostomi* 3, ed. A.-M. Malingrey and P. Leclercq, 2 vols., SC 341–2 (1988), i. 76. See Stewart, *Cassian*, 13–15.

[12] S. Marsili, *Giovanni Cassiano ed Evagrio Pontico*, StAns 5 (Rome, 1936), and H.-O. Weber, *Die Stellung des Johannes Cassianus zur ausserpachomischen Mönchstradition* (Münster, 1961) remain landmark studies, but require revision in light of subsequent discoveries about the Evagrian corpus. For an introduction to these, and for Evagrius and Origenism, see

deposed bishop of Constantinople.[13] From such masters, Cassian had learnt bitter lessons in the political and social tensions involved in ascetic claims to public attention. He settled in the West as a refugee from the storms that had engulfed both Evagrius and Chrysostom, and in the *Institutes* and *Conferences* there is barely a mention of Church politics,[14] but Cassian did not always trouble to keep his own head low. In 431, at the invitation of Archdeacon (soon to be pope) Leo, Cassian wrote a vehement refutation of the Christological teachings of Nestorius, patriarch of Constantinople.[15] In contrast to Augustine of Hippo—who had even been presumed dead by Nestorius' predecessor Atticus—John Cassian thus gained a reputation that was not so easily forgotten around the late Roman Mediterranean.[16]

Modern historiography usually hails Cassian as the messenger who brought 'the wisdom of the desert' to the West. In the *Institutes* and the *Conferences*, he is seen to have relayed to a Latin audience the teaching on the ascetic life that he himself had received at first hand from the desert fathers. The conventional account of the development of the western monastic tradition then sees Cassian's teachings themselves to have been definitively codified in the sixth-century *Rule of St Benedict*.[17] The explicit dependence of the *Rule* on Cassian has

E. Clark, *The Origenist Controversy* (Princeton, 1992), esp. pp. 43–84. Stewart, *Cassian, pass.*, sustains a commentary on the extent and the limits of Cassian's use of Evagrius (see esp. pp. 11–12, 36–7, 42–3, 90–4, 115–22).

[13] Cassian's first appearance in the historical record is as a loyal disciple of John Chrysostom at the moment of his deposition as bishop of Constantinople in 403: see Palladius (above, n. 11). Over twenty-five years later, Cassian himself explicitly acknowledged his discipleship to Chrysostom in his condemnation of his master's successor as patriarch of Constantinople, Nestorius. See *De Inc.* 7. 31. 3, CSEL 17, 390, and for a general assessment of the treatise in these terms, M.-A. Vannier, 'L'influence de Jean Chrysostome sur l'argumentation scripturaire du *De Incarnatione domini* de Jean Cassien', *RSR* 69 (1995), 453–62.

[14] The famous exception to this is the reference to the anthropomorphic controversy at *Conl.* 10. 3, SC 54, 76–8. As noted by Stewart, *Cassian*, 7–8, 10–12, this reference is extremely truncated and misleading.

[15] For the western context of Cassian's re-entry into Constantinopolitan politics, see E. Amann, 'L'Affaire Nestorius vue de Rome', *RSR* 23 (1949), 3–37, 207–44; 24 (1950), 28–52, 235–65, and J. Plagnieux, 'Le grief de complicité entre erreurs nestorienne et pélagienne: D'Augustin à Cassien par Prosper d'Aquitaine?', *REAug* 2 (1956), 391–402. Rousseau, *Ascetics, Authority, and the Church*, 227–31, and Stewart, *Cassian*, 96–7, suggest ways in which the treatise connects to the preoccupations of the *Institutes* and *Conferences*. (For a brief discussion and ample further references on the treatise, see Stewart, *Cassian* 22–4 and nn. 198–218).

[16] In our own era, the situation is, of course, reversed: the precise date of Cassian's death is unknown to us.

[17] See below, Ch. 5, for further discussion. Benedict, having drawn heavily on Cassian, in the conclusion to his *Rule*, refers interested readers back to Cassian's texts themselves: *RB* 723. 5, SC 182, 672. There has been much discussion as to whether Benedict is drawing

ensured his place in the canon of western spirituality, but it has also encouraged the assumption that the regular monastic tradition is an accurate guide to Cassian's intentions as an ascetic teacher. In particular, Cassian has been held to have anticipated Benedict in promoting the cenobitic life at the reluctant expense of the eremitic life of solitude.[18] As we shall see, however, the cenobitic interpretation of Cassian given in the *Rule of St Benedict* was only one among several readings of Cassian possible in the sixth-century West: neither Caesarius of Arles, nor Gregory the Great, for example, regarded Cassian as an exclusively 'monastic' writer. Cassian, it will be suggested here, did not regard himself as such: he took immense care not to restrict the meaning of his work to the monastery, or to any single institutional context.

More recently, study of Cassian has shifted away from his teaching on monastic institutions towards his analysis of ascetic purity. A tantalizing essay on Cassian's discussion of nocturnal emissions and their prevention—the outer limits of male celibacy—represents the last published section of Michel Foucault's unfinished *History of Sexuality*. Several scholars (including the present author) have subsequently been tempted to develop Foucault's approach to late Roman asceticism and to Cassian in particular.[19] This more recent work, however, often shares with traditional patristic scholarship the unnecessary assumption that Cassian wrote for cloistered male communities, and that he was more concerned with probing the depths of the psyche than with the outside world. To his contemporaries and to his readers in the fifth- and sixth-century West, however, Cassian was a figure of compelling moral authority on the widest public stage.

directly on Cassian, or indirectly via one of his sources. See e.g. A. de Vogüé, 'De Cassien au Maître et à Eugippe: le titre du chapitre de l'humilité', *StMon* 24 (1982), 247–61.

[18] See e.g. J. Leroy, 'Les Préfaces des écrits monastiques de Jean Cassien', *RAM* 42 (1966), 157–80, followed by the same author's 'Le Cénobitisme chez Cassien', *RAM* 43 (1967), 121–58; P. Rousseau, 'Cassian, Contemplation and the Cenobitic Life', *JEH* 26 (1975), 113–26; modified in id., *Ascetics, Authority, and the Church*, 177–83. Thus also Stewart, 31, who, while critical of the overly institutional approach of Leroy, none the less concludes that, in practice, 'Cassian's audience was probably almost entirely cenobitic from the outset, as it certainly was by the time of Benedict's recommendation of Cassian's writings'.

[19] M. Foucault, 'Le Combat de chasteté', *Communications* 35 (1982), 15–25; tr. in P. Ariès and A. Béjin (eds.), *Western Sexuality: Practice and Precept in Past and Present Times* (Oxford, 1985), 14–25. For a critique, see E. Clark, 'Foucault, the Fathers, and Sex', *JAAR* 56 (1988), 619–41. No less influential in this field has been A. Rousselle, *Porneia: De la maîtrise du corps à la privation sensorielle* (Paris, 1983), tr. F. Pheasant, *On Desire and the Body in Late Antiquity* (Oxford, 1988). See below, n. 67, for further references.

The benefits of living in a monastic community were, in fact, far from obvious to Cassian. In the *Conferences*, he lets it be known that his companion Germanus and he have both left their monastery in Palestine, and that, despite some qualms, they do not intend to return there.[20] Communal living on the pattern of the Jerusalem community of the sort that Augustine had so passionately endorsed was not for everyone in the Church, Cassian suggested. Where Augustine had seen in the monastery a place in which worldly differences could be resolved, Cassian was more impressed by the impossibility of living the ascetic life with others of differing spiritual abilities. The attempt to do so could actually accentuate tensions between Christians rather than resolving them.[21]

Ambivalent about the terms for true community, Cassian put his trust in a science of moral authority, 'the business of the Lord'.[22] The *Institutes* and the *Conferences* instructed readers in how to achieve spiritual purity—what they should wear, eat, or read, for example— and, more importantly, supplied them also with a system of analysis for publicly assessing their own moral progress. The pure in heart could be known in part through their bodies, which betrayed not even the trace of sexual desire, but still more significant was their speech, the oldest medium in the ancient world for the assessment of a person's moral worth. If heart was to speak to heart, Cassian suggested, it would not be because of community of property, but through the honing of the voice to a pitch of near perfection. This was precisely the kind of science Augustine had come to reject: whether conscious or not, the effect of Cassian's work was to make viable for western ascetics the ethical wisdom threatened by Augustine's renunciation of moral certainty. A discourse of expertise, Cassian suggested, would stand public surety for the behaviour of ascetics not hitherto known for their temperance. He laid before his Gallo-Roman readers the holy life as a process of education: it called for unremitting effort, promised only gradual progress, and carried the constant risk of immediate failure—but it conferred expertise of the sort that any educated person would have to acknowledge.[23] For asceticism, Cassian argued, like rhetoric or philosophy, partook of a Great Tradition.

[20] See in particular *Conl.* 17. 1–12, SC 54, 248–58.
[21] See the discussion below (pp. 56–8) of *Conl.* 16.
[22] *De Inc.* pref., CSEL 17, 235.
[23] On temperance and its political uses in the ancient world, see H. North, *Sophrosyne* (Ithaca, NY, 1966); and now Cooper, *The Virgin and the Bride*.

ASCETIC AMBITION IN FIFTH-CENTURY GAUL

If the drama of Cassian's intervention as an ascetic teacher in Gaul has escaped us, this is because we have not clearly understood why it was required. We have grown accustomed to picturing early fifth-century Gaul as the locale above all others where the monastic movement in the West first realized its cultural and political potential, in the shape of a brilliant generation of aristocratic monk–bishops and ascetic men of letters.[24] According to this widely accepted view, Christian monasticism readily answered the needs of ruling élites in Gaul to rethink and regroup, bewildered as they were by the barbarian incursions (starting with the crossing of the Rhine in the winter of 406–7) and the rending of imperial structures of government. In the context of the secular world's perceived disintegration, monk–bishops, above all from Lérins, showed how ascetic renunciation of the world could provide a new style of civic leadership. The barbarian invasion thus created the opportunity for 'the ascetic invasion',[25] as witnessed in a glittering array of sermons, panegyrics, treatises, and lives. The very ebullience of these Gallic texts, however, might lead us to suspect that ascetics were less than fully secure or unanimous in their seizure of political or cultural power.

Cassian is always included in the throng of 'invaders', but with little sense of his distinctiveness: both classic and more recent historiography has promoted the assumption that 'Provencale monasticism' spoke with one voice. The possibility that Cassian was out of sympathy with the ascetic company he kept in southern Gaul—in particular the

---

[24] See e.g. F. Prinz, *Frühes Mönchtum im Frankenreich: Kultur und Gesellschaft in Gallien, den Rheinländern und Bayern am Beispiel der monastischen Entwicklung (4. bis 8. Jahrhundert)* (Munich, 1965; 2nd edn., 1988); M. Heinzelmann, *Bischofsherrschaft in Gallien: Zur Kontinuität römischer Führungsgeschichten vom 4. bis zum 7. Jahrhundert*, Beihefte der Francia 5 (Munich, 1976); R. Van Dam, *Leadership and Community in Late Antique Gaul* (Berkeley/Los Angeles, 1985). On ascetics and their *litteratura*, see J. M. Vessey, 'Ideas of Christian Writing in Fifth-Century Gaul' (Oxford Univ. D. Phil. thesis, 1988), a study to which I owe much. For critiques of the received position that the ascetic takeover in Gaul was swift and unproblematic, see P. Brown, 'Relics and Social Status in the Age of Gregory of Tours', repr. in id., *Society and the Holy in Late Antiquity* (London, 1982), 223–50, especially at 246–7; J. Harries, 'Bishops, Senators and their Cities in Southern Gaul' (Oxford Univ. D. Phil. thesis, 1978), from which is descended ead., *Sidonius Apollinaris and the Fall of Rome* (Oxford, 1994); and now B. Jussen, 'Über "Bischofsherrschaften" und die Prozeduren politisch-sozialer Umordnung in Gallien zwischen "Antike" und "Mittelalter"', *HZ* 260 (1995), 673–718; id., 'Liturgie und Legitimation, oder Wie die Gallo-Romanen das römische Reich beendeten', in R. Blänkner and B. Jussen (eds.), *Institutionen und Ereignis: Über historische Praktiken und Vorstellungen gesellschaftlichen Ordnens* (Göttingen, 1998), 75–136.
[25] The phrase is Robert Markus's; see *End of Ancient Christianity*, 199 ff.

Lérinians—has not been widely considered.[26] In a traditional, theo-
logically-driven, perspective, the ascetics of Provence are ranged
against Augustine and his disciples in Gaul, notably Prosper of
Aquitaine, in the 'semi-Pelagian controversy'.[27] Scholars have presumed Cassian to be the ringleader of the unnamed 'servants of Christ
at Marseilles' referred to by Prosper as dissenting from Augustine's
increasingly articulate stance on predestination.[28] Cassian's thirteenth
Conference, which considers the interaction of grace and free will in
human salvation, has been read since the seventeenth century as a
response to Augustine's *On correction and grace*, and as the founding
charter for 'semi-Pelagianism' . Over the past two generations, however, the broad critique of this kind of history of dogma has gone hand
in hand with a more accurate understanding of Cassian's purpose in
writing this *Conference*. It is now largely agreed that Cassian was quite
as concerned as Augustine and his disciples by the persistence of
Pelagian error, and wrote *Conference* 13 to contribute to a papally-
sponsored campaign to affirm orthodoxy in southern Gaul.[29] To speak
of a tradition of 'monastic semi-Pelagianism' will lead us no closer
to understanding relations between Augustine, Cassian, and the
Lérinians—which is not to say we need lose sight altogether of
Prosper's disquiet at the activities of ascetics in Marseilles.

---

[26] See, however, Stewart, *Cassian*, 17 and esp. 28, developing the observation of A. de
Vogüé, *Césaire d'Arles: Oeuvres Monastiques*, i. 114–17, that Cassian was critical of Lérinian
liturgical practice.

[27] For a classic survey in these terms, see É. Amann, 'Semi-pélagiens', art. *DTC*, 14, 2,
1796–1850; and now R. Weaver, *Divine Grace and Human Agency: A Study of the Semi-
Pelagian Controversy* (Macon, Ga., 1996). Revisionist accounts include R. A. Markus, 'The
Legacy of Pelagius: Orthodoxy, Heresy and Conciliation', in R. Williams (ed.), *The Making
of Orthodoxy* (Cambridge, 1989), 214–34; and T. Smith, *'De Gratia': Faustus of Riez's
Treatise on Grace and Its Place in the History of Theology* (Notre Dame, 1990); Vessey, *'Opus
imperfectum'*; C. Leyser, 'Semi-Pelagianism', in A. Fitzgerald (ed.), *Augustine through the
Ages: An Encyclopedia* (Grand Rapids, Mich., 1999), 761–6.

[28] Augustine, *Ep.* 225. 2, CSEL 57, 455.

[29] Markus, *End of Ancient Christianity*, 177–9, where it is suggested that Cassian's
rebuttal in the Conference followed from papal condemnation of Pelagian views in 425. So
also Stewart, *Cassian*, 18 n. 161; the same author (19–22 and 76–81) judiciously insists upon
interpreting the thirteenth Conference in the context of the discussion of sexual purity
initiated by Cassian in the previous Conference. Other contexts for Cassian's knowledge of
Augustine are proposed by A. de Vogüé, 'Les Sources des quatres premiers livres
des Institutions de Jean Cassien: Introduction aux recherches sur les anciennes règles
monastiques latines', *StudMon* 27 (1985), 241–311, and B. Ramsey, 'John Cassian: Student
of Augustine', *Cistercian Studies Quarterly* 28 (1993), 5–15. However, J. Fleming, 'By
Coincidence or Design: Cassian's Disagreement with Augustine Concerning the Ethics of
Falsehood', *AugStud* 29 (1998), 19–34, suggests that *Conference* 17 picks an argument with
Augustine.

A more recent view of Cassian and his environment contrasts southern with northern Gallic monasticism. The province of Gaul is seen to have been divided between, on the one hand, the monastic culture associated with Tours and the cult of St Martin, and on the other the 'Rhone monasticism' emanating from the island of Lérins, of which Cassian is figured as a prominent but by no means unique representative.[30] Touraine monasticism is perceived to have taken its character from the Pannonian soldier turned monk–bishop, St Martin (d. 397): a rough-hewn asceticism, relying on charismatic displays of miraculous power. By contrast 'Rhone monasticism' is seen as smoothly organized, both institutionally and rhetorically sophisticated in character.[31] The two monastic cultures are seen as operating in quite separate spheres of emphasis, until the arrival, in the late sixth century, of a third party in the shape of Columbanus.

In its concern, perhaps, to offer a coherent alternative to the history of dogma, this view substitutes a clarity of cultural as against theological definition. Whether or not such a strongly-drawn contrast between Tours and Lérins is viable later on, it is surely premature so to characterize the highly volatile situation of the early decades of the fifth century. We have too little information about the regimes of monastic observance in either the north or the south. Although much effort has been expended on identifying 'the Rule of Lérins', the results have not have not proved entirely convincing.[32] The same is

[30] See Prinz, *Frühes Mönchtum*, esp. pp. 449–84. This monumental account has become standard: see e.g. Klingshirn, *Caesarius of Arles*, 3. Cautions were early expressed, however: see J. M. Wallace-Hadrill's review of *Frühes Mönchtum*, *EHR* 83 (1968), 370–1, on the limitations of Prinz's 'cartographical approach'. Less polarized approaches have long been available: see e.g. J. Fontaine, 'L'Ascétisme chrétien dans la littérature gallo-romaine d'Hilaire à Cassien', in *La Gallia Romana*, Accademia Nazionale del Lincei 153 (1973), 87–115; and I. Wood, 'Avitus of Vienne' (Oxford Univ. D. Phil. thesis, 1975). S. Loseby, 'Marseille and the Pirenne Thesis, I: Gregory of Tours, the Merovingian Kings and "Un grand port"', in R. Hodges and W. Bowden (eds.), *The Sixth Century: Production, Distribution and Demand* (Leiden, 1998), 203–29, demonstrates the abiding importance of Marseilles to the Merovingians, a point to be born in mind in the discussion of the 'Tours/Lérins' dichotomy.

[31] Thus the contrast is an archetypal one, between 'shaggy' and 'smooth' cultural styles; see Gen. 26: 25–34 on Esau and Jacob, and M. Douglas, *Natural Symbols: Explorations in Cosmology* (London, 1970), 102.

[32] See Pricoco, *Isola*, 77–91, on the poverty of the Lérinian sources in this context, and on the unlikelihood of there being a 'Rule of Lérins' before 450. A. de Vogüé has subsequently argued that the anonymous *Rule of the Four Fathers* and the *Second Rule of the Fathers* are the work of the early Lérinians. See his *Les Règles des saints Pères*, 2 vols., SC 297–8 (1982). The identification is, however, circumstantial and not universally accepted: see M. Carrias, 'Vie monastique et règle à Lérins au temps d'Honorat', *RHEF* 74 (1988), 191–211; S. Pricoco, 'Il primo monachesimo in Occidente: Alcune considerazioni su un dibattito attuale', *Studi e*

true for Marseilles: all we know (from a late fifth-century witness) is that Cassian founded two communities in the city, one for men and one for women.[33] The male community is traditionally identified with that of St Victor at Marseilles, but secure evidence for this identification dates no further back than the eleventh century, at which point the monks of the refounded community of St Victor's were keen to claim descent from Cassian's foundation: in our period, however, the presumption that either the male or the female monastery founded by Cassian enjoyed a continuous history is based on the rarely punctuated silence of the historical record. Nothing at all is known about the organization of these communities or their reception of Cassian's writings.[34]

Ascetics in early fifth-century Gaul were both more united and more divided than the 'Marseilles/Hippo' or the 'Tours/Lérins' dichotomies would allow: their situation was more chaotic than we conventionally assume. The collapse of secular government in Gaul invited bids for power from an assortment of Roman generals. In the mêlée of coup and counter-coup, prominent ascetics were at one and the same time accused of dereliction of civic duty, and of flattering the tyrants who had seized office.[35] It was in the interests of all ascetics to support each other, as they worked out strategies for the survival of their movement.[36] This is not to say, however, that they enjoyed unbounded solidarity: rivalries between, or within, local centres could

---

ricerche sull'oriente cristiano XV (1992), 25–37. See below, Ch. 4, for the question of whether it is possible to identify the 'Rule of Lérins' at the time that Caesarius was there.

[33] Gennadius, *De viris illustribus* c. 62, TU 14, 82.

[34] There is little basis for the assumption that either the male or female community at Marseilles functioned as venues for the implementation of Cassian's teachings, certainly not after his lifetime. The evidence for the survival of these monasteries is inconclusive. Caesarius of Arles sent his sister to a convent at Marseilles (*Vita Caesarii* 35, MGH SRM 3, 470, and see below, Ch. 4); and Gregory the Great attempted to protect the nunnery of St Cassian (Gregory, *Ep.* VII. 12, CCSL 140, 461). It is possible, although by no means certain, that this is the same community as that founded by Cassian. See S. Loseby, 'Marseille in Late Antiquity and the Early Middle Ages' (Oxford Univ. D. Phil. thesis, 1993), 138 ff. For a more traditional assertion of the link between Cassian and the male community of St Victor at Marseille, refounded in the 11th cent., see J.-C. Moulinier, *Saint-Victor de Marseille: les récits de sa passion*, Studi di Antichità Cristiana 49 (Vatican City, 1993), 385–405, esp. 390; and P. Amargier, *Un Âge d'or du monachisme: Saint Victor de Marseille (990–1090)* (Marseilles, 1990). My thanks to Simon Loseby for his advice on this point.

[35] See Pope Zosimus, *Epp.* 1–7, CSEL 35, 103–108, and the account of Mathisen, *Factionalism*, 27–74.

[36] See e.g. Heros of Arles, a disciple of Martin of Tours, who made his way south after Martin's death to join the circle of Proculus, as witnessed by Prosper of Aquitaine, *Chronicon*, MGH AA IX, 466; and noted by Prinz, *Frühes Mönchtum*, 112–13.

flare all the more intensely because of the threat of extinction. As I have argued elsewhere, the early Lérinians were by no means a unified group: thrown into bewilderment by their success in capturing control of key sees in southern Gaul, they were apt to wrangle bitterly among themselves.[37] The force of Cassian's writings—his injunctions against anger and vanity for example—will not be apparent unless we bear this fissiparous, polemically charged context in mind.[38]

This is nowhere more apparent than in Marseilles. In the letter of admonition with which we began, Pope Celestine singled out for condemnation the bishop of Marseilles. Although not named, this is likely to have been Proculus, Cassian's patron and the unofficial leader of the ascetic party in Gaul over the past generation.[39] Proculus' role in this latter capacity merits further study: it is clear that his reputation and connections spanned the length and breadth of the Mediterranean.[40] But the man was also notorious. In 426, his great rival Patroclus of Arles had been assassinated: the bishop of Marseilles was said to have 'rejoiced so much at the death of his brother that he rushed to meet one who arrived spattered with his blood in order to share it with him'.[41] The Pope commanded an investigation into his shameful conduct. If the story was true, then Cassian will surely have shared with Prosper of Aquitaine, his theological opponent, a grave concern about the servants of Christ living at Marseilles.

It was in an effort to persuade local ascetics to temper their zeal that

[37] See Leyser, '"This Sainted Isle"', 188–201.

[38] See e.g. *Inst.* 8, SC 109, 334–66; *Conl.* 16. 6–7, SC 54, 227–30 on anger; *Inst.* 11, SC 109, 426–46 on vanity.

[39] No writings and no *Life* of Proculus are known to have existed. His sole surviving monument may be the remains of the magnificent baptistery and episcopal complex excavated on the north side of the port at Marseilles. See Loseby, 'Marseille in Late Antiquity and the Early Middle Ages', p. 126ff. The same author's 'Marseille: A Late Antique Success Story', *JRS* 82 (1992), 165–85, gives an account of the Christian life of the city in which Cassian is refreshingly incidental: Proculus takes centre stage.

[40] From his home in Bethlehem, Jerome did not hesitate to recommend the bishop of Marseilles as the man to whom young ascetics in southern Gaul should turn for guidance. Jerome, *Ep.* 125. 20, ed. J. Labourt, 7 vols. (Paris, 1949–63), vi. 133. See also H. Crouzel, 'Jerôme et ses amis toulousains', *BLittEcc* 73 (1972), 125–47. The connection between Jerome and Proculus may not have been altogether comfortable for Cassian. Although paying tribute to Jerome (*De viris illustribus*, 8, 11, PL 23, 654A–B, 658B–659B), Cassian had cause to distrust him for his role in the condemnation of Origenism, and of his teacher Evagrius. See now S. Driver, 'From Palestinian Ignorance to Egyptian Wisdom: Cassian's Challenge to Jerome's Monastic Teaching', *ABR* 48 (1997), 293–315.

[41] *Cuperemus quidem* 10, PL 50, 435C–436A: 'Massiliensis vero ecclesiae sacerdotem, qui dicitur, quod dictu nefas est, in necem fratris taliter gratulatus, ut huic qui eius sanguine cruentus advenerat, portionem cum eodem habiturus occurreret.'

Cassian first resolved to leave the 'harbour of silence'.[42] In the preface to his first work, the *Institutes*, he warns his dedicatee, Bishop Castor of Apt, that he will be no flatterer of his patrons: 'I do not believe that a recent foundation could have found in the Gallic West observances more perfect than those to which the holy and spiritual fathers have remained faithful since the start of the apostolic mission'.[43] Cassian's first move was to present himself as the critical expert. He consistently argued that ascetics could not simply improvise their lives as they pleased. Spiritual discipline was an acquired technique, and Cassian named the places where it was best learned—Egypt and Syria, deriving in turn from the apostolic community of Christians at Jerusalem.

This was an initial line of defence, giving Cassian room to manoeuvre in a way that seemed relatively impartial. A stringent critique of all Gallic monasticism (not just that of the North) meant that he would not be seen to favour Castor's monastery over, say, Lérins. Another means of achieving a similar effect was to co-opt his readers into sharing the premise of Egyptian superiority. In 427, as he dedicated his second set of *Conferences* to the Lérinians Honoratus and Eucherius, Cassian presumed their assent to his own perspective:

You, O holy brothers Honoratus and Eucherius, are so stirred by the great glory of these splendid men from whom we received the first principles of the anchoritic life, that one of you, presiding as he does over a large monastery of the brethren, is hoping that his congregation . . . may be instructed in the precepts of these fathers, while the other has been anxious to make his way to Egypt to be edified by the sight of them in the flesh.

Cassian imagined that Eucherius would take wing 'like some pure turtle dove', leaving behind the icy chill of Gaul, to head for the land 'on which the sun of righteousness looks, and which abounds in the ripe fruits of virtues'.[44] Eucherius, however, in what it is tempting to read as a direct reply to Cassian, did not stint in his promotion of Lérins as a site of ascetic living to rival those of the East.[45]

---

[42] *Conl.* 1, pref., SC 42, 75; also *De Inc.* pref., CSEL 17, 235.

[43] *Inst.* pref. 8, SC 109, 30.

[44] *Conl.* 11, pref., SC 54, 98. Honoratus is the cenobitic leader, Eucherius the recluse.

[45] See Eucherius, *De laude eremi* 42, ed. S. Pricoco (Catania, 1965), 75–7, and for further discussion, Leyser, ' "This sainted isle" ', 195–6. It is possible also that a rivalry existed also between Proculus of Marseilles and Leontius of Fréjus as rival patrons of Cassian and of the Lérinians: according to Honoratus' disciple Hilary, Proculus had failed to attract Honoratus to stay in Marseilles, and he had eventually gone to Lérins (Hilary, *Sermo de vita sancti Honorati* 13. 1, SC 235, 102–4).

Cassian's point was not to initiate a competition between holy sites of Egypt and Gaul, however. The significance of the desert for Cassian lay in its being the only place where authentic apostolic living still persisted. Seeking to make explicit the connection between his own experience of the desert in the East with the life of the earliest Christians, Cassian turned, like Augustine, to the text of Acts of the Apostles. Eusebius of Caesarea had long ago suggested that monks were direct descendants of the Jerusalem community.[46] Briefly in the *Institutes*, and at greater length in the *Conferences*, Cassian rearticulated this version of monastic history.

The system of cenobites arose at the time when the apostles were preaching. The crowd of believers in Jerusalem were of this sort, as it is described in the Acts of the Apostles: 'The multitude of believers were of one heart and one soul, neither said any of them that any of the things which he possessed was his own, but they had all things in common'. The whole Church lived then as the cenobites lived; they are now so few that it is difficult to find them.[47]

For Cassian, this was a story about the onset of *tepor*, initial fervour growing lukewarm.[48] The decline in standards began when the leaders of the Jerusalem community offered concessions to gentile converts, and then adopted these less exacting standards themselves. The fervent few who faithfully preserved the original pattern of the community were forced to leave the city, and live in the desert: 'Marked out from most of the faithful by their celibacy and their separation from relatives, they came to be known as *monachi*, or *monazontes*, because they led a disciplined life alone'.[49] This account turned the flight into the desert upside down. It was not ascetics, but the rest of the community, who had split off and moved away in the more important, spiritual sense. *Monachi* could claim a virtual monopoly of the apostolic life. The deserts of Egypt and Syria were the only place

---

[46] Eusebius, *Historia Ecclesiastica* II. 16–17, II. 24; itself an adaptation of Philo, *De vita contemplativa* 13, 18–25. Eusebius' account is followed in turn by Jerome, *De viris illustribus* 8, 11. My thanks to Derek Krueger for his advice on this point.

[47] *Conl.* 18. 5, SC 64, 14–15. Cf. *Inst.* 2. 5. 1–3, SC 109, 64–6. These two passages are much discussed. See e.g. A. de Vogüé, 'Monachisme et Église dans la pensée de Cassien', *Théologie de la Vie Monastique*, 213–40, and id., 'Les Sources des quatres premiers livres des Institutions de Jean Cassien', *StudMon* 27 (1985), 241–311, esp. 268–72, both noting the differences between the *Institutes* and the *Conferences* in their accounts of the origins of monasticism. See also Rousseau, *Ascetics, Authority and the Church*, 200–5; Markus, *End of Ancient Christianity*, 165–8.

[48] S. Pricoco, '*Tepidum monachorum genus* (Cassian., *conl.* 18. 4. 2)', *Scritti classici e cristiani offerta a Francesco Corsaro* (Catania, 1994), 563–73.

[49] *Conl.* 18. 5, SC 64, 15–16.

where Jerusalem *communitas* still existed. Cassian's reading of Acts 4 was thus the basis for a monastic genealogy. The cenobites, he continued, gave rise to the 'eremites', as the flower is followed by the fruit.[50] (Where this left the rest of the faithful Cassian did not here explain.)

In sketching an apostolic genealogy for contemporary monasticism in the deserts of the East, Cassian's purpose was not to incite his readers to travel there. On the contrary, he wished to enable western ascetics to stay where they were—in the 'icy chill' of their surroundings—by offering to initiate them in the lore of ascetic sanctity.[51] His account of the Jerusalem community offered his readers a commentary on that of Augustine, and an alternative conception of the apostolic life (whether or not this dialogue with Augustine was exactly Cassian's intention).[52] To both men, the memory of the apostolic Jerusalem served as a reminder that, whatever the romance generated by Antony and the elders of the desert, it was not in fact necessary to seek out the wilderness in order to lead a Christian life. The city could serve as an equally enchanted venue: as the truly committed would know, the question of site was unimportant for serious ascetic purposes. In strong contrast to Augustine, however, Cassian did not necessarily propose the Jerusalem community as a living model for ascetic community in the present. He was relatively uninterested in the ways in which community of property might set up community of hearts and minds (and tended to refer more to Matthew 19: 22 on the renunciation of property than to Acts 4 on its sharing). The giving up of material possessions was only a preliminary gesture in the work of driving out avarice, and the other vices, from the soul. For Cassian, in short, the Jerusalem community was less an anticipation of the future community of the blessed than a point of reference in a history of ascetic expertise.

If a replica of the Jerusalem community was not Cassian's ultimate goal as an ascetic teacher then neither was his immediate concern the speaking of heart to heart. No one could hope to experience such transparency in relationship with another unless they had first purified their own soul, Cassian argued. For him, charity necessarily began as

---

[50] *Conl.* 18. 6, 17.

[51] The importance of this point for the expansion of monasticism in the cities of Gaul is well brought out by C. Courtois, 'L'Évolution du monachisme en Gaule de St Martin à St Columban', *Settimane* IV, 47–72, at 58.

[52] See above, Ch. 1, n. 102, and Markus, *End of Ancient Christianity*, 165–8.

self-scrutiny, prior to any genuine social interaction or contemplation of God. Where Augustine had looked to the ways in which humans might relate to each other, across differences of class in particular, Cassian looked at how a man might resolve his interior differences, and at the stages of moral progress he might attain. His focus was on the individual in his struggle with the vices considered abstractly, not on how 'the rich' and 'the poor' or 'the weak' and 'the strong' might co-exist.[53] If, for the bishop of Hippo, asceticism without charity was meaningless, for Cassian the equation was at least partially reversed: charity without asceticism was, if not without meaning, at best merely adequate, or lukewarm. A community made up of ascetics of differing levels of moral achievement could not hope to function effectively. The ascetic life properly executed, however, was a life of fervent communion with God and with fellow Christians: this was the life that Cassian sought to offer his readers.[54]

MASTERY OF THE MIND

From the moment he began to write in Gaul, Cassian had in mind the terrain he intended to cover. His exposition, however, like his journeys around the Nile delta, takes a meandering course. 'He was partial to schemata, though he was not a systematic thinker', as his most recent commentator has acutely remarked.[55] According to (one of) Cassian's own designs, his first text, the *Institutes*, deals with the outer man—what he should eat, sleep, wear—before moving to an inventory of the stages of temptation that the inner man had to surmount. The *Conferences* cross and recross much of this same interior ground, while expanding its frontiers in its discussions of the reading of Scripture to promote interior stability and wordless prayer.[56] In making their way across his work, modern students of Cassian are, perhaps, bound to alight on his analysis of what would become 'the deadly sins': for his earliest readers, however, it was the moral and spiritual language

---

[53] e.g. the interior reading of Ps. 132: 1 in *Conl.* 12. 11, SC 54, 138. Cassian takes the verse—'How good and pleasant it is for brethren to dwell together as one'—to refer to the harmony of the well-trained body and soul.

[54] Stewart, *Cassian*, 43–4, on the relation between purity of heart and charity.

[55] Stewart, *Cassian*, 37. Exactly the same could be said of Gregory the Great: see below, Ch. 7.

[56] Stewart, *Cassian*, 29–39, gives a helpful overview of Cassian's programme in the *Institutes* and *Conferences*.

Cassian provided—more, perhaps, than any single system—that held their attention.[57]

The force of Cassian's arguments lay not in novelty, but in their profound adherence to traditional moral philosophy. Cassian's immediate point of reference was his teacher Evagrius: the hierarchy of the eight sins, the idea that the most advanced form of temptation was interior, the problem of the restless energy of the mind—all of these Cassian reworked from his master's Greek into Latin, sometimes ostentatiously reminding his western audience of his bilingualism.[58] In the longer perspective, what Evagrius passed on to his pupil was the wisdom of the Christian Platonic tradition, which looked to Origen as its founding father.[59] This tradition in turn was framed in dialogue with pagan moral philosophy. To an educated Classical reader, the ideals of passionlessness and of stability which Cassian described as the preliminary to the contemplative life would have been familiar from the works of Cicero, or from any of the philosophical handbooks in wide circulation.[60] In *Conference* 14, to which we turn in a moment, Cassian, using himself as a model, insisted that the Christian reader block out the various 'fables' that he has learnt as a child, but this rejection of the contents of the Classical literary tradition coexisted—in Cassian as in so many other late Roman Christian intellectuals—with an equally strong appropriation of its moral goals.[61]

Cassian's attention was dominated by what he saw as the first stage of the process of spiritual cleansing: the expurgation of sin. This he

[57] For the medieval future of Cassian's typology of sin, see the classic M. Bloomfield, *The Seven Deadly Sins: An Introduction to the History of a Religious Concept, with Special Reference to Medieval English Literature* (East Lansing, Mich., 1952); L. K. Little, 'Pride goes before Avarice: Social Change and the Vices in Latin Christendom', *AHR* 76 (1971), 16–49; and more recently, R. Newhauser, 'Towards modus in habendo: Transformations in the Idea of Avarice. The Early Penitentials through the Carolingian Reforms', *ZSSR* CVI, *Kan. Abt.* 75 (1989), 1–22; id., *The Treatise on Vices and Virtues in Latin and the Vernacular*, Typologie des Sources du Moyen Age Occidental 68 (Turnhout, 1993).

[58] Cf. *Conl.* 7. 4, SC 54, 248, for a display of Greek learning by Cassian. See C. Stewart, 'From λόγος to *verbum*: John Cassian's Use of Greek in the Development of a Latin Monastic Vocabulary', in E. R. Elder (ed.), *The Joy of Learning and the Love of God: Studies in Honor of Jean Leclercq* (Kalamazoo, Mich., 1995), 5–31.

[59] On Origen in this context, see H. Crouzel, *Origène et la "connaissance mystique"* (Toulouse, 1961); Stewart, *Cassian*, 35–7, 44, 99.

[60] M. Colish, *The Stoic Tradition from Antiquity to the Early Middle Ages*, ii. 114–22. P. Courcelle, *Late Latin Writers and their Greek Sources*, 228–9, and see below n. 73.

[61] *Conl.* 14. 10. 12, SC 54, 199, for Cassian's fables. On the theme in general, see A. Cameron, 'Paganism and Literature in Late Fourth Century Rome', in *Christianisme et Formes Littéraires de l'Antiquité Tardive en Occident*, Fondation Hardt pour l'Étude de l'Antiquité Classique, Entretiens XXII (Geneva, 1977), 1–30.

called the 'active' or the 'practical' life, following the standard philosophical distinction between *praxis* and *theoria*, or contemplation.[62] The whole of the *Institutes* and the bulk of the *Conferences* were essentially structured as a series of 'practical' discourses on how to avoid temptation. It was simple enough for an ascetic enthusiast to make the outward gestures of holiness; what fascinated Cassian was the inward disposition of the mind. In the first *Conference*, he stressed: 'You do not attain the perfect life simply by throwing away your money or your rank. There must go with it that charity which the apostle Paul described, consisting in purity of heart alone.'[63] The achievement of purity—here coterminous with charity—involved the subduing of the passions and the abandonment of self-will. It was not the retreat into the desert, but the gaze into one's own soul which marked the beginning of a relentless struggle against the array of diabolic temptations that threatened to pollute it.

In the *Institutes*, having described the patterns of observance in the desert—details of dress and liturgy, or entry procedures, for example (Books 1–4)—Cassian then turned to the interior disposition of the ascetic. In a further eight books, he treated each of the eight sins that were likely to beset the soul. The sequence went from the most basic (gluttony) to the most advanced (pride), implying the possibility of gradual and cumulative progress. If the ascetic were to eliminate gluttony, that would reduce his susceptibility to lust; he could then move to eliminate avarice, anger, melancholy, *ennui*, and vain glory. The final challenge was pride: the more the ascetic advanced, the more likely he was to succumb to pride in his own achievements (or envy of another's)—and all would be lost.[64]

Here, again, Cassian set himself against Augustine, in proposing that a man could systematically improve his moral condition through ascetic labour. Where Augustine had identified the sin of Adam and

---

[62] From an extensive literature, see A. Guillaumont and C. Guillaumont, *Evagre le Pontique: Traité pratique ou le moine*, 2 vols., SC 170–1 (1963), 38–53, for an overview of ancient thought on the active and contemplative lives. For Cassian's reception and use of these traditions, see M. Olphe-Gaillard, 'Vie contemplative et vie active d'après Cassien', *RAM* 16 (1935), 252–88; Markus, *End of Ancient Christianity*, 184–7; Stewart, *Cassian*, 47–61.

[63] *Conl.* 1. 6, SC 42, 84, referring to 1 Cor 13: 3 ff. Cf. ibid. 2. 2. The ascetic may fast, pray, and give alms, but none of these will preserve him from diabolical deception. On purity of heart, see M. Olphe-Gaillard, 'La Pureté de coeur d'après Cassien', *RAM* 17 (1936), 28–60; Stewart, 42–7.

[64] *Inst.* 12. 2–3, 15, SC 109, 452, 470. Cassian on the vices is, intentionally, an aspect not covered by Stewart (see *Cassian*, p. vii). See below, Ch. 7, for Gregory the Great's reception of Cassian's list.

Eve as pride—gluttony or lust being mere consequences of their disastrous bid for autonomy from their creator—Cassian argued that it was, in fact, the desire to eat of the fruit which caused the Fall.[65] In locating original sin in physical desire, and in outlining a programme to track down and to eliminate desire in the body and then in the mind, Cassian's account departed from the basic premises of the *City of God*. The advantages of this analysis were not lost on Cassian's ascetic readers. Where Augustine had argued that to discipline the body was epiphenomenal to the deep flaw in the soul, Cassian now affirmed the conventional wisdom that, through regulation of his diet in particular, the ascetic could hope to alter the balance of his body's humours, thus 'chemically' reducing his vulnerability to desire.[66] In the opening books of the *Institutes*, Cassian expounded a reassuringly scrupulous regime of fasting, prayer, and reading designed to prevent the body from leading the soul astray.

An especial test was the battle against the sin of fornication.[67] Unlike gluttony, this was a temptation completely to be eliminated (some desire for food being necessary), and Cassian organized much of his analysis of moral purification around this theme. Victory over the spirit of fornication involved far more than mere abstention from sexual intercourse or from masturbation: the man seeking purity should track down sexual desire to its lair in the mind. His success in so doing could be indexed in the manner in which he emitted semen during the night. A man who seemed, in the daytime, to present the

[65] *Conl.* 5. 4, SC 54, 191.

[66] Compare *Conl.* 4. 10–11, SC 42, 174–6, with *Civ.Dei* XIV. 1–3, CCSL 48, 414–17, on conceptions of mind and body. From a survey of its uses in Scripture, Augustine in the *City of God* had decided that 'the flesh' connotes the whole person by synechdoche. To live 'according to the flesh' is thus not simply to indulge in bodily pleasures: the 'vices of the soul' are also involved. In a parallel discussion about the meanings of 'the flesh' in Scripture, Cassian had specifically rejected Augustine's reading. However, while refusing to understand by 'flesh' the whole person, Cassian does not follow the opposite course of equating 'flesh' with 'body'. He offers instead a looser definition of a 'will of the flesh, and the worst kinds of desires'. A 'carnal' nexus of will and desire implicates both body and soul in the production of sin. Only ascetic technology can liberate body and soul from their perceived subjection to 'the flesh'.

[67] Cassian's discussion of fornication begins at *Inst.* 6; it continues in *Conl.* 12 and 13; and concludes at *Conl.* 22 (*de nocturnis inlusionibus*). It has received extensive recent discussion, much of it inspired by Foucault, 'Combat de chasteté'. See e.g. Brown, *Body and Society*, 218–24; D. Brakke, 'The Problematization of Nocturnal Emissions in Early Christian Syria, Egypt, and Gaul', *JECS* 3 (1995), 419–60; Stewart, *Cassian*, 62–84 (see, in particular, n. 91). C. Leyser, 'Masculinity in Flux: Nocturnal Emission and the Limits of Celibacy in the Early Middle Ages', in D. Hadley (ed.), *Masculinity in Medieval Europe* (Harlow, 1999), 103–20, develops at greater length the argument presented here. See below, Chs. 3 and 8, for the reception of Cassian on *fluxus* by Pomerius and Gregory the Great.

outward signs of holiness, could, through nocturnal emission, betray the real contents of his heart. Reducing nocturnal emission to a physiological minimum, if not eliminating it altogether, became for Cassian the ultimate ascetic challenge—and provided his readers with a graphic means by which to measure their moral progress.

How could the ascetic eliminate even the thought of fornication?[68] Cassian implied that such control was indeed possible—but it is not until the *Conferences* that his thinking on this question is entirely clear. It was in their reading that ascetics could attain to mental purity, he came to argue. If regulating diet could protect the body from sinful excess, then precisely organized consumption of text could surely immunize the mind from diabolic attack. This was an idea fundamental in Evagrius, but Cassian found his own vivid imagery in which to expound it.[69] In the first *Conference*, a dialogue with Abba Moses, the full logic of this method becomes apparent. Cassian's companion Germanus put to Abba Moses the question:

How do you explain that, against our own will, and what is more even without our knowledge, superfluous thoughts creep into our minds, arriving by subtle and secret routes? It becomes no small task to spot them and pin them down, let alone to expel them. Can the mind ever be free of these distractions, or be rid of their intrusion?[70]

Moses replies that the mind will always suffer the invasive onrush of thought:

The churning of the mind is not unlike the movement of millstones: water rushes round a channel, powering them around and around. In fact millstones cannot stop turning, ceaselessly driven as they are by the force of the water.[71]

In this life, the human mind is bludgeoned around, under relentless pressure from a torrent of thoughts, whirling under possible temptation. This was a given for Cassian: the motion of the mind could not

---

[68] See e.g. *Inst.* 6. 1, SC 109, 262; ibid. 6. 20, 284.

[69] On Evagrius in this context, see M. O'Laughlin, 'The Bible, the Demons, and the Desert: Evaluating the *Antirrheticus* of Evagrius Pontus', *StMon* 34 (1992), 201–15. On this theme in the desert more broadly, see D. Burton Christie, *The Word in the Desert: Scripture and the Quest for Holiness in Early Christian Monasticism* (New York, 1993), 122–9. For an early 5th-cent. western parallel to Cassian, see G. Morin, 'Pages inédites de deux pseudo-jérômes de l'environ l'an 400', *RBen* 40 (1928), 293–302, at 298. The female addressee of the letter *Quamlibet sciam* is urged: 'sicque clausa sit ianua arcae ex obliquo facta, id est, aurium tuarum introitus vel egressus, ut ne modica quidem ex fabulis saecularium, quae sunt velut aqua decurrens in diversa ad penetralia cordis tui stilla perveniat.'

[70] *Conl.* 1. 16, SC 42, 98. Cf. Caesarius of Arles, *Sermones* I. 3, CCSL 103, 2–4.

[71] *Conl.* 1. 18, SC 42, 99. Cf. *Caes.Serm.* 8. 4, CCSL 103, 44, discussed below, Ch. 4.

be stopped, it could only be exploited to the advantage of the ascetic.[72] In terms of the metaphor of the mill, the man in charge of the mill could decide what he wanted to grind, be it grain, barley, or tares: 'It is largely for us to raise the tone of our mental activity.'[73]

The reading and praying of Scripture thus took on its especial importance for Cassian.[74] If ascetics were engaged in poring over the sacred text, then they would supply grist to the psychic mill. Grinding the Scriptures would bring the mind to recall its desire for perfection and hope for the blessed life to come: in this way, ascetics could sustain purity of heart. On the other hand, Abba Moses continues: 'If we capitulate to apathy and carelessness, we shall find our minds crammed with sinful thoughts and idle chatter, bound up in worry and anxiety over worthless trivia'.[75] The root cause of all sin, Cassian argues, is the uncontrolled 'wandering of the mind': the antidote to sin is mental 'stability' or 'tranquillity' achieved by studious preoccupation of the mind with sacred matter.[76] The spirits of the vices would find no point of entry into the heart of a man who was rapt with sacred scripture.

The recommendation of Scripture as a talisman receives more attention from Cassian than the business of interpreting the actual meaning of passages of Scripture. While his commitment to the spiritual sense behind the letter of Scripture is pervasive, Cassian devotes only briefest consideration to the various allegorical senses of the scriptural text.[77] This reticence seems out of place for one working so strongly within the tradition of Origen, the founding father of the practice of allegorical exegesis—until we remember the fraught status

[72] This was a premise derived directly from Evagrius, *Praktikos* 48, SC 171, 608; ibid. 15, 248, and behind him, the Stoic tradition. See e.g. the 5th-cent. pseudo-Plutarchan *Epitome*, in H. Diels (ed.), *Doxographi Graeci* (Berlin, 1879); at 386 the idea of the perpetual mobility of the mind is attributed to Thales. For the medieval future of the image of the mill, see M. Carruthers, *The Craft of Thought: Meditation, Rhetoric, and the Making of Images, 400–1200* (Cambridge, 1998), 81–100.

[73] *Conl.* 1. 18, SC 42, 99.

[74] On prayer, Stewart, *Cassian*, 84–130: this is the main focus of his study.

[75] *Conl.* 1. 18, SC 42, 99: Cf. *HEz.* I. 11. 5–6, CCSL 142, 170–2: Gregory's declaration of vulnerability to idle words, discussed below, Ch. 8.

[76] See e.g. *Inst.* 2. 14, SC 109, 84; 5. 21. 3, 226 on vainglory; 7. 9. 1, 302–4 on avarice; 10. 6, 390 on *acedia*; 10. 23, 422; 11. 15, 440. Cf. Augustine, *De doctr. chr.* II. 7. 9, Green, 63 on fixing, as though to the wood of the cross, the *superbiae motus* with the apprehension of God through Scripture, and for discussion, D. Dawson, 'Sign Theory, Allegorical Reading, and the Motions of the Soul in *De doctrina christiana*', in Arnold and Bright (eds.), *De doctrina christiana*, 123–41. To the best of my knowledge, Augustine does not employ the metaphor of the millwheel in this context.

[77] Ibid. 14. 8, SC 54, 189–92.

of Origen's legacy in the early fifth century. Cassian's immediate teacher, Evagrius, at the very centre of the Origenist controversy, was still more silent on the senses of Scripture, diplomatically choosing to lay stress instead on the power of the word of God to ward off demons.[78] Although his own position was relatively more secure, Cassian may have calculated the importance of demonstrating that his teaching on exegesis was bound in with his discussion of moral purity. In a tantalizingly opaque sequence, he implies that the struggle for purity through 'mental occupation', *of its own accord*, gives on to a contemplative experience of spiritual meaning:

While we are going over and over sections of Scripture as we strive to commit them to memory, the mind is so busy that it does not have time to consider their meaning: it is only later on, especially at night-time, when we are free from all disturbance from action and vision, that in silently turning them over in our mind, the most hidden meanings, whose presence we would scarcely suspect when we are awake, come to the surface—when we are resting, and as though in a deep sleep.[79]

Night-time was a time for revelation: while the impure man is betrayed by the emission of his semen while he sleeps, the pure in heart are vouchsafed the meaning of the texts on which they have been focused during the day.[80] In a similar way, they might find their use of a single verse of Scripture in prayer dissolve into a wordless 'prayer of fire'.[81]

Cassian's was a compelling, supple analysis of moral purity that persuaded generations of ascetic readers in a variety of institutional contexts. We shall see that it suggested to an ascetic bishop—Caesarius of Arles—how he should approach the problem of evangelizing the countryside,[82] and to cenobitic leaders such as St Benedict how they should structure the daily routine of their monks.[83] What truly caught and held the attention of Cassian's readers, however, was the way that his argument moved from its premises concerning the achievement of

---

[78] See McLaughlin, 'The Bible, the Demons, and the Desert'.
[79] *Conl.* 14. 10, SC 54, 196–7: 'deinde quod ea, quae creberrima repetitione percursa, dum memoriae tradere laboramus, intellegere id temporis obligata mente non quivimus, postea ab omnium actuum ac visionum inlecebris absoluti praecipueque nocturna meditatione taciti revolventes clarius intuemur, ita ut occultissimorum sensuum, quos ne tenui quidem vigilantes opinatione percipimus, quiescentibus nobis et velut soporis stupore demersis intelligentia reveletur.'
[80] *Conl.* 22. 3–5, SC 64, 116–20.
[81] See *Conl.* 10. 11, SC 54, 93; Stewart, *Cassian*, 117–22.
[82] Below, Ch. 3.
[83] Below, Ch. 4.

inner purity and contemplative peace towards its conclusions about the moral authority conferred by ascetic expertise. The route Cassian took was an indirect one. He claimed repeatedly to be moving from the 'practical' life of struggle with the devil to a discussion not of authority, but of the 'theoretical' enjoyment of divine contemplation. Yet the momentum of the argument brought Cassian to articulate how it was that the contemplative could become a teacher. At its most basic, he imagined ascetic development as a passage from 'sacred reading' to 'sacred knowledge' and thus to 'sacred speech'. The elegance of Cassian's logic was that the ascetic who had assiduously filled his whirling thoughts with sacred matter would himself become a source of such matter. In his plain and wholesome speech he would provide others with 'good grain' to grind.

Cassian's discussion of the authority of plain speech is made most explicit in *Conference* 14, given by Abba Nestoros.[84] Cassian approaches Nestoros with an 'advanced' question: having memorized much of Scripture, he finds himself unable to concentrate on any single verse, and instead lurches from verse to verse as though intoxicated. Nestoros tells him that if he truly immerses himself in the words of the Fathers, the rovings of his mind will be converted into a 'holy and unceasing rumination on the sacred law'.[85] He will himself become a 'perpetual fount', a wellspring of spiritual discourse for others.[86] As ever, Cassian is at pains to stress that reading does not of itself produce understanding of Scripture, or experience of contemplation. True knowledge is only obtained by those who have first achieved purity of heart. 'Jews, heretics, and even some catholics' are named as impostors who lay claim to an understanding of Scripture which, in not meriting, they do not actually possess.[87] There are two kinds of reading, which give rise to two kinds of speech: an empty facility with words, and an ascetically grounded, spiritually productive mode. 'Rhetorical know-how' cannot long pass for the authentic coin of moral expertise.[88]

Cassian's promotion of a true expertise (*peritia*) over worldly wisdom has often been taken to mean that he advocated a charismatic approach to biblical exegesis, and, more broadly, that he believed the 'sweat of ascetic experience' to be a more authentic path to enlighten-

---

[84] For parallel discussions of this Conference, see Vessey, 'Ideas of Christian Writing', ch. 2, and Markus, *End of Ancient Christianity*, 184–8.

[85] *Conl.* 14. 10, SC 54, 195.

[86] *Conl.* 14. 16, 206.

[87] Ibid. 14. 15, 202–3.

[88] Ibid. 14. 9, 194; 14. 16, 203.

ment than 'book learning'. This, however, is to misconstrue the specific sense of *peritia*, which we have translated as 'expertise' rather than 'experience';[89] and again to mistake the highly mannered conventions of the dialogue genre Cassian was using. Even as he presented himself as the disciple of the venerable fathers of the desert, Cassian issued a warning to his readers: old age does not guarantee a man the authentic expertise of 'the elders'.[90] He had no truck with the romanticization of illiteracy.[91] The very purpose of casting asceticism as a technique and a tradition was to safeguard against the possibility of aberrant charismatic leadership, which had dogged the ascetic movement in Gaul.

As his audience knew, the claim to plain and unadorned speech was archly rhetorical. In speaking from the desert, Cassian showed how this most ancient, and most hollow, of the tropes of political discourse could be given the sting of authenticity. His readers in the fifth and sixth centuries took as axiomatic his recommendations about 'mental preoccupation' with sacred text, and his designation of the purity of a man's words as the most revealing sign of his spiritual expertise. The care taken minutely to control the appetites of the body ascetics now also lavished upon their every word, read or uttered. They challenged themselves with the 'discipline of the tongue', striving vigilantly to avoid 'sins of the mouth', all to demonstrate that they were men who could be trusted with power.

EXPERTS AND BEGINNERS

To offer his public a language of authority without some kind of explicit instruction as to its social use would have been to undermine his own argument: Cassian took some care in attempting to specify who could avail themselves of the expertise he described. His first

[89] *Pace* P. Miquel, 'Un homme d'expérience: Cassien', *CollCist* 30 (1968), 131–46, and H. Holze, *Erfahrung und Theologie im frühen Mönchtum: Untersuchungen zu einer Theologie des monastischen Leben bei den ägyptischen Mönchsvätern, Johannes Cassian und Benedikt von Nursia* (Göttingen, 1992). D. Illmer, '*Totum namque in sola experientia ususque consistit*: Eine Studie zur monastischen Erziehung und Sprache', in. F. Prinz (ed.), *Mönchtum und Gesellschaft im Frühmittelalter* (Darmstadt, 1976), 430–55, emphasizes the rhetorical element in Cassian's programme.

[90] *Conl.* 2. 13, SC 42, 125; a point well made by Rousseau, *Ascetics, Authority and the Church*, 189–94.

[91] See *Conl.* 10. 3, SC 54, 76–8, on the misguided Serapion, unable to pray in anything other than corporeal images; discussed by Stewart, *Cassian*, 85–90.

thought was for his readers, those who attentively followed his teachings in the *Institutes* and *Conferences*. At a crucial point in his argument
the 'teachings of the elders' are discreetly inserted as 'good grain' suitable for mental consumption. No less than the word of God, the
'words of the Fathers' should command the humble and silent attention of the disciple.[92] This provided at once the basis of Cassian's claim
to pedagogic authority, extended the same to his readers, and offered
to each a self-defence against the charge of imperfect understanding.
Meanwhile, the rhetorical authority of rival speakers could be disabled
by a counter-accusation of *imperitia*—lack of expertise, meaning moral
impurity. The discourse of *peritia* served as the title to cultural legiti-
macy of which Gaulish ascetics stood so badly in need. At its most
confident moments, Cassian's work envisages an expanding ascetic
élite, dispensing true wisdom to an ever widening circle.

At the same time, however, Cassian could not easily conceal the
unresolved tensions in his approach. How was the community of
expertise to be formally organized? What relation did experts bear to
ascetic *ingénus*, their less advanced colleagues? Were there, in fact, any
real experts in Gaul? So rigorous was Cassian's discussion of technique, so palpable his sense of a fervent tradition of expertise gone
lukewarm, that he threatened at times to exclude the possibility that
any of his contemporaries could truly master the ascetic art. The
strengths of his analysis were therefore also its weaknesses. On the one
hand, his description of technique applied to all situations because it
was conceived at a spiritual, rather than an institutional, level. On the
other, because his conception of the ascetic life was so spiritually
demanding, and precisely because his moral discussion had slipped
institutional anchorage, Cassian threatened to condemn his work to
wander 'on the immense ocean', without a permanent home.[93] Aware,
perhaps, of the possible dangers, in the final set of *Conferences* he
attempted to bring his language of expertise back to a well-defined
monastic harbour.

In *Conference* 16 on friendship, Cassian squarely faced the question
of monastic communal living, and how it could be achieved. What he
found, however, was that he could not easily convert the discourse of
expertise into a language of community. It was simple enough to set
out with the canonical texts of both the Classical and the Biblical
traditions on true friendship, juxtaposing references to Cicero's *On*

---

[92] *Conl.* 14. 9, SC 54, 193–4; 14. 10, 195.   [93] Ibid. 1, pref., SC 42, 75.

friendship with, for example, the opening verse of Psalm 132, 'How good and pleasant it is for brethren to live in harmony'. However, the immediate conclusion, drawn impeccably from the philosophical tradition, must be that true friendship and charity can only exist between those of similar moral standing.[94] The logic of Cassian's discussion demands that he parses charity in two different senses. Although 'we should accept all men as brothers', *frater* actually denotes not so much a fellow human as 'one who shares in our way of life'.[95] The universal charism of charity resolves into *agape*, the loving disposition showable to anyone, and *diathesis*, the precise affect given and received by the few who enjoy moral kinship.[96]

Cassian's definition of the monastery follows from these exacting premises. To repeat the fundamental point: in ascetic relationships as Cassian envisages them, apostolic community of property of itself avails nothing. Because of his insistence on moral purity as the precondition of true charity, Cassian is forced to demand a community of expertise. The *coenobium*, the monastic community, is meant to constitute such an environment. Everything here depends upon equality of virtue and consonance of wills. All the members of the community should of course strive to advance, but there is to be no racing ahead, and no lagging behind. There is ultimately no possibility of supporting weaker brethren. Cassian sketches out a theory of different needs and capacities within the community, but abandons it almost immediately. In theory, experts could cohabit with the *ingénus*—but in practice the latter would inevitably prove too weak to accept correction from their more qualified brethren. Their faults no sooner pointed out, they would become proud, and hard of heart.[97] Thus the community can only function at a shared level of ascetic competence. It becomes difficult for Cassian to envisage a monastic institutional

---

[94] *Conl.* 16. 2–3, SC 54, 138. For an overview of the Classical tradition, see D. Konstan, *Friendship in the Classical World* (Cambridge, 1997); C. White, *Christian Friendship in the Fourth Century* (Cambridge, 1992); and for late fourth century debates among ascetics as to the reception of this tradition, E. Clark, 'Friendship between the sexes: Classical Theory and Christian Practice' in ead. *Jerome, Chrysostom and Friends* (New York, 1986), followed by 'Theory and Practice in Late Ancient Asceticism: Jerome, Chrysostom, and Augustine', in *Journal of Feminist Studies of Religion* 5 (1989), 25–46. On Cassian's Conference 16 and the Classical tradition: K. A. Neuhausen, 'Zu Cassians Traktat *De amicitia* (Coll. 16)', in C. Gnilka and W. Schetter (eds.), *Studien zur Literatur zur Spätantike*, *Antiquitas* Reihe I, Band 23 (Bonn, 1975), 181–218.

[95] Ibid. 16. 17, SC 54, 237.

[96] Ibid. 16. 14, 233.

[97] Ibid. 16. 23–26, 242–4.

context for the exercise of the moral authority, the spiritual grounds of which he has so clearly articulated. If the community cannot include weaker brethren, on what terms can any monk break rank and claim the authority to correct his peers? The *coenobium* for Cassian becomes a place of paced competition, a 'wrestling arena' for monks, and he cannot imagine a monastic community on any other terms.[98]

Cassian's first premises were thus often his conclusions. In some senses, he did not move far beyond the meticulous exposition of the necessary conditions for a life of apostolic charity. On occasion, he was tempted to argue that these conditions were also sufficient. In the final *Conferences*, he attempted to arrive at a definitive statement on the relation and relative value of the cenobitic and eremitic lives—but without success.[99] Indeed he seems deliberately to have refused to adjudicate the question of which life was preferable, preferring instead to argue for the validity of many paths. Encouraging his readers not to be distracted by the spiritual achievements of others,[100] Cassian returned their attention again and again to the purification of the mind, thus leaving it for them to find a social place for themselves as best they could.

Of course, there had been a community of expertise in the desert, and in the past; and it was in evoking these halcyon days and nights that Cassian gave the clearest sign of his hopes for ascetic community in the present. The twenty-four elders who gave the *Conferences* were meant to constitute for his readers an image of the perfectly balanced society of spiritual masters. (To alert readers of Scripture they would call to mind the twenty-four elders in the Apocalypse.[101]) Frequently, Cassian's desert fathers would in turn recall the fathers before them—the meetings these still more venerable elders had held to decide the number of psalms that monks should sing, or how best to discern the deceptions of the devil.[102] The elders of bygone days might express different opinions—and on one occasion, an angel intervenes to arbitrate their discussion[103]—but the consensus that emerges from

---

[98] *Conl.* 18. 11, SC 64, 22. Cf. Gregory the Great in a different context: *RP* III. 37, SC 382, 522: 'Et gravis quidem labor praedicari est, et in communis praedicationis voce, ad occultos singulorum motus causasque vigilare, et palaestrarum more in diversi lateris arte se vertere.'

[99] Thus the promotion of the cenobitic life in Conferences 18 and 19 is offset by continuing advice for solitaries (such as Cassian and Germanus), and for lay people. See *Conl.* 18. 14, SC 64, 26–8; 19. 11–16, 48–55.   [100] *Conl.* 14. 6–7, SC 54, 187–8.

[101] *Conl.* 24. 1, SC 64, 171, referring to Apoc. 4: 4.

[102] See *Inst.* 2. 6, SC 109, 69, on psalms; *Conl.* 2. 2, SC 42, 112–14, on discretion; cf. *Inst.* I. 2. 2, SC 109, 41, on private property.

[103] *Inst.* 2. 5. 5–6, SC 109, 68.

their debate stems from the fundamental equilibrium that they enjoy with each other. As we have suggested, Cassian's nostalgia for a past era of shared spiritual fervour was a means of exercising restraint on his intemperate peers; at the same time, its function was to instil a decorous enthusiasm among them, that they might, after all, continue the Great Tradition.

An ascetic community in the present was constituted by Cassian's readers, wherever they might be—a *coenobium* of letters. In a sense, this was the natural expectation for Cassian to hold of his audience. The Classical literary community had managed to survive and prosper across the various physical, dynastic, and institutional boundaries separating members of the educated élite one from another: how much the more should the new Christian *litterati* of the Latin West be able to sustain each other. Cassian imagined some of his dedicatees 'receiving into their cells the authors of the *Conferences* together with the actual volumes of the *Conferences*'. In this way they would be able, even while living alone, to follow the paths of 'ancient tradition, industry, and expertise'.[104] The epitomes of Cassian in circulation in the Latin West suggest that his expectations were not disappointed.[105]

THE REPUBLIC OF CHRISTIAN LETTERS

That it may be Cassian, not only Augustine, who presides over the Christian transformation of the ancient rhetorical heritage prompts a reconsideration of a long-held understanding of cultural change in late antiquity. Erich Auerbach, in the course of his classic investigation into the development of the vernacular in the early middle ages, pointed to the formation in this period of Christian 'plain speaking', or *sermo humilis*.[106] Auerbach's concern was to trace the decline of Latin as a literary language, in other words, the gestation of the romance vernaculars. This philological transformation, Auerbach argued, was

---

[104] *Conl.* 18, pref., SC 64, 8–9.

[105] K. Honselmann, 'Bruchstücke von Auszügen aus Werken Cassians: Reste einer verlorenen Schrift des Eucherius von Lyon?', *Theologie und Glaube* 51 (1961), 300–4. A. de Vogüé, 'Un morceau célèbre de Cassien parmi des extraits d'Evagre', *StMon* 27 (1985), suggests otherwise (12 n. 24), but the attribution is accepted by W. Dunphy, 'Eucherius of Lyons in unexpected (Pelagian?) company', *Augustinianum* 37 (1997), 483–94, esp. 489–90, which studies the 6th-cent. reception of Eucherius' epitome of Cassian.

[106] See E. Auerbach, *Literary Language and its Public in Late Latin Antiquity and the Middle Ages*, tr. R. Mannheim (London, 1965), 25–66, baldly summarized here.

the work of late antique Christian rhetoricians, in particular Augustine and his later disciples Caesarius and Gregory the Great.

In Auerbach's account, it was Augustine who definitively initiated the new rhetoric of *sermo humilis* by reordering the relation between style and content demanded in classical canons of rhetorical deportment. For an orator trained in the Ciceronian tradition, the linguistic register of a speech had to correlate and adjust to its subject matter: thus high style for lofty subject matter, middle style for 'middling subjects', and colloquial style for mundane subjects. Himself a product of this tradition, Augustine turned against it to develop a new aesthetic of Christian public speaking. All topics of discussion were equally revealing of the presence of God, Augustine argued, and thus the code enforcing distinctions between levels of style no longer applied. Christian speech should be simple and unadorned, aiming only to edify its hearers.

Auerbach thought that Caesarius was a plain speaker in the augustinian tradition, and that Gregory the Great was another:

Caesarius the energetic preacher, and the Pope with his miraculous tales [in the *Dialogues*] have in common the importance they attached to the concerns of everyday life. . . . Their purpose—to teach Christianity—enabled them to raise the simplest matters to a new style level and to speak of them in a tone that would not formerly have been possible.[107]

For Auerbach, the 'homespun eloquence' of the bishop of Arles and Gregory's 'popular short stories' in the *Dialogues* reveal the character of the new rhetorical dispensation of *sermo humilis*.[108] These characterizations are open to question, as we shall see below, in part because the whole premises of Auerbach's approach invite re-examination.

If we step aside from a philological perspective, and approach the issue of 'plain' or 'pure speech' in its social context and in the context of ascetic tradition, then a quite different picture emerges. When a late antique speaker claims to be using unadorned language, this does not necessarily have to do with his being understood by 'the people': instead, the speaker's rhetorical goal may be to vouchsafe the purity of his persuasive intentions. 'Plain speech' in this sense is a self-conscious (and often ornately eloquent) renunciation of 'fickle rhetoric', a public gesture well understood by all those wishing to claim moral authority

---

[107] Auerbach, *Literary Language*, 102–3.

[108] Ibid., 85–103; quotations at 95, 100. See C. A. Rapisarda, 'Lo stile umile nei sermoni di S. Cesario d'Arles', *Orpheus* 17 (1970), 117–59; and below, Chs. 4, 7.

in the ancient world. Socrates, after all, was seen to have staked his life on his credibility as a purveyor of the unvarnished truth—while his failure to dissociate himself sufficiently from the duplicitous talk of the sophists had ensured his condemnation. Like the 'rhetoric of vulnerability', the plain speech of late antique Christianity, which Auerbach saw as revolutionary, was a mode of discourse espoused by ascetics precisely because of its hallowed place in the culture of the ruling élite.

In the light of this, Augustine's purposes and his originality as an advocate of *sermo humilis* may need reassessment.[109] As we have seen, the initiative in drawing up a code of ascetic speech had been taken not by Augustine, but by Cassian. It was in Cassian's *Conferences* that language had become a principal object of ascetic attention.

The community of Cassian's readers was not constituted solely by recluses or by cenobites. His emphasis upon language as a medium for sanctification at once encouraged and made more dangerous the assumption of pastoral responsibilities by ascetics. As Cassian argued, to speak as a trained ascetic was in itself a means of exerting moral authority. Simply in manifesting through his speech his spiritual purity, the ascetic expert began to teach others to follow his example. But to speak was also to risk pollution, to grasp (or to be seen to grasp) at power for worldly purposes. With the slightest slip of the tongue, a would-be moral expert might reveal that he had not, after all, purged his mind of profane careerist intent. The safest ascetic state might thus be silence—and we might pause to remember the voiceless majority whose choice of ascetic lifestyle did not lead to their advancement in the Church hierarchy, but rather ensured their immediate and perpetual anonymity. In contrast, those like Caesarius of Arles and Gregory the Great, who had shunned the path of obscurity, were always at risk from the dangers inherent in the use of language in public. Once they had begun to speak, there was no turning back, charged as they were to 'cry out without ceasing' (Isa: 58: 1).

---

[109] For a discussion of the complexity of Augustine's language in his sermons, see S. Pôque, *Le Langage symbolique dans la prédication d'Augustin d'Hippone* (Paris, 1984).

PART II

Sixth-Century Alternatives

3

The Pastoral Arts of the Rhetor Pomerius

A bishop comes in a state of consternation to his spiritual advisor. The setting is the unspecified space of philosophical dialogue: all we know is that we are in 'Christian times'.[1] As the bishop considers the weight of his tasks, and in particular his responsibility to preach to his flock, he regrets ever having taken office. He wants to flee, to live as a recluse—but, as his advisor points out, this is hardly a moral solution. The bishop must confront the reality of his dilemma: 'You can neither discharge your office nor abandon it without sin', and the moral risks of abdication are in fact the greater, warns the advisor. Bishop and advisor together recall the words of the Lord to the prophet Ezekiel on the inalienable responsibility of the watchman to announce to the Israelites their sins: if he fails to do so, their blood will be on his hands. The bishop discovers, albeit in terror, a renewed enthusiasm for his pastoral duties: 'Who, I ask, will have so stony a heart, who will be so unfeeling, that this judgement [of the Lord's] does not frighten him?'[2]

Such is the scene painted for us by the North African rhetor Pomerius, in his *On the Contemplative Life*, composed in southern Gaul in the early years of the sixth century. Although rarely recognized as such, the work is cast as a dialogue:[3] Pomerius plays the advisor, and names as his interlocutor one Bishop Julianus, whose

---

[1] Pomerius, *De vita contemplativa* I. 16. 4, PL 59, 461B, 'Nunc autem, quod Christiani temporis sacerdotes magis sustinent quam curant possessiones ecclesiae . . .'. II. 4, PL 59, 448A has Pomerius in the process of composition (*dictamen*) but the location is unspecified. The text in PL 59 reprints the edition of J.-B. Le Brun des Marettes and D. Mangeant (Paris, 1711), together with Mangeant's editorial *Admonitio* (PL 59, 411–14).

[2] Pomerius, *De vita cont.* I. 20, PL 59, 435B, tr. M. J. Suelzer, *Julianus Pomerius: The Contemplative Life*, ACW 4 (Westminster, Md., 1947), 43.

[3] The work is usually described as a treatise (see e.g. M. Schanz, C. Hosius and G. Krüger, *Geschichte der römischen Literatur*, IV. 2 (Munich, 1920), 554–6), but Pomerius casts it as a dialogue with Bishop Julianus, in an uneven combination of reported and direct speech. In the Preface, Pomerius sets out questions that Bishop Julianus has asked him. In Book I. 1–14, Pomerius begins to reply to these; I. 15–25 recalls in direct speech an interchange between Pomerius and Julianus. II. 1–3 reverts to Pomerius' response to the questions. II. 4–5 is an interruption reported in direct speech. In II. 6–24 and III in its entirety, Pomerius answers Julianus' questions without further interruption. The effect of this disposition is to direct attention to I. 15–25 as the most important in the work: see below, pp. 71–2.

historical identity remains uncertain.[4] Their encounter concerns the dilemma of the ascetic in power, and in particular the morally dangerous duty of public speech. What Pomerius teaches the anxious bishop, however, is that to fall silent carries its own risks, and that there are words the pure in heart can use without fear of contamination.

To moderns, Pomerius himself seems a relatively obscure figure.[5] We do not know when he came to Gaul from Africa: he may have been a refugee from Vandal persecution. He seems to have been ordained a priest in Gaul.[6] He appears in our sources as an occasional correspondent of bishops in Provence and Northern Italy,[7] and a teacher of grammar and rhetoric at Arles. In this capacity, he stands inevitably in the shadow of his most famous pupil: Caesarius, the future bishop of Arles.[8] His own literary renown, however, was sufficient to earn him honourable mention in two catalogues of Christian authors. A contemporary acquaintance records that, in addition to *On the Contemplative Life*, Pomerius composed a dialogue—also with Bishop Julianus—on the origins of the soul (fragments of which survive),[9] two treatises of moral instruction (lost), and 'other things which have escaped my notice'.[10] In the following century Isidore of Seville gives

---

[4] Bishop Julianus may be an imaginary figure; equally, Pomerius may have had in mind Bishop Julianus of Carpentras (present at the Council of Epaon of 517, as noted by Mangeant, *Admonitio*, PL 59, 414B), or Julianus of Vienne (on whom see A. C. F. Arnold, *Caesarius von Arelate und die gallische Kirche seiner Zeit* (Leipzig, 1894; repr. 1972), 210 n. 666). Following Isidore of Seville, Pomerius' early modern editors conjoined the name 'Julianus' to the *cognomen* 'Pomerius' (see Isidore, *De viris illustribus* 25. 31, PL 83, 1096A), with the consequence that the author of *On the contemplative life* has been known ever since as 'Julianus Pomerius'. However, the 6th-cent. evidence (see below, nn. 6 and 9) knows only the name 'Pomerius'. It seems likely that Isidore assimilated without warrant Pomerius to his interlocutor Bishop Julianus, and I have therefore adopted the practice of the earlier witnesses in referring simply to 'Pomerius'.

[5] For an introduction and bibliography, see A. Solignac, art. 'Julien Pomère', *DSp* 8, 1594–1600; R. Kaster, *Guardians of Language: The Grammarian and Society in Late Antiquity* (Berkeley/Los Angeles, 1988), 342–3, assembles the biographical data, placing Pomerius in the company of other known grammarians.

[6] According to Pseudo-Gennadius (see below, n. 9). Ruricius of Limoges (n. 7) calls Pomerius 'abbas' repeatedly, but this does not necessarily indicate that Pomerius was an abbot: the term was also a commonplace to denote a spiritual father.

[7] See the letters to Pomerius of Ruricius of Limoges, *Epp.* 1. 17, 2. 10 and 11, CSEL 21, 369–70, 385–9 (see also ibid. 2. 8 and 9, 383–5 to Bishop Aeonius of Arles, urging him to send Pomerius to Italy), and Ennodius of Pavia, *Ep.* 2. 6, CSEL 6, 44.

[8] *VCaes.* 1. 9, MGH SRM, 3, 460, discussed below.

[9] See A. Solignac, 'Les Fragments du "De Natura Animae" de Julien Pomère (fin Ve siècle)', *BLE* 75 (1974), 41–60.

[10] See Pseudo-Gennadius, *De viris illustribus* 99, ed. E. C. Richardson, TU 14.1 (Leipzig, 1896), 96. The two lost works are *De contemptu mundi et rerum transitarium*, and *De vitiis*

a slightly different list of Pomerius' works, including a text (now also lost) on the organization of the ascetic life for virgins.[11] By the eighth century, however, Pomerius' reputation had faded, and *On the Contemplative Life* had been reascribed to Prosper of Aquitaine—an attribution unchallenged until the early modern period.[12] Thus submerged in medieval libraries, Pomerius has attracted scant critical attention from modern scholars.[13]

In his own day, however, Pomerius' services as a grammarian were much in demand. Ennodius of Pavia, and, still more, Ruricius of Limoges were as eager as is Bishop Julianus in *On the Contemplative Life* to benefit from Pomerius' instruction; both went to some lengths to persuade him to move to their own cities.[14] Pomerius evidently refused, content with or perhaps reluctant to disrupt, his situation in Arles, where he enjoyed the patronage of the 'illustrious Firminus and his kinswoman Gregoria'.[15] It was these notables who brought their distinguished rhetor into contact with the young aristocrat Caesarius, a precocious ascetic, already being groomed as a future bishop of the city. Taken together, the evidence generated around Pomerius reveals a network of rich and cultured clerics and laity in southern Gaul and beyond, with particular interests in the ascetic life and its promotion throughout the Church.[16]

et virtutibus. It appears that *De vita cont.* is one of the works unknown to Gennadius' continuator.

[11] Isidore, *De vir. illust.* 25. 31, PL 83, 1096A. Isidore attributes to Pomerius the following: a treatise on the soul, the *Libellum de virginibus instituendis,* and *De vita contemplativa.* The loss of the *De virginibus* deprives us of the opportunity to compare this text with Caesarius' *Regula ad virgines.*

[12] Chrodegang of Metz, *Regula canonicorum* 31, ed. J.-B. Pelt, *Études sur la cathédrale de Metz,* i. *La Liturgie* (Metz, 1937), 24–5, is the first recorded instance of this reattribution. For others in the Carolingian period, see Suelzer, ACW 4, 74 n. 19. Four of the oldest manuscripts of *De vita cont.,* however, ascribe the work to Pomerius. See M. W. Laistner, 'The Influence during the Middle Ages of the Treatise "De vita contemplativa" and its Surviving Manuscripts', most accessible in id., *The Intellectual Heritage of the Early Middle Ages* (Ithaca, NY, 1957), 49–56.

[13] Exceptions being Arnold, *Caesarius von Arelate,* 79–84, 124–7; and more recently, Kaster, *Guardians of Language,* 70–97; and Markus, *End of Ancient Christianity,* 189–92. For dismissal of Pomerius relative to Caesarius, see e.g. P. Riché, *Education et culture dans l'Occident barbare, VIe–VIIIe siècles* (Paris, 1962) 131–2.

[14] See above, n. 6.

[15] *VCaes.* 8–9, MGH SRM 3, 460. The precise nature of the relationship between Firminus and Gregoria is unclear: W. E. Klingshirn, *Caesarius of Arles: Life, Testament, Letters,* TTH 19 (Liverpool, 1994), 13, suggests they are husband and wife, while Kaster, *Guardians of Language,* 343, sees Gregoria as Firminus' mother (and notes also suggestions that Firminus was related to Ennodius of Pavia).

[16] W. E. Klingshirn, *Caesarius of Arles: The Making of a Christian Community in Late*

Pomerius was their Cassian: while more confident than they had been three generations previously, prominent Christians in Gaul still looked for moral authentication from a qualified expert.[17] As Cassian had discovered, this was not an altogether comfortable position; as a grammarian, however, Pomerius would have been accustomed to negotiating the tension between the authority conferred by his own expertise and the undeniable social power of his patrons.[18]

If we seek an explanation for why the great and the good, in particular among the episcopate, turned to Pomerius as their latter-day Cassian, we need look no further than *On the Contemplative Life*. Disclaiming, of course, any intention to offer his ecclesiastical superiors advice,[19] Pomerius demonstrates to Bishop Julianus that there is a persuasive language of moral authority available to ascetics in a position of power. The language is a synthetic one: as a North African rhetor resident in southern Gaul, Pomerius was able not only to exploit his status as an 'outsider' as Cassian had done, but also to bring together the contrasting approaches of Augustine and Cassian on questions of ascetic authority. As we have seen, Augustine had refused to supply ascetics in power with a secure science of moral improvement: he had offered them only language to express the contrast between their official status and their human fallibility. Cassian had devised just such a science, but had been wary of specifying where or by whom it might be exercised. The singular achievement of *On the Contemplative Life* was to join the augustinian 'rhetoric of vulnerability' with the techniques of pure speech established by Cassian. These became the two principal gestures of good faith available to sixth-century ascetics in public office, the one involving the disclaimer of all interest in power, the other a demonstration of constant purity of heart and hence spiritual expertise. Pomerius' contribution was to

Antique Gaul (Cambridge, 1994), 75–82, for an overview of the 'reforming party' and its texts at the turn of the 6th cent.; see Vessey, 'Ideas of Christian Writing', and Wood, 'Avitus of Vienne', for the preceding generation.

[17] See e.g. *De vita cont.* II. 4, PL 59, 448B on the abuse of ascetic authority: Pomerius, like Cassian, sought to establish his expertise through a critique of the practice of others.

[18] See Kaster, *Guardians of Language*, p. xi, contrasting 'the self-image [evoked by the texts of the grammarian] of a man immersed in his expertise and the sense of authority he draws from his skill. The grammarian in these texts is the master, buoyed up by his profession's tradition, refining it, laying down the laws of language with a confidence verging on complacency. . . . [But the grammarian was also] a dependant. The grammarians' patrons sustain them in their professional lives and affect for good or for ill most other areas of their lives beyond the strictly professional.'

[19] *De vita cont.* pref., I. 14; PL 59, 415B, 430C. J. C. Plumpe, 'Pomeriana', *VC* 1 (1947), 227–39, emphasizes that, in speaking of *sacerdotes*, the treatise is addressed to bishops.

insist that these perspectives be mutually reinforcing, so that ascetics might carry moral conviction in their assumption of pastoral responsibility. Ascetics in power could present themselves at one and the same time as reluctant to hold office, and as expertly qualified to do so.

We should note that Pomerius does not present *On the Contemplative Life* as a work of synthesis, but as a supplement to the writings of Augustine. In a manner highly characteristic of the sixth-century construction of patristic tradition, Cassian is never mentioned by name, and Pomerius presents himself instead as a faithful disciple of Augustine. The dialogue ends with fulsome homage for the bishop of Hippo:

The holy bishop Augustine, keen in mind, charming in eloquence, skilled in human learning, zealous in ecclesiastical labors, celebrated in daily disputations, self-possessed in his every action, catholic in his exposition of our faith, penetrating in the solution of problems, prudent in the refutation of heretics, and wise in explaining the canonical writings—it is he, I say, whom I have followed in these little books to the best of my ability.[20]

Impressed by these gestures, scholars have tended to cast Pomerius as the thinker who brought augustinian doctrine to 'semi-Pelagian' Gaul, a process crowned by Caesarius of Arles' affirmation of the primacy of grace in human salvation at the Council of Orange in 529.[21] While more recent work has emphasized the moderate character of Gallic augustinianism in the early sixth century,[22] it has only hinted at the possibility of Cassian's influence on Pomerius.[23] It is here suggested that Pomerius' devotion to Augustine must be considered alongside his equally thorough appropriation of the work of Cassian. *On the Contemplative Life* showed exactly how to harness the numinous authority of Augustine to Cassian's language of moral purification, all in the service of ascetic leadership of the Church. The lesson was not lost on Caesarius of Arles and his generation—and it may equally have

---

[20] *De vita cont.* III. 31. 6, PL 59, 516C–517A, tr. ACW 4, 165. This enthusiastic augustinianism is one of the features which suggested to Carolingian readers of *De vita cont.* that its author was Prosper of Aquitaine.

[21] See e.g. Arnold, *Caesarius von Arelate*, 83, 125–9, 312–62. For Pomerius as a slavish augustinian in an ethical (rather than a theological) context, see H. Hagendahl, *Latin Fathers and the Classics: A Study on the Apologists, Jerome, and Other Christian Writers* (Göteborg, 1958), 345–6.

[22] C. Tibiletti, 'La teologia della grazia in Giuliano Pomerio: alle origini dell'agostinismo provenzale', *Augustinianum* 25 (1985), 489–506; reiterated by Markus, *End of Ancient Christianity*, 192–3.

[23] Markus, *End of Ancient Christianity*, 189 n. 27.

been absorbed by a later reader of Pomerius' dialogue, Pope Gregory the Great.[24]

SCRIPTURAL CONTEMPLATION AND RHETORICAL ACTION

Pomerius' title for his work threatens to mislead its modern readers, who will find there neither a discussion of beholding the divine in paradise, nor of 'contemplative' prayer, nor even of the monastic life in general. As Robert Markus has emphasized, what Pomerius in fact composed was a handbook for pastors, encouraging them to participate in an ascetic understanding of moral authority and pastoral responsibility.[25] These priorities are announced at once: having promised to define 'in a few words' the nature of the contemplative life, Pomerius offers to consider 'whether one charged with ruling a Church can become a sharer in contemplative virtue'. This question in turn leads on to a host of others, all of which presume a concern with the moral exercise of episcopal office. Pomerius will discuss:

> whether it is expedient to hold the goods of the Church to provide for the community life of the brethren and their support, or to spurn them through love of perfection; what should be regarded as perfection in abstinence, and whether it should be regarded as necessary only for the body or for the soul as well; to what extent simulated virtues differ from true virtues; from what prior causes and by what later additions vices are usually engendered and increased, and by what remedies, as by so many medicines, they can with God's help be lessened or corrected.[26]

Community of property on the Jerusalem model, physical and mental purity, accuracy in spiritual correction: it would be difficult more succinctly to identify the issues involved in Augustine's and Cassian's discussions of the assumption of public office by ascetics. As a pastoral

---

[24] On the probability of Gregory's knowledge of Pomerius, see Markus, *Gregory*, 19. For the reception of Pomerius in Italy, see also *RM* 91. 70, SC 106, 410, citing *De vita cont.* II. 16. 2, PL 59, 460B (as noted by de Vogüé, SC 105, 221 and n. 2). Ennodius of Pavia may have assisted the diffusion of Pomerius' work in Italy. It is also possible, given Pomerius' connections with the well-placed laity in Arles, that Liberius (*c.*465–*c.*554) may have taken an interest. As Praetorian prefect in Gaul and Italy, main ally of Caesarius at the Council of Orange, and founder of a monastery in Campania (see Gregory, *Dial.* 2. 35. 1, SC 260, 236) he was certainly in a position to act as a prominent intermediary. For an overview of Liberius' career and significance, see J. J. O'Donnell, 'Liberius the Patrician', *Traditio* 37 (1981), 31–72.

[25] Markus, *End of Ancient Christianity*, 189–91.

[26] *De vita cont. prol.* 3, PL 59, 416C–417A, tr. ACW 4, 15.

handbook, the work is, more specifically, an attempt to work out how the ascetic expert as described by Cassian should conduct himself in ecclesiastical office. Where Cassian had been reluctant to specify the institutional context for the deployment of his spiritual science, Pomerius did not hesitate to commend it to the attention of all bishops.[27]

In the extraordinary Book One of *On the Contemplative Life*, Pomerius manages to move from a discussion of contemplation of God in the heavenly Jerusalem to the programme of rhetorical action that bishops should deploy in the exercise of their ministry. As Markus has observed, in so doing Pomerius shifts from an augustinian frame of reference, to take up a position closer to that established by Cassian.[28] Augustine had defined contemplation in an eschatological sense: any experience of beholding the divine in the present was a shadowy inti-mation of the face-to-face encounter to take place at the end of time. Cassian, however, had led the discussion away from the field of sacred history, towards the technical aspects of contemplative prayer. In Conference Fourteen, Cassian had gone still further, defining contem-plation simply as the understanding of Scripture vouchsafed to the pure in heart, those with spiritual expertise. And it is of contemplation in this sense that Pomerius is thinking when he asks if those holding office can partake in contemplative virtue.[29]

Such a definition of contemplation puts it clearly in the purview of those entrusted with the task of expounding Scripture to the people: such is the first stage of Pomerius' argument. Exposition, how-ever, is a heavy burden, and Pomerius summons Bishop Julianus to dramatize the point, and behind Julianus, Augustine. In terms strongly reminiscent of the bishop of Hippo's consecration anni-versary sermon, Book I of *On the Contemplative Life* becomes a sus-tained meditation on the watchman of the house of Israel. Bishop Julianus begins:

If I am not mistaken, this is what the Lord states through the Prophet Ezekiel under the threat of some fear, when he says to him: 'So thou, O Son of man, I have made thee a watchman unto the house of Israel.' [Ezek. 3: 17] Nor should we give passing heed to the fact that he calls a priest a 'watchman'. It is the work of a watchman to look out from a higher place and to see more than all others: so, too, a priest should stand out above all by the sublimity of his pattern of life and should

[27] *De vita cont. prol.* I. 14, PL 59, 430C.
[28] See above, n. 21.
[29] See esp. *De vita cont.* I. 8, PL 59, 425–6.

have the attraction of a superior knowledge of the way of life whereby he may be able to instruct those who live under him.[30]

Distraught at his inadequacy as a preacher, Bishop Julianus regards himself not as a watchful shepherd, but as an abusive tyrant. He confesses his desire 'to withdraw and to flee, to remain in solitude for the Lord to save me'.[31]

Pomerius shows him that this is not the only way to conceive of the episcopal burden. It is enough if the bishop announces to the people their sins, and there is a language that he can speak. Julianus had found the imperative that a preacher's life must mirror his words to be impossibly daunting. Pomerius reverses the equation: the fact that deeds speak louder than words is a source of rhetorical liberation.

Not in the glitter of his words then, but in the virtue of his deeds let him place all his confidence in preaching. . . . The purpose of rhetoricians is one thing, and that of teachers another. The former with all the force of their eloquence aspire to the display of studied declamation; the latter by moderate and ordinary language seek the glory of Christ. The former clothe empty subject matter with extravagant verbal ornamentation; the latter adorn and grace simple words with true ideas. . . . The former put all their glory in the favor of the people; the latter, in the assistance of God.[32]

Here, the ideology of plain speech, drawn powerfully from Cassian, comes to the rescue of the vulnerable bishop. Pomerius gives a moral charter for the exercise of power by bishops, a public platform for their word.[33] The remainder of the dialogue is concerned with the consequences of this: with what bishops shall say, and with the effect of their utterance on their listeners and themselves.

VIRTUES AND VICES

The moral language that Pomerius maps for bishops is, like his language of authority, a product of synthesis, established by working through the tensions in the texts of Augustine and Cassian. Augustine

---

[30] *De vita cont.* I. 20. 2–3, PL 59, 434C–435A, tr. ACW 4, 42–3. See Arnold, *Caesarius von Arelate*, 122 n. 364a, on Pomerius' influence on Caesarius here, and below, Ch. 4.

[31] *De vita cont.* I. 21. 4, PL 59, 437C, tr. ACW 4, 47.

[32] Ibid. I. 23–24, PL 59, 439A–C, tr. ACW, 49–50. Cf. *De doctr. chr.* IV: Augustine had specifically not foresworn the use of rhetoric.

[33] *De vita cont.* I. 25. 1, PL 59, 439C–440B, tr. ACW, 50–1: 'If holy priests—not such as the divine threat declares are to be sentenced and condemned, but such as the apostolic teaching commends—convert many to God by their holy preaching . . . who will be such a stranger to faith as to doubt that such men are sharers in contemplative virtue?'

had insisted that a measurable science of moral progress was impossible. Pomerius was committed from the outset to just such a science—he had asked, 'Is perfection necessary for the body, or only for the soul'—and he knew that Cassian's texts would guide him. The challenge, however, was not simply to follow the path of perfection as Cassian had mapped it, but also to attract augustinian sanction for this course. By paying close attention to augustinian arguments, he located those points at which it was possible to move the analysis in an ascetic direction not countenanced by Augustine.

The most important example of this is in the treatment of original sin. Augustine's account of the Fall turned on the flaw in the soul: the sin of pride, for which there could be no ascetic remedy. At the same time, the very vividness with which Augustine had evoked the broken condition of humankind expelled from Eden proved an irresistible challenge to his ascetic readers. *On the Contemplative Life* shows that Augustine's account of original sin could, in fact, provide a warrant for asceticism. In twice describing the Fall in his dialogue, Pomerius each time follows Augustine's path of reasoning, only to veer aside in the ascetic direction indicated by Cassian.[34] He begins:

Let us see how those first human beings committed so great a sin which cast them from paradise into this exile of a life full of grief . . . Now, they would not have eaten of the forbidden tree, so it seems to me, if they had not been desirous to do so.[35]

Pomerius, as a good augustinian, is not seduced into imagining desire to be the fundamental problem: no desire without temptation, he reasons, no temptation 'if they had not been deserted by God'; no desertion by God if they had not first deserted him; nor would they have deserted God if they had not been proud and damnably craved likeness of God'. Open concupiscence would not have moved them, he says of Adam and Eve, unless hidden pride had first seduced them: thus far, very augustinian.[36]

[34] *De vita cont.* II. 19, III. 2–4, PL 59, 433–4, 476–80. The former starts with a discussion of abstinence, which then becomes a discussion of pride; the latter starts with pride, to which is then assimilated avarice. Tibiletti, 'Teologia della grazia', 498–503, emphasizes the augustinian character of these passages, while noting Pomerius' avoidance of Augustine's most controversial themes such as predestination—and, it is here suggested, Augustine's view of the human will.

[35] *De vita cont.* II. 19. 1, PL 59, 463A, tr. ACW 4, 89. Pomerius is brought to consider the fall via a discussion of the apostolic community of property, on which see below.

[36] *De vita cont.* II. 19, PL 59, 464A, tr. ACW 4, 89. See Tibiletti, 'Teologia della grazia', 498–500.

Absent from the discussion, however, is Augustine's precision about the will and its turning away from God: in Pomerius, it is the 'appetite' which the devil ensnares:[37]

Concupiscence of the flesh was satisfied by them because they tasted of the forbidden tree; concupiscence of the eyes, because they wished for their eyes to be opened; and pride of life, because they could become the same as God. Seduced then by the pleasure of the flesh and the curiosity of the eyes, and the pride of life, they were cut off from the tree of life.[38]

At one moment Pomerius precisely identifies 'the desire of the flesh' as the 'punishment for sin'; but in the next he cites the Pauline dictum 'Desire is the root of all evil' (1 Tim. 6: 10). His resolution of these apparently contrary points is the most direct possible: he argues that the first sin arose out of a combination of pride and desire, as has all sin since. Thus coupled, pride and desire make 'one evil', and an ascetic programme must be devised accordingly.[39]

Pomerius' manipulation of augustinian language in an ascetic direction does not amount to unequivocal endorsement of Cassian. Just as Pomerius evades the precision of Augustine's theology of the will, so he shirks also the physiological rigour of the *Institutes* and the *Conferences*. Cassian had moved in a relatively orderly way from the disciplining of the body to the purification of the mind.[40] What characterized Pomerius' discussion of bodily and mental purity, however, was not its analytical clarity, but its rhetorical flourish.

The basic outlines of Cassian's analysis are still in place in Pomerius. Moral purification begins for Pomerius with the fight against gluttony, the first sin Cassian discussed in the *Institutes*, as the first sin in the garden of Eden.[41] Fasting is thus the *sine qua non* of any

[37] *De vita cont.* II. 19, PL 59, 464C. 'nec eis per serpentem diabolus propinaret tam ferale consilium, nisi prius eorum deprehenderet appetitum'. See also III. 4. 1, 479C, where *appetitum* again stands in for *voluntas* in the discussion of pride in the garden of Eden.

[38] Ibid. II. 19. 2, PL 59, 465A, tr. ACW 4, 90.

[39] Ibid. III. 2–4, PL 59, 476–80, esp. III. 4. 1, 479c: 'Porro cupiditas atque superbia in tantum est unum malum, ut nec superbus sine cupiditate, nec sine superbia possit cupidus inveniri.' The reconciliation of pride as the root of all evil (Eccl. 10: 15) with the text of 1 Tim. has good augustinian precedent: see above Ch. 1, n. 30 (also Newhauser, 'Towards modus in habendo', 2–3 and n. 5.) My point here is that the same reconciliation of Scriptural proof texts is used to different ends by Augustine—who wanted to argue for the priority of pride—and by his 6th-cent. ascetic readers, for whom it was important to assimilate pride with desire. See e.g. Caesarius, *Serm.* 48. 5–7, CCSL 103, 219–21, and Gregory, *HEv.* 1. 16, PL 76, 1136, and the discussions below, Chs. 4 and 6.

[40] e.g. *Conl.* 1. 6, SC 42, 84, and see above, Ch. 2. For Pomerius' assent to the need to purify the mind, see e.g. *De vita cont.* II. 17, PL 59, 462.

[41] *De vita cont.* II. 18, PL 59, 463–4. Cf. Caesarius, *Vereor* 3. 1–3, SC 345, 302: a reminder

ascetic commitment. Pomerius avoids, however, the level of physical detail sustained in Cassian's discussion. Nowhere does he attempt to describe how much water, or how many salted fish or leeks the ascetic should ideally consume, for example.[42] Instead, following the overall logic of Cassian's analysis, Pomerius concentrates on the elimination of the desire for food. He imagines at mouth-watering length the pheasants and fish and liqueurs that the ascetic must regard (and read about) with as much indifference as anything else: only then can a man claim to have achieved 'true renunciation'.[43] Similarly, Pomerius recognizes that, in the war against sexual desire, control of discourse is as important as regulation of diet. Men who make 'details about women' their habitual conversation—'this one is awkward, that one coquettish; this one is homely, that one, beautiful'—inflame their own desires. Their mental pollution is likely to show itself in the emission of semen, not only while asleep (which Pomerius took to be guilt-free), but in the daytime.[44] While suggesting some familiarity with Cassian's discussion, this is a terse abridgement, however, of what, as we have seen was a major theme across the *Institutes* and *Conferences*.

If the terms of Cassian's physical regimen for purity are blurred by Pomerius, his psychic prescriptions are altogether ignored. Although enthusiastic about the reading of Scripture as a mode of contemplation for active bishops, Pomerius has nothing to say about the use of Scripture as a psychic shield against the onslaught of temptation. The armature of Cassian's entire analysis is removed in *On the Contemplative Life*. As a result, Cassian's network of causal relations between body and soul dissolves into a looser rhetorical play with metaphor; and his meticulous system for assessing moral progress is itself subject to rhetorical diversion.[45] Ascetic progress need not only be figured as becoming physically colder and drier, and so eliminating lust: one can speak of the heat of spiritual desire, the gushing fertility of the soul; and by the same token, of spiritual coldness and dryness. This is a thick, rich language mixing physical with emotional, literal with

---

to nuns in Arles that every soul who wishes to lead the religious life must first conquer gluttony, 'lest by an abundance of delicacies, one is provoked into lustful desire'.

[42] e.g. *Inst.* IV. 22, SC 109, 152.

[43] *De vita cont.* II. 23. 2, PL 59, 469B–470A.

[44] Ibid. III. 6. 5, PL 59, 481C, ACW 4, 115–16.

[45] The same is true in the work of Gregory the Great: Straw, *Gregory*, 18, draws a distinction between a 'metonymic' asceticism, operating on a cause-and-effect model for body and soul, and the more 'metaphorical' approach of Gregory. See below, pp. 167–8.

figurative. Body and soul have here a plastic quality: they can be shaped and reshaped according to the demands of the rhetorical moment. Pomerius, for example, describes the spiritually pure thus:

One who is dead to sin . . . does not, being given over to drink, enkindle his thirst more and more by drinking; he does not take fire from the torch of hatred. . . . He is not seized by restless curiosity, nor stretched by anxiety over household business; he does not swell with pride; windy ambition does not drive him headlong.[46]

Conversely, Pomerius offers a vivid, but, in Cassian's terms, unscientific procedure by which to recognize sinners. 'I show the signs whereby pride can be recognized and avoided', he claims. Of the very proud, he writes: 'Their unbending neck, harsh expression, piercing eyes, and frightening manner of speech shout undisguised pride.'[47] A sixth-century doctor would find these texts impossibly confused. While continuing to use physiological language, they have hyperextended its range. The methodical lists of vices in the _Institutes_ and _Conferences_ are turned by Pomerius (and other sixth-century readers of Cassian) into declamatory catalogues of moral disturbance.[48]

The very power of this language created new moral dangers for its users. Once every physical trait or movement was understood as a sign of spiritual condition, once corporal language itself had become so insistently metaphorical, it was difficult to speak plainly about the body, or indeed the soul. Both were engulfed in denunciation of the sins of 'the flesh'. Bishops had to watch what they said: their own moral language might become infected with the kind of excess against which they were preaching. To the perennial temptation to abuse their position were now added new questions concerning the politics of correction. Of these risks, Pomerius was well aware, even if he was unable to secure against them.

---

[46] _De vita cont._ II. 21, PL 59, 466–7.

[47] Ibid. III. 8–10, PL 59, 484–90. Cf. Caesarius, _Serm._ 233. 5, CC 104, 927–8, on the covertly proud, when their true nature is discovered: 'effrenato ore et erecta cervice superbia, quae in corde tegebatur, ex ore profertur.'

[48] See e.g. _Monita_ of Porcarius, abbot of Lérins at the end of the 5th cent., and the spiritual master of Caesarius before he came to Pomerius at Arles: 'Iram superbiam contumaciam maledicta extingue et detestare. Odia avaritiam vanitatem et omnem sermonem malum extingue et detestare. Scurrilitates et verbositates vel cogitationum malarum initia et spiritum fornicationis extingue et detestare. Haec sunt quae te inimicum Dei faciunt et exculcerant et computrescere faciunt animam tuam', A. Wilmart, 'Les _Monita_ de l'abbé Porcaire', _RBen_ 26 (1909), 475–80, at 479, ll. 46–54.

ECCLESIAL COMMUNITY AND EPISCOPAL AUTHORITY

On the Contemplative Life is set in the timeless space of philosophical dialogue. Certainly the questions asked by Bishop Julian are characteristic of what Pomerius calls 'Christian times', but the conventions of his genre do not compel him to be any more specific.[49] On the other hand, the logic of Pomerius' argument leads him to sketch, at least in outline, the kind of social and institutional context for the language of authority he offers to Julian.[50] Here, again, we witness a balancing act between earlier authorities: Pomerius' augustinianism demands of him a clarity of institutional vision, especially where monastic community is concerned. As a reader of Cassian, however, he will have been careful to avoid specifying too precisely the context for the implementation of his discourse of authority, in order to retain a degree of flexibility.

Pomerius begins Book Two of the dialogue with a clear vision of the kind of community a bishop will address, which he derives from the internal logic of the language of correction:

If all suffered together from the very same trouble of mind and, being afflicted with identical disorders of the soul, did not differ from one another, it would be necessary to tolerate all or reprove all. But, as it is, some are to be borne with, others are to be chastised because according to the difference in sinners the type of prescription also differs.[51]

Pomerius here aligns himself with an augustinian vision of the community as a place of difference, requiring different remedies. Like Augustine in the *Praeceptum*, Pomerius is prepared to envisage a community where different standards of virtue are countenanced:

It is ineffective to scold all, as it is to treat all mildly. Holy priests will know and be able to discern whom they should correct with a carefully moderated strictness, and whom they should tolerate out of the magnanimity appropriate to their office. . . . The presence of those who, because of their own frailty, are unable to bear the rebuke of another, is to be born with mildness and a sense of duty.[52]

This was, as it were, a clear rebuke to Cassian. As we have seen, the

---

[49] *De vita cont.* I. 16. 4, PL 59, 461B: 'Nunc autem, quod Christiani temporis sacerdotes magis sustinent quam curant possessiones ecclesiae . . .'. II. 4, PL 59, 448A has Pomerius in the process of composition (*dictamen*) but the location is unspecified.

[50] Plumpe, 'Pomeriana', is a scrutiny of Pomerius' vocabulary aimed at exacting a measure of institutional clarity from the text, and guides my own discussion here.

[51] *De vita cont.* II. 1, ACW 4, 57.

[52] Ibid. II. 5, PL 59, 449B, 450A. My translation.

ascetic experts of the *Conferences* know only one kind of remedy for all conditions. Pomerius brushed aside Cassian's sense that there is only one kind of remedy and his contention that a community with differing levels of spiritual ability is impossible to sustain. He affirmed instead Augustine's hope that a (monastic) community could accommodate difference.

This augustinian vision of community appears to relate to an equally augustinian model of how the episcopal household ought to be organized. Bishop Julian had asked, 'Is it expedient to hold the goods of the Church to provide for the community life of the [priestly] brethren and their support, or to spurn them through love of perfection?' In other words, should the bishop and his clerical *familia* seek to recreate the apostolic Jerusalem, as envisaged by Augustine—or was it better to follow the path of perfection advocated in Jesus' answer to the rich man (the path advocated by Cassian)? Pomerius' answer was, unhesitatingly, that the bishop's household ought to live with their property in common.[53]

Absent from Pomerius' discussion, however, is any explicit reference to the earliest community of Christians at Jerusalem, and to the unity of hearts established by the community of property.[54] His discussion of the episcopal household turns instead into an analysis of avarice—unlike Augustine, he was even prepared to tolerate priests who were too weak to renounce their possessions—and from there into the analysis of gluttony which we have followed above.[55] In other words, the shape of the community gathered around the bishop as Pomerius has defined him remains unclear.

What remains in focus is episcopal authority. Pomerius implies that the community of clerics in the episcopal household, and the wider community of the Church are formed by the expertise of the bishop.[56] A discussion towards the end of *On the Contemplative Life* about 'social virtue' devolves rapidly into a condemnation of those endowed with pastoral gifts 'who shun the work of a burdensome administration for the sake of enjoying repose'.[57] The bishop, through a combination of

[53] *De vita cont.* II. 9–12, PL 59, 453–6. This was the passage cited by Chrodegang of Metz, as above n. 12; and for discussion, see Ganz, 'Ideology of Sharing', 22–4.

[54] Elsewhere, Pomerius offers an ascetic definition of charity as a 'right will turned completely from all earthly and present things, joined and united inseparably to God' (*De vita cont.* III. 13, PL 59, 493B, ACW 4, 131).

[55] On weak priests, see ibid. II. 12, PL 59, 455D–456A.

[56] *De vita cont.* II., PL 59 449B.

[57] See ibid. III. 28, PL 59, 509–11, ACW 4, 156.

compassion and rhetorical expertise, is able to cater for the needs of the faithful, both physical and spiritual.[58] This is a momentous insight, glimpsed, but not fully worked out in *On the contemplative life*: it will be for Gregory the Great to develop the premiss that the ascetic expert in power can bind up and resolve the tensions and differences of the community.

There were risks involved in such a view of moral authority: an extra burden of expectation attended the ascetic ruler, and new possibilities arose for abuse and corruption of power. Pomerius knew that his proposals required an extra vigilance concerning the character of those who came to power.[59] He deliberately interrupts his own celebration of the relationship between a holy bishop and the flock who benefit from his correction in order to signal his awareness that this relationship could sour. 'I had not yet completed my discussion about holy priests, when one of our friends came in and curiously asked me what I was dictating.' Having read what Pomerius has to say, the unnamed friend explodes into a tirade against bishops whose familiarity with ascetic discourse leads them only to pander to those in their flock who exploit the display of moral virtue to take advantage of virgins, widows, and orphans. The friend's outburst allows Pomerius to expand upon the dangers of favouritism and hypocrisy on the part of the bishop, and above all, of rhetorical pride. 'It is not for me to say anything of those who, prompted by slight suspicion, rebuke men who live uprightly so that they confuse and discourage them through ungrounded correction and thereby seek for themselves the glory of an ill-considered severity.'[60] Pomerius was certain that one who reproves, 'not to correct, but to vaunt himself insultingly, will not escape the anger of God', but he opens an alarming vista of authoritarian abuse.[61] His confidence that episcopal corruption will be exposed obscures the case of the bishop who, in good faith, was too harsh in correction—the very case Augustine had considered in the *Rule*. Pomerius gave to bishops a moral voice, but he made it in some ways more difficult for bishops and their subjects to tell when either had crossed the line.

The best evidence for the institutional working through of Pomerius' rhetorical instruction is furnished, perhaps, by Caesarius of Arles. In Caesarius we find a bishop who had absorbed and strove to

---

[58] *De vita cont.* I. 12, PL 59, 428B.
[59] See ibid. I. 21, PL 59, 435–7: *luctuosa descriptio sacerdotis carnaliter viventis*.
[60] Ibid. II. 8, PL 59, 452C, ACW 4, 71.
[61] Ibid. II. 8, PL 59, 453A, ACW 4, 72.

implement Pomerius' ideas about the ascetic expert in power. Pomerius himself and his correspondents make no mention of Caesarius, but the bishop's *Life* gives a memorable account of his encounter with his teacher. The rhetor's patrons in the city, Firminus and Gregoria, asked him to take charge of Caesarius, then a young man recently arrived in the city. It was a challenging assignment, as the youth had already fallen out with his previous mentor, the abbot of Lérins, for his excessive ascetic zeal. Pomerius' task was to complement this (abbreviated) spiritual training with 'worldly knowledge'. The pupil, however, seemingly rejected what his teacher had to offer. Asleep at his studies one day, Caesarius had a terrifying vision of a dragon twisting itself around his arm and shoulders as he leant on his books. Drawing the moral that he should not be bound in the coils of earthly wisdom, the future bishop put his trust in an untutored, spiritually pure speech. He understood, according to his biographers, 'that the gift of perfect eloquence would not be lacking in one who shone with spiritual understanding'.[62]

To readers of Pomerius, then and now, the moral of this story can hardly be that Caesarius rejected his education in rhetoric: to the contrary, it demonstrates the enduring influence of Pomerius' lessons, not only on Caesarius, but also on Caesarius' biographers.[63] The antitheses in this episode from the bishop's *Life*—between pure and monstrous speech, and between true teachers and false rhetoricians— are articulated in terms drawn almost verbatim from the scene of Pomerius' counselling of Bishop Julianus in *On the contemplative life*. In this sense, the story of Caesarius' dream as a student reveals the transmission of Pomerius' pastoral rhetoric across three generations in sixth-century Gaul—from Pomerius to Caesarius, and thence to Caesarius' younger episcopal colleagues who were to act as his biographers.[64] This is not to say, of course, that Caesarius himself was simply the mouthpiece for his master's voice. But as we turn to hear the extraordinary rhetorical performance of the Bishop of Arles, we ought to bear in mind the man who taught him. The date of Pomerius' death is unknown to us, but it is at least possible that he witnessed his disciple in action as a speaker.

---

[62] *VCaes* I. 9, MGH SRM 3, 460. Cf. Jerome's famous account of his dream in a cave in Syria, *Ep.* 22. 30 (in which God told him 'Ciceronianus es, non Christianus', and for comparative discussion of both Jerome and Caesarius, Kaster, *Guardians of Language*, 70–1, 81, 93–5.   [63] *Pace* Solignac, 'Julien Pomère', 1594.

[64] Cyprian of Toulon, Firminus of Uzès, and Viventius of unknown see, are responsible for part I of the *Vita Caesarii*. See Klingshirn, TTH 19.

4

The Pure Speech of Caesarius of Arles

A bishop addresses his episcopal colleagues in southern Gaul. 'If we weigh it well and carefully in our hearts, there is a grave danger and a huge burden pressing on the necks of all bishops', he begins.[1] They are to be called to account for the sins of those in their charge. Bishops should think of themselves in the most morally exalted terms. It was not their part to spend time in the administration of Church property: delegating such routine tasks to parish priests, bishops should devote their energies to preaching. The episcopal burden is thus a rhetorical one; it falls on watchful bishops to 'cry out, without ceasing' (Isa. 58: 1). The speaker anticipates, only to brush aside, the objection that special rhetorical gifts are required for this. 'We know that the Lord our God did not choose scholars or rhetors; he chose illiterate fishermen and shepherds, the poor and ignoble to preach the word.'[2] Untrained speech was indeed morally safer, claimed the bishop, being untainted by worldly rhetoric. Here we have Caesarius of Arles, Pomerius' star pupil, in full flight: the anxieties given voice to by Bishop Julianus in *On the contemplative life* are boldly resolved in this address, composed in the late 520s, at the height of Caesarius' influence over the Church in southern Gaul.

Caesarius of Arles is seen by scholars to have followed his own exhortations. He has the reputation of a popular preacher of great fervour and enduring influence. Nearly 250 of his sermons 'to the people' have survived, and there may be more to discover.[3] William

---

[1] *Caes.Serm.* 1. 3, CCSL 103, 2. See Klingshirn, *Caesarius*, 228–9, for a summary and discussion of this address and its date (it seems to have been written rather than actually delivered), emphasizing the issues of clerical status involved in Caesarius' call for the delegation of powers to parish priests. My concern here is with the moral tradition invoked by Caesarius in his discussion of episcopal authority, and in particular, his recasting of themes and motifs learnt from Pomerius.

[2] Ibid. 1. 20, CCSL 103, 16. Cf. Pomerius *De vita cont.* I. 23.

[3] The reconstitution of the Caesarian homiletic corpus was the life's work of Dom Germain Morin; he collected 231 sermons which he attributed to Caesarius (*Sancti Caesarii Episcopi Opera Omnia*, 2 vols. (Maredsous, 1937), i, *Sermones*, repr. in CCSL 103–4 (Turnhout, 1953); and see his manifesto, 'Mes principes et ma méthode pour la future édition de saint Césaire', *RBen* 10 (1893), 62–78). Since the appearance of Morin's edition, at least ten more sermons have been attributed to Caesarius; see e.g. R. Étaix, 'Deux nouveaux sermons de saint Césaire d'Arles', *REAug* 11 (1965), 9–13; id., 'Nouveau sermon pascal de saint

Klingshirn's study of Caesarius—the first full-length treatment for nearly a century—has reinvigorated our sense of Caesarius' extraordinary ambition and energy in attempting to Christianize the citizens and peasants in his diocese.[4] Klingshirn argues that Caesarius' missionary attempt fell short of its goals precisely because of its impossibly visionary quality: peasant communities literally did not have time to undertake the kind of devotional regime urged on them by their urban and aristocratic bishop.[5] In the longer term however—as Klingshirn shows—Caesarius' achievement was to bequeath to later churchmen an example of what it was to bring standards of Christian perfection associated with the monastic cloister out into the world of the laity. The sheer force of his initiative was unequalled until the Carolingians, rich farmers of his textual legacy, or indeed the reformers and missionaries of the early modern period.[6]

Caesarius also has the reputation of being the faithful champion of Augustine in the early middle ages. At the Council of Orange in 529, he is traditionally seen to have carried the day for the augustinian

Césaire d'Arles', *RBen* 75 (1965), 201–11; id., 'Les épreuves du juste. Nouveau sermon de saint Césaire d'Arles', *REAug* 24 (1978), 272–7. On the other hand, some of the works included in the second volume of Morin's edition ('Coegisti me', and *De gratia, Opera omnia*, ii. 129–34, 159–64) have been shown to be later texts transmitted under Caesarius' name (See R. Etaix, 'Trois notes sur S. Césaire', *Corona Gratiarum*, i Instrumenta Patristica 10 (Steenbrugge, 1975), 211–27). In light of the growing critique of the reliability of Morin's attributions in other contexts, a reassessment of his reconstruction of the Caesarian homiletic corpus may be necessary: see B. Axelson, *Ein drittes Werk der Firmicus Maternus? Zur Kritik der philologischen Identifierungsmethode* (Lund, 1937), Kungl. Humanistika Vetenskapssamfundets i Lund, Årsberättelse, IV; K. Cooper, 'Concord and Martyrdom: Gender, Community, and the Uses of Christian Perfection in Late Antiquity', 2 vols. (Princeton Univ. PhD. thesis, 1993), ii. 345–85; and E. Lowe, 'Asceticism in Context: The Anonymous *Epistolae sangallensis 190*' (Manchester Univ. M.A. thesis, 1998). On Morin himself, see G. Ghysens, P.-P. Verbraken, *La Carrière scientifique de Dom Germain Morin (1861–1946)* (Steenbrugge/La Haye, 1986); and J. M. Vessey, 'After the Maurists: the Oxford Correspondence of Dom Germain Morin OSB', in J. Fontaine, R. Herzog, and K. Pollmann (eds.), *Patristique et Antiquité tardive en Allemagne et en France de 1870 à 1930: Influences et échanges. Actes du Colloque franco-allemand de Chantilly (25–27 octobre 1991)* (Paris: Institut des Études Augustiniennes, 1993), 166–90.

[4] The earlier studies are Arnold, *Caesarius von Arelate*, and A. Malnory, *Saint Césaire, Eveque D'Arles* (Paris, 1894; repr. Geneva, 1978). See also H. C. J. Beck, *The Pastoral Care of Souls in South-East France during the Sixth Century* (Rome, 1950); Beck promised to treat Caesarius' monastic activities in another volume, but this never appeared. See Klingshirn, *Caesarius*, 3–5, for an overview of work on Caesarius since the 1890s.

[5] See esp. Klingshirn, *Caesarius*, 199–200.

[6] Ibid. 242–3, 271–86. See also R. A. Markus, 'From Caesarius to Boniface: Christianity and Paganism in Gaul', in J. Fontaine and J. Hillgarth (eds.), *The Seventh Century: Change and Continuity* (London, 1992), 250–76; R. McKitterick, *The Frankish Church and the Carolingian Reforms, 789–895* (London, 1977), esp. 45–79, 90–2.

theology of grace against its 'semi-Pelagian' opponents. The demise of this view of dogmatic history notwithstanding, Caesarius' special affiliation with Augustine remains an accepted point of reference in a variety of other contexts. Thus Augustine's writings are seen to have profoundly shaped Caesarius' vision of human community, both inside and outside the cloister;[7] and Caesarius' prowess as a popular preacher is understood to follow from his close attention to the example of the bishop of Hippo. In his eagerness to learn how to emulate the master of the charismatic appeal, Caesarius would happily redeliver a homily of Augustine's verbatim;[8] and he would urge other priests to do the same.[9] Caesarius' overall project has thus been understood as an attempt to realize in his diocese the City of God.[10]

The received image of Caesarius as an augustinian popular preacher need not, however, carry all before it. There is reason to suppose that, as a pastor, Caesarius was more focused on the city than on the rural parishes.[11] More surprisingly, we find that his discipleship of Augustine notwithstanding, Caesarius organized his programme of Christianization around the premise that it was Cassian who had best defined the means and ends of Christian perfection.[12] The rhetor Pomerius had already indicated some of the advantages a bishop could gain as a preacher from attention to Cassian: his pupil dramatically exploited this suggestion. Striving to construct an image of the heavenly Jerusalem on earth, Caesarius drew inspiration less from the augustinian community of charity, and more from Cassian's vision of a citadel of pure speech. He sought not so much to awaken a sense of the workings of divine grace in the lives of his hearers, as to catch their attention with his words, so as to fix their minds on the divine word. The mental preoccupation of the whole flock with sacred Scripture was an all-demanding pastoral ambition. In pursuit of it, Caesarius never hesitated to go to any lengths—and could never rid himself of the sense of incompletion.

---

[7] Klingshirn, *Caesarius*, 26–32.

[8] e.g. *Caes.Serm.* 231, 232, CCSL 104, 915–21: *Aug.Serm.* 339, 340 (the former being the consecration anniversary sermon discussed above, Ch. 1).

[9] Ibid. 2, CCSL 103, 18–19.

[10] Klingshirn, *Caesarius*, 32.

[11] See *Caes.Serm.* 1. 6–7, CCSL 103, 5.

[12] For an initial discussion of this view of Caesarius, see P. Christophe, *Cassien et Césaire, prédicateurs de la morale monastique* (Gembloux, 1969).

THE CAESARII OF ARLES

The icon of Caesarius as a popular preacher is not the creation of twentieth-century historiography: the bishop and his biographers went to great lengths to promote such an image. Caesarius' sermons monumentally attest to his effort to expand the boundaries of the ascetic community of letters. We see him in Arles and in the country-side, relentlessly stating and restating his commitment to the moral safety of his hearers. The *Life*, meanwhile, composed shortly after his death, shows the bishop bestriding his diocese, and other territories, like a colossus. Wherever he goes, 'it is hardly possible to approach him to say hello because of the sheer number of poor people making their requests to him.'[13] Our own access to Caesarius is equally restricted, thanks to the rhetorical screen thrown up by him and his disciples. We have no means of describing Caesarius' development as a preacher, because almost none of the sermons can be dated with any certainty: his own editor, he specifically erased markers of time in his texts because he wanted to enable others to use his sermons, just as he reused those of Augustine. Indications as to place are as fragmentary and unreliable: sometimes he indicated whether the countryside or the town was the more suitable venue, but more often than not, we are in the dark.[14]

Clearer, perhaps, is the civic context for this concerted fashioning of Caesarius. The depiction of the bishop with his flock in the countryside is there; but behind it we see the struggle of Caesarius, his relatives and the close associates, a group we might call 'the Caesarii', to face down their rivals in the city of Arles. This was not simply a competition for power or status. At stake across the four decades of Caesarius' episcopate was the nature and purpose of authority itself, as the bishop attempted to reshape the city and its élite into an ascetic community. The audience for whom the image of Caesarius as 'the people's bishop' was projected was not, therefore, the peasant farmers of Provence, but the rich and urbane clergy and laity of Arles.[15] If

---

[13] *VCaes.* I. 37, MGH SRM 3, 471, tr. Klingshirn, TTH 19, 28. On crowds of the poor and civic leaders, see Brown, *Power and Persuasion*, 71–117.

[14] See Klingshirn, *Caesarius*, 9–15, for discussion of Caesarius' homiletic corpus, and further references to the few sermons we can date and locate.

[15] On the material conditions of Arles in this period, see S. Loseby, 'Arles in Late Antiquity: *Gallula Roma Arelas* and *urbs Genesii*', in N. Christie and S. Loseby (eds.), *Towns in Transition: Urban Evolution in Late Antiquity and the Early Middle Ages* (Aldershot, 1996), 45–70. My point here is that Caesarius calculated that his hearers thought of themselves as rich.

Caesarius mentions the poor, or the rustics, it is frequently in order to shame his own peer group. In a sermon on almsgiving for example, Caesarius evokes the poor man who makes space for a little bed in the corner of his house for a stranger. 'What excuse do we have—with our large and spacious houses—for hardly ever offering such hospitality?'[16] Such an appeal to the propertied is not surprising in a homily on alms-giving, but it is repeated in other, less obvious, contexts. In condemn-ing sexual intercourse on holy feast days, for example, he warns that the children born of such unions are either epileptics or lepers; and that such miscegenation happens especially among the 'rustics'.[17] This is a frank appeal to the urbane self-image of his listeners to induce their continent behaviour. 'The people', in short, often served Caesarius as a rhetorical foil with which to prick the consciences of the civic élite, whose allegiance the bishop could not afford to neglect.

The vicissitudes of the Caesarii in Arles emerge directly in the bishop's *Life*. This text was commissioned and produced by Caesarius' immediate circle of family, his closest episcopal colleagues, and his attendants in the years immediately following his death in 542.[18] Under threat themselves from the bishop's enemies and detractors, they knew that Caesarius had found his fellow clerics and the citizens of Arles more intractable than the drunken 'rustics' whom he sought to civilize. Accordingly, Caesarius' biographers seek to present him as a man who spurned the privileges of his station. Of noble birth, Caesarius began and could have maintained a career as a cleric in his home town of Châlons, but in his mid-twenties he abandoned this course. Drawn by its magnetic reputation,[19] he sought and gained entry to the community at Lérins. Although the *Life* presents this move as a renunciation of family ties, the narrative reveals in spite of itself the extent to which Caesarius' career at Lérins and then at Arles

---

[16] *Caes.Serm.* 199. 3, CCSL 104, 804.

[17] Ibid. 44. 6, CCSL 103, 197.

[18] The *Vita* has been edited by B. Krusch, MGH SRM 3 (1896), 457–501; and again by Morin, *Opera Omnia*, ii. 293–349; see now the trans. by W. E. Klingshirn, TTH 19, 9–65. The text itself is composed in two parts. The first, which tends to concentrate on Caesarius' public career, is the work of Bishops Cyprian of Toulon, Firminus of Uzès, and Viventius (his see unknown); the second, focused on Caesarius in his household and as a miracle-worker, is composed by Stephen, a deacon, and Messian, a priest, both of them members of the bishop's entourage. On the circumstances of its composition, see W. E. Klingshirn, 'Caesarius' Monastery for Women in Arles and the Composition and Function of the *Vita Caesarii*', *RBen* 100 (1990), 441–81.

[19] Cf. *Caes.Serm.* 236. 3, citing 1 Kings 10: 6: 'It was a true report that I heard in mine own land.' Addressing the Lérins community from Arles, Caesarius reminds the monks of their responsibility to live up to their reputation.

depended upon the successful exploitation of family connections.[20] It was, perhaps, the very strength of these connections which drove Caesarius into repeated and extravagant demonstrations of his ascetic otherworldliness. Such a relentless show of moral superiority may have safeguarded the bishop and his family from the crude accusation of feathering their own nest—but it was hardly calculated to appease the concerns of the clergy and the laity who were excluded from the moral circle of the Caesarii. As the *Life* records, his opponents were not slow to level the charge that the bishop's stewardship of the Church of Arles was driven by an excessive and damaging zeal.

The issue of Caesarius' stewardship is present in the *Life* from the very start of his ascetic career at Lérins.[21] The account of the young neophyte at the island monastery is constructed as a case study in ascetic zeal and its measured correction. Appointed as cellarer, Caesarius showed himself to lack precisely the expertise required to exercise responsible stewardship of the monastery's resources. He succeeded only in antagonizing his peers with the miserliness of his rations, and in inducing his own physical collapse. His headstrong fasting recalled the early days of the ascetic movement in Gaul, betraying proud lack of self-control rather than humble temperance.[22] Taking advantage of Caesarius' debilitated condition, Abbot Porcarius sent the hothead to Arles to convalesce. Here, he was received into the prominent household of Firminus and Gregoria. As we have seen, they found for him the best rhetorical instruction available in the shape of Pomerius, and introduced the young man to his relative, Bishop Aeonius. In circumstances that are not entirely clear—because of the reticence of Caesarius' biographers—Aeonius began to groom

---

[20] A point well made by Klingshirn, *Caesarius*, 72.

[21] There has been much speculation as to the monastic regime observed at Lérins when Caesarius arrived there *c*.495. Caesarius later referred to the *regula Lirinensis* in the liturgical section of his *Rule for Virgins* (*Reg. virg.* 66. 2, SC 345, 254), and many attempts have been made to reconstruct this rule. For a brief discussion of whether the 'rule of Lérins' in the late fifth century can be identified with the *Regula Macarii*, see Klingshirn, *Caesarius*, 24–6, resuming A. de Vogüé, *Les Règles des saints Pères*, SC 297, 298. The main piece of evidence customarily invoked is the mention in the 7th-cent. *Life of John of Réomé* of a *regula Macarii* implemented by John in his monastery of Reomanus near Langres, after an eighteen-month stay at Lérins (Jonas of Bobbio, *Vita Iohanni* 4–5, MGH SRM 3, 508–9). While it is plausible to argue that John had encountered this *Rule of Macarius* at the island monastery, there is no reason to assume either that this text was in force as the 'Rule of Lérins'; or that it is identical with the text that has been transmitted as the *Rule of Macarius* (hardly an uncommon name in ascetic circles in this period).

[22] *VCaes.* I. 7, MGH SRM 3, 459–60; Klingshirn, *Caesarius*, 30 (following Sr. Mary Kealy) points out that the episode is constructed as an illustration of Cassian's teachings on fasting at *Inst.* 5. 23, SC 109, 230–2; *Conl.* 2. 17–24, SC 42, 132–5.

Caesarius as his successor, giving him charge of a monastery in Arles.[23] The sudden appearance and promotion of the newcomer did not endear him to the local clergy. Like Hilary of Arles before him, Caesarius was exactly the kind of untried ascetic stranger whose assumption of episcopal office had so concerned Pope Celestine and other observers three generations previously. It is, perhaps, an index of the advances made by the ascetic party in Gaul that, on Aeonius' death, Caesarius was able to best the rival local candidate for the office, and to curry favour with Rome;[24] it is equally the case that he could never take his tenure of power for granted, as the local clerical party strove obstinately to undermine him. In this treacherous institutional context,[25] much depended upon Caesarius' prowess as a public speaker. If he could persuade the Arles patriciate of his credentials as a disinterested servant of the common good, then his opponents could be kept at bay.

Caesarius and his supporters engaged in a running battle with his clergy about the proper disposition of the resources of the Church of Arles. In a city facing famine and siege, and in the relative absence of secular government, his was the responsibility of feeding the poor,[26] caring for the sick,[27] and feeding and housing refugees and the large number of prisoners whose ransom he had paid.[28] A good student of Pomerius, Caesarius doubtless saw his patronage of the poor and redemption of prisoners in ascetic terms—as an exaltation of the bodies of the symbolically defenceless.[29] In the eyes of the city clergy, these projects may have seemed an alarming and self-promotional exorbitance, and Caesarius made no effort to avoid confrontation on this issue.[30] In 508, for example, following the Gothic recapture of Arles from the Franks, he took drastic measures to raise the ransom for the large number of Frankish and Burgundian prisoners held in the city. Having disposed of all the Church plate, Caesarius proceeded to

[23] *VCaes.* I. 12, MGH SRM 3, 461.

[24] For the probable existence of a rival candidate, see W. E. Klingshirn, 'Church Politics and Chronology: Dating the Episcopacy of Caesarius of Arles', *REAug* 38 (1992), 80–8, resumed in id., *Caesarius*, 85–7.

[25] Treachery is not too strong a word: Arles was thick with accusations of treason, and Caesarius was usually implicated, especially in the early years of his episcopate. See *VCaes.* I. 21, 29, MGH SRM 3, 465, 467–8, and Klingshirn, *Caesarius*, 93–7, 107–10.

[26] *VCaes.* I. 20, MGH SRM 3, 464. Cf. ibid. I. 37, MGH SRM 3, 471.

[27] Ibid. I. 20, MGH SRM 3, 464.

[28] Ibid. II. 7, MGH SRM 3, 486.

[29] Cf. Pomerius, *De vita cont.* I. 12, PL 59, 428B, and above, p. 79.

[30] For a full discussion, see W. E. Klingshirn, 'Charity and Power: Caesarius of Arles and the Ransoming of Captives in Sub-Roman Gaul', *JRS* 75 (1985), 183–203.

remove and to sell all its consecrated ornaments. Three decades later his biographers report that 'even today the blows of axes are visible on podiums and railings from which the silver ornaments . . . were cut away'.[31] The axe-marks had evidently become a kind of ascetic graffiti in Arles—read as a sign of desecration by the city clergy, but in the eyes of the Caesarii and their followers, a forthright statement of the need of the church to renounce its worldly ornamentation.[32]

Caesarius' most ostentatious ascetic projects were his monasteries. There were three ascetic communities in the city for which he was responsible, two male and one female. Caesarius continued to oversee the male monastery which Aeonius had assigned to his charge; probably near the end of his career, he wrote a brief *Rule* for the monks.[33] The other male community Caesarius maintained was his episcopal household: women were barred from entering, and as his biographers make clear, the bishop held his clerical *familia* to the strictest ascetic standards.[34] Caesarius' especial pride—and the focus of opposition towards him—was the convent that he founded early in his episcopate (*c*.506/512),[35] dedicated to St John the Baptist, and located in the south-east corner of the city, tucked against the city walls. In naming his sister Caesaria as abbess of the community (having sent her to Marseilles for a training in the ascetic arts)[36] Caesarius no doubt hoped to maintain the strength of his family's presence and connections in Arles. When his sister died *c*.524, she was succeeded by the bishop's niece, also called Caesaria, who was to out-

[31] *VCaes*. I. 32, MGH SRM 3, 469, Klingshirn, TTH 19, 25.

[32] Similarly, the *Life* presents the captives redeemed by Caesarius as the true temple of the Lord, worth any of the treasures of the Church at Arles, I. 33, MGH SRM 3, 469. The practical wisdom of the vast expense on the redemption of captives is illustrated at II. 8, MGH SRM 3, 486–7, when the Burgundian king returns the favour done to him by Caesarius.

[33] Caesarius, *Regula monachorum*, ed. J. Courreau and A. de Vogüé, *Césaire d'Arles: Oeuvres Monastiques*, ii. *Oeuvres pour les moines*, SC 398 (Paris, 1994), 204–26. The order of composition of Caesarius' monastic *Rules* is disputed. It was generally assumed that the *Regula monachorum* preceded the *Regula ad virgines* until A. de Vogüé, 'La Règle de Césaire d'Arles pour les moines: un résumé de sa Règle pour les moniales', *RAM* 47 (1971), 369–406, argued to the contrary, a conclusion now widely accepted. Albrecht Diem (Univ. of Utrecht) proposes anew the priority of the *Regula monachorum*.

[34] *VCaes*. I. 62, MGH SRM 3, 483.

[35] See *VCaes*. I. 28, 35, MGH SRM 3, 467, 470. The original foundation of *c*.506, located probably outside the city walls, was destroyed in the siege of the city in the winter of 507–8. Four years later, Caesarius refounded the community in a more secure location inside the city walls. See Klingshirn, *Caesarius*, 104–7, 117–18 (and the further references given there to the much-debated religious topography of the city).

[36] *VCaes*. I. 35, MGH SRM 3, 470. See above Ch. 2 n. 34 for speculation as to whether this convent is the same as the female community founded by Cassian.

live her uncle and take the lead in preserving his memory. (It was she who commissioned his *Life*.) Caesarius lavished attention on the nuns. He wrote a letter to the community, and then a *Rule*, and then a *Recapitulation* to the *Rule*, setting out an increasingly meticulous devotional regime;[37] in his *Testament*, he attempted to bind relations between the convent and his successor.[38] Of all the ascetic groups in the city, the consecrated virgins—whom few would ever see again once they had entered the convent enclosure—were to serve as the most potent emblem of the moral purity evoked so fervently by the bishop in his homilies to the people. His biographers duly report that in building the convent for the nuns, Caesarius 'like a latter-day Noah ... fashioning an ark' adorned and protected the Church and the city.[39]

As the convent was the vessel of Caesarius' most cherished hopes, so it may also have been the object of the bitterest opprobrium from his enemies. The sequence of texts relating to St John's, and in parti-cular the increasingly nervous clauses of the *Recapitulation* to the *Rule* and the *Testament*, thus register the fluctuations in Caesarius' political credit in the city—his anxious sense of its dwindling towards the end of his life. For example, to the clauses in the *Rule for Virgins* ensuring the strict enclosure of the nuns, Caesarius added the extraordinary stipulation that 'The hair of the women shall be tied no higher than the mark we have made in this place with purple ink'.[40] Although we have no evidence concerning the enforcement of this unusual clause, a mark is faithfully reproduced, in varying lengths, in the Carolingian exemplars of the rule.[41] As we have suggested elsewhere, such a mark was meant to underscore the claustration of the holy virgins, serving as a sign that theirs was a life of consummately regulated purity, fully deserving of the church's financial support.[42]

The same concern to demonstrate probity runs through the *Life*, commissioned *c*.546 by Caesaria the Younger. While the convent did not come under direct attack after Caesarius' death, its future in Arles

[37] For the text of the letter, known as *Vereor*, see SC 345, 294–338, tr. Klingshirn, TTH 19, 129–39. For the *Regula virginum* (*RV*), with the *recapitulatio*, see SC 245, 170–272; Eng. tr. M. C. McCarthy, *The Rule for Nuns of St Caesarius of Arles* (Washington DC, 1960). These texts are ed. and trans. in J. Courreau and A. de Vogüé, *Césaire d'Arles: Oeuvres Monastiques, i. Oeuvres pour les moniales*, SC 345 (Paris, 1988).

[38] Caesarius, *Testamentum*, SC 345, 380–96; tr. Klingshirn, TTH 19, 71–6.

[39] *VCaes*. I. 35, MGH SRM 3, 470.

[40] *RV* 56, SC 345, 240.

[41] SC 345, 241 n. 8.

[42] See C. Leyser, 'Long-haired Kings and Short-haired Nuns: Writing on the Body in Caesarius of Arles', *Studia Patristica* 24 (1993), 143–50.

was threatened by the foundation with Frankish royal patronage of
another convent and a monastery in the city.[43] The new bishop,
Aurelian, sought to wrest control of the memory and the cult of
Caesarius from the nuns: lacking adequate finances and political back-
ing, Abbess Caesaria and her well-wishers responded, as their revered
master had done, by exploiting to the full the rhetorical resources at
their disposal. The narrative of the bishop's *Life*, like the relics of
his body, was meant to serve as a protective talisman. If Caesarius'
disciples could tell his story, perhaps he would continue to act as their
patron. In the event, the Merovingians moved in on Arles, and the
convent was swamped by other foundations. Tempting as it may be to
hail this as the start of a regime of early medieval royal monasteries in
Arles, it is as well to recognize that the Merovingian *adventus* put an
end to forty years of the virtual monopoly of the Church by Caesarius
and his family members. That they managed to survive for so long is
in no small part due to his bravura as an orator.

MORAL SURVEILLANCE

Caesarius' ministry was dominated by vigilant attention to detail. As
he urged his flock towards an economy of fasting and almsgiving,
the bishop admitted that his own conduct had not always been as
scrupulous as it should have been: 'I blame and condemn myself, however, because it has sometimes happened that clothes of mine which I
should have given to the poor, have been devoured by moths.'[44] At the
Last Judgement, the bishop fears, his moth-eaten clothing will be used
as evidence against him. We may applaud here a classic instance of the
pastoral use of the 'rhetoric of vulnerability': the bishop's confession
was doubtless intended to set exacting standards of perfection for his
flock. At the same time, we ought not to ignore the concrete issue of
the bishop's clothes. This rhetorical flourish is one among a number of
signs that the distribution of Caesarius' garments was in fact a subject
of public scrutiny and debate.[45] Such expectations of the bishop came

---

[43] Klingshirn, 'Caesarius' Monastery for Women in Arles'; also id., *Caesarius*, 262–4.
[44] *Caes.Serm.* 199. 5, CCSL, 806, in response to James 5: 1–2: 'Your garments are moth-
eaten.' Note the possible augustinian parallel: *Aug.Serm.*, Mayence 27/Dolbeau 10, ch. 13,
ll. 301–3, *RBen* 102 (1992), 61, on the *detestabilis tinea*. Moth-eaten clothing was evidently a
problem in late antiquity.
[45] In the 540s in particular, Caesarius' garments seem to have become key tokens in
discussing the bishop's stewardship of the Church. In his will, Caesarius twice disposes

as much from his supporters as his enemies: the *Life* shows that Caesarius' biographers were keenly aware of the politics of their master's wardrobe.[46] What may appear to a modern audience as the minutiae of style speak to the bishop's temperament as an orator—and to the aristocratic milieu in which Caesarius was operating, where mastery of detail could be everything. To appreciate this, we need only turn to the convent. Caesarius' nuns epitomize the Christianity of the rich laity of Arles: they will presume to have slave-girls, they will want to hang waxed curtains, tapestries, and pictures, decorate the oratory with silk and other expensive fabrics, wear purple or embroidered clothes, and dress their hair.[47] No further explanation is needed for the ascetic bishop's invocation of his moth-eaten clothing that ought to have been given as alms.

The determination to establish a regime of strict surveillance in an élite culture of ostentation conditioned Caesarius' assimilation of the writings of Augustine. Time and again, we find Caesarius using augustinian texts and motifs, but in ways that were some distance from their context in Augustine himself. Caesarius' resolve to use Augustine's words for his own purposes is perhaps nowhere more evident than in a monastic context. It has been amply demonstrated that Augustine's *Rule* structures the whole of the middle section of Caesarius' *Rule for Virgins*;[48] but it is equally clear that community of property forms neither the economic nor the spiritual basis of the community along the lines envisaged by Augustine. At the start of his *Rule*, Caesarius quotes Matt. 19: 21, 'Go sell all you have and give to the poor', and

of his clothes, *Testamentum* 14–15 and 42–4, SC 345, 384, 394. At the beginning, he leaves the best garments to his successor, and the remainder to his household; at the end of the text, he redirects his finest coat and belt to Bishop Cyprian, and his fur coat to Abbess Caesaria, who had made it. While it is possible that these bequests were made at different times (see SC 345, 362–4 for a possible chronology of composition) that there should be two provisions is a measure of the pressure on Caesarius to account in detail for his management of ecclesiastical resources.

[46] As a boy, the precociously ascetic Caesarius is shown returning home having given all his clothes away to beggars: *VCaes*. I. 3, MGH SRM 3, 461–2. As bishop, Caesarius' clothes are invested with powers of healing, giving rise to a strong concern on the part of his attendants to control access to these powers. The deacon Stephen in particular seems to have used his proximity to Caesarius' miraculous garments to weave ties with the secular élite: see the stories of the patrician Liberius and his wife Agretia, both of them healed by touching the bishop's clothes at ibid. II. 10–15, 42–4, MGH SRM 3, 487–90, 498–9.

[47] For slave girls, *RV* 7. 1, SC 345, 186. For fabric, *Vereor* 7. 9–10, SC 345, 322; *RV* 44–5, 60. 1, SC 345, 228–30, 244. For hair, *RV* 56, SC 345, 240, and for discussion, Leyser, 'Long-haired Kings and Short-haired Nuns'.

[48] *RV* 20–35, SC 345, 194–218. For a full survey, see L. Seilhac, 'L'Utilisation par s. Césaire d'Arles de la Règle de s. Augustin', *StAns* 62 (Rome, 1962).

this is nowhere countermanded.[49] The convent is not a place where the differences of social class will be abrogated: the daughters of the poor are not expected as inmates. The poor, in fact, are not to come near the monastery, as they may create a disturbance at the door: the abbess is to supervise all almsgiving activities.[50] Caesarius systematically edits the augustinian *Rule*, removing the clauses dealing with the poor.[51] The convent in Arles is no anticipation of the heavenly Jerusalem as Augustine had imagined it. The community can only serve as a receptacle for the bishop's authority.

Caesarius' imagination of the eschatological community itself is a clear measure of his likeness and dissimilarity from Augustine—and the extent to which this is determined by the pastoral exigencies of his situation in Arles. Directly paraphrasing Augustine, Caesarius describes two cities, Jerusalem and Babylon, humble and proud, built by Christ and the Devil respectively.[52] In the conclusion to the sermon, however, he imagines an objection from the audience: 'Perhaps someone is thinking to themselves why has there been no mention of charity and desire in this sermon?' In response, Caesarius stresses that humility derives from charity, the mother of all virtues, and pride from desire, the 'root of all evils'. 'Whenever in sacred Scripture you hear . . . the condemnation of pride, you should understand the execration of desire.'[53] Thus he suggests to his congregation at Arles that if they hear mention of pride, they should immediately call to mind its association with desire.[54] On several other occasions, he does not trouble to legitimate or to mark his departure from augustinian premises: he simply takes as axiomatic the Pauline dictum on desire as the root of all evils.[55]

Caesarius here shows himself a true pupil of Pomerius. He takes for

[49] *RV* 5, SC 345, 182–4 cites Matt. 19: 21, from *Inst* 4. 3–5, 7. 16, SC 109, 124–8, 314. Cf. *Vereor* 8, SC 345, 324–8: girls should not give their fortunes back to their parents. They may give their parents little presents, but should aim to give as much as possible in alms. Fifteen short chapters later, *RV* 20. 4, SC 345, 194, cites Acts 4: 32, conjoined with 4: 35. In this sense, *RV*, like the contemporary rules for cenobites in Italy, is a florilegium. See below, Ch. 5, for discussion of the opportunities afforded by the genre of the florilegium for synthesizing different traditions.

[50] *RV* 42. 1–7, SC 345, 224.

[51] See the omission at *RV* 21. 2 (SC 345, 196) of *Praec* 1. 5–6, Verheijen, i. 419, ll. 17–22, on the pride of the poor in being in the company of the rich. On illness, *Praec* 3. 5, *Règ.Aug.* i. 422, ll. 69–72, is removed at *RV* 22. 3–4, SC 345, 198.

[52] *Caes.Serm.* 48. 5–7, CCSL 103, 219–21; cf. 120. 7, CCSL 103, 503; 233. 3–4, CCSL 104, 926–7.   [53] Ibid. 48. 5–7, CCSL 103, 219–21.

[54] Ibid. 48. 7, CCSL 103, 220.

[55] e.g. ibid. 22. 2–3; 23. 1; 39. 3; 120. 7.

granted the antitheses structuring the argument in the *City of God*—spirit and flesh, will and refusal, heavenly heights and earthly degradation—but his very familiarity with this vocabulary enables him to use it without the precision of meaning intended by Augustine. Caesarius does not imagine the prelapsarian condition in any analytic detail, and simply avoids any discussion of the precise relation of will and desire in Eden. He arrives at generalizations about the Fall in the context of particular exegeses or exhortations, and one generalization need not exactly resemble another. On these occasions, he is not setting out his theological views on the Fall, so much as deploying a language of spiritual encouragement; he is thus able to bypass what might appear to be contradiction as he repeatedly assimilates pride and desire, and advises his audience how to avoid them.

Caesarius was not content to defer all his hopes for a pristine community until the end of time; nor was he content to think of the task of spiritual correction as 'stabbing in the dark'. He depicted himself as imposing the 'law of heaven' on the 'law of the forum'.[56] Concubinage, prostitution, and casual violation were evidently still normal civic practice in the sexual culture of the male élite. Caesarius sought to render them as shameful adultery and fornication. He evokes the boasting of noblemen over their exploits with slave-girls—their own, or their neighbours'—in order to ask what these same men would do if their wives behaved in the same way, or if a 'famous whore' came and embraced them in full view in the market-place.[57] 'They confess their exploits jokingly with an asinine cackle', he observes, the more formidably to imagine a future where their laughter will be turned into eternal weeping.[58]

The bishop of Arles aspired to a literal policing of desire in his city. He encouraged a regime of mutual correction and the denunciation of adulterers to himself.[59] Well aware that many priests colluded with the sexual habits of their peers, and that offenders were too many to excommunicate, Caesarius may have hoped none the less to lend psychological credence to the idea of moral surveillance. The notional army of loyal informers to whom Caesarius appealed for help embodied his drive to reveal secret thoughts of sex, that is, 'fornication' in the interior sense that most interested Cassian.[60] Adulterous talk, adultery in the gaze, in fantasy:[61] in the effort to uncover these

---

[56] *Caes.Serm.* 43. 4, CCSL 103, 192.
[58] Ibid. 42. 3, CCSL 103, 187.
[60] See above, Ch. 2.

[57] Ibid. 45. 2, CCSL 103, 202.
[59] Ibid. 42. 2, CCSL 103, 186.
[61] *Caes.Serm.* 41. 4–5, CCSL 103, 183.

elusive sins—indeed, to render them as sin—Caesarius takes the language of pollution to an unrestrained pitch:

> Tell me, I beg you, is there anyone who can stand above a latrine or a cesspit full of worms, and breathe in the smell? Compare now the atmosphere of the latrine with thoughts of lust, and see which gives off the greater stench.[62]

In the world of Caesarius' sermons, Arles is to become, like Calvin's Geneva, or Borromeo's Milan, a disciplined city of godly confession.

If we return to Caesarius' address in the 520s to his episcopal colleagues with which we began, we may observe him identifying his place within the tradition of moral language in which he had been schooled. The sermon is a reforming tract which sets out his view of pastoral responsibility as he ideally would wish it to be exercised. With a number of his supporters installed as his suffragans, the bishop of Arles was finally able to promote the ascetic understanding of episcopal and more broadly clerical office in which he had been trained:

> Bishops are called watchmen because they are placed in a higher position, as if at the highest citadel of the Church, namely the altar. From this place, they must watch over the city and the field of God, that is the whole Church. They must not only guard the disposition of the great gates—that is, prevent capital sins with their most wholesome preaching—they must also guard the small doors behind, the little underground passages. In other words, they must continually warn the people to watch the tiny sins that creep up every day, and to purge them with fasting, almsgiving and prayer.[63]

The cities of Provence had been frequently under siege: Caesarius could hardly have chosen a more graphic image with which to evoke the character, material and moral, of episcopal leadership in early sixth-century Gaul. In the same moment, he defined his position with regard to his mentors. Augustine and Pomerius had taken the Ezekiel passage as an opportunity to meditate upon the exposed condition of those in power: by contrast, the anxiety of authority for Caesarius resided in the possibility that in his role as a watchman a detail might escape him.

---

[62] *Caes.Serm.* 45. 3, CCSL 103, 203. [63] Ibid. 1. 3, CCSL 103, 3–4.

THE CITY OF PURE SPEECH

'Cry aloud, without ceasing', Caesarius enjoined his episcopal colleagues.[64] The instrument of episcopal vigilance was the voice, Caesarius had learnt from Pomerius, and he demanded that his words be heard. He shut the church doors at Arles so that no one could leave while he was preaching.[65] Conversely, he ensured that his texts were as widely disseminated as possible, thrusting copies into the hands of any interested visitors to Arles.[66] Caesarius condemned those who kept their books all shiny on the shelves—books were to be used, borrowed, passed around.[67] He aimed to secure the circulation of his words not merely in written form, but by word of mouth. His sermons were to be read out by priests and lay people alike. Caesarius brushed aside objections of illiteracy: surely in any group, there would be at least one person who could read to the rest, he argued.[68] He did everything possible to enforce the memorization of what he said, recapitulating the main points of his sermons in his perorations. If individuals could not remember a whole sermon, they should each remember a part of it, so that together they could reconstitute the complete body of his text.

Someone should say to someone else: 'I heard my bishop talking about chastity.' Another should say, 'I remember that he said we should cultivate our souls as we cultivate our fields.' Yet another should say, 'I recall that my bishop said that whoever can read should make an effort to read Scripture; whoever cannot read should find someone who can.' While they remind one another in this fashion what they heard, they are able not only to recall in their memories the whole word, but with Christ's help to fulfil it.[69]

Caesarius thus imagined the body of the faithful as a permanent audience, always attentive to his word—in fact, continuing to exist as a communal body because entrusted with his word.

This was a dramatic realization of Pomerius' insight into the sustaining social power of a well-trained voice. But where Pomerius

---

[64] *Caes.Serm.* 1. 2, CCSL 103, 2.
[65] *VCaes.* I. 27, MGH SRM 3, 466–7.
[66] Ibid. I. 55, MGH SRM 3, 480.
[67] *Caes.Serm.* 2, CCSL 103, 18–19.
[68] Ibid. 6. 2, CCSL 103, 31; 8. 1, CCSL, 103, 42.
[69] Ibid. 6. 8, CCSL 103, 35–6. In outlining a scenario of repetition by others, Caesarius was of course finding another device to repeat himself. For other recapitulations, see 99. 3, 117. 6, 124. 6; CCSL 103, 406, 489–90, 518. For further references, see A. Ferreiro, '*Frequenter legere*: The Propagation of Literacy, Education, and Divine Wisdom in Caesarius of Arles', *JEH* 43 (1992), 5–15.

had, in outline, envisaged that the bishop would minister to all indi-
vidually as they had need, Caesarius aimed to purify the minds of the
faithful with one basic strategy—that of the occupation of the mind
with sacred text. This was a lesson learned directly from Cassian,
whose work Caesarius may first have encountered at Lérins, before
his tutelage under Pomerius.[70] In sermon after sermon, Caesarius
hammered home Cassian's prescriptions on how to take in sacred
Scripture in order to drive out the suggestion of sin. Saturation with
Scripture was the answer to the problem of physical and rhetorical
excess. The holy word should penetrate to the marrow of the bone
beneath 'the flesh'. In his diagnosis of sin and in the remedy proposed,
Caesarius wanted the body to be completely taken up into sacred discourse.[71]

Caesarius' use of Cassian to develop a model of episcopal authority
is, at points, entirely unmediated (in contrast to his carefully tended
relation with Augustine). In a homily 'On reading assiduously', for
instance, he explains:

Every person, whether good or bad, cannot be empty; whoever fills their soul with
the love of the world cannot receive the sweetness of Christ . . . On the other hand
a holy and spiritual person . . . who frequently reads or hears sacred Scripture is
speaking with God. See if the devil can find his way in to anyone he sees continually talking to God.[72]

This is to follow Cassian's logic as outlined in the *Conferences* exactly.[73]
Caesarius does not hesitate to call upon Cassian's most powerful image
for the process of 'mental preoccupation':

Our mind seems to be like a millwheel, continually turned by the power of flowing
water; and just as mills cannot rest idle, so human minds cannot possibly be still.
However, with the help of God it is in our power to decide what it is we grind in
these mills of stone or in our minds.[74]

The millwheel was no empty metaphor: the townspeople of Arles
could immediately have called to mind the huge and ancient water-

---

[70] See above, Ch. 3 n. 48: the *Monita* of Caesarius' abbot Porcarius are redolent with
Cassian.

[71] The *Life* obliges him—he is described near his death as the radiant embodiment of
legibility, his inner virtues, most notably of speech, made plain on his face: *VCaes.* II. 35,
MGH SRM 3, 497.

[72] *Caes.Serm.* 8. 3, CCSL 103, 43.

[73] See above, Ch. 2.

[74] *Caes.Serm.* 8. 4, CCSL 103, 44. Cf. Caesaria the Younger, *Dicta* 3. 8, SC 345, 474: 'Quia
omnino numquam mens humana otiosa esse non potest . . .'

mill operating ten miles away from the city.[75] In grinding good grist—
holy and honest thoughts—Caesarius continues, 'we prepare a meal
for Christ who has honoured us by staying for supper'.[76] Like Cassian,
Caesarius reasoned that his own speech, in mediating the word of
God, could itself be used as good grist to the psychic mill: hence his
frequent use of repetition.

The logic of this programme demanded that Caesarius concern
himself not only with what his flock heard, but also with what they
said. One of his first actions as bishop was to make the laity prepare
psalms, hymns, and antiphons, 'to be chanted in a high modulated
voice, some in Greek, some in Latin . . . so that there would be no time
for telling stories in Church'.[77] Against the image of the community of
sanctified speech, Caesarius set the image of the ungodly society of the
alehouse, with their 'sins of the mouth'[78]—lies, boasts, flattery, insults,
obscenities, jokes, pagan songs. In any list of faults these are always
more prominent than anything else.[79] And the prime site of unclean
speech is the 'people', especially in the countryside: they are the
singing, laughing, dancing bodies.[80] However close this image was to
the realities of rural life, it does not make of Caesarius a 'popular
preacher'. He is rather the preacher who constructed 'the people' in
terms that became standard for the medieval and even more the
Reformation Churches. Caesarius is a Tridentine figure, defining a
'popular culture' to destroy.[81]

If the laity had to sing the office and to memorize their bishop's
sermons, in the monastery there could be no excuse for unclean
speech. The monastic life for Caesarius was defined by the intensity of
its vigilance for sins of the mouth. 'For if we do not restrain our
tongue, then our religious profession is not true, but false.'[82] The consequences of a tepid commitment were graphically laid out in the
Apocalypse: 'So then, because you are lukewarm, I shall spew thee out

[75] See Klingshirn, *Caesarius*, 41 and n. 73.
[76] *Caes.Serm.* 8. 4, CCSL 103, 44.
[77] *VCaes.* I. 19, MGH SRM 3, 464: '. . . ut non haberent spatium in ecclesia fabulis
occupari'.
[78] For *peccata oris*, see *Regula Magistri* 11. 30, SC 106, 14. See also ibid. 8–9 on *taciturni-
tas*, and 16. 53. These passages are discussed below in Ch. 5.
[79] See e.g. *Caes.Serm.* I. 10–12, CCSL 103, 7–8 (addressed to clerics); 14. 3 (to the
people), CCSL 103, 71; 234. 4, CCSL 103, 935 (to monks). All of these passages include a
citation of Wisdom 1: 11 'Os quod mentitur occidit animam.'
[80] e.g. ibid. 6. 3, CCSL 103, 32; 13. 4, CCSL 103, 67.
[81] P. Burke, *Popular Culture in Early Modern Europe* (London, 1978), 'The Triumph of
Lent', 207–44.
[82] *Caes.Serm.* 233. 7, CCSL 103, 931.

of my mouth.'[83] In his household, Caesarius could make certain that there was no lukewarm response to the word of God, as the *Life* records:

The noon meal and dinner were always accompanied with reading, so that the inner and outer man being well fed, both might doubly rejoice. I admit that in this enclosed and shut up atmosphere the listeners were sweating and many were greatly mortified when, in front of [Caesarius] they were found to have forgotten what they had heard read.[84]

In the *Rule for Virgins*, Caesarius sought to prescribe hour by hour the utterance of the nuns. Their strict enclosure within the walls of the convent is a prelude to the claustration of their own tongues. Having entered the convent, and 'escaped the jaws of the spiritual wolves', Caesarius urges his charges 'to strive to shun and avoid swearing and cursing as the poison of the devil'. Their own mouths, in other words, may be as dangerous to them as the jaws of the world.[85] No loud voices, no murmuring, no story-telling, no harsh words, no answering back:[86] against this litany of garrulousness, Caesarius sets the incessant rumination of the word of God, through reading, meditation in the heart, recitation from memory, performance in the liturgy.[87] The text of the the *Rule* itself Caesarius strove to make a vessel of the kind of immaculate rhetorical purity he is describing. He becomes increasingly anxious to assert that what he says comes not from his own presumption, but from Scripture and the Fathers.[88] He urges present and future abbesses not to change or diminish any aspects of the *Rule*—and enjoins the community to resist any abbess who does so.[89] The *Recapitulation* devolves into a series of repetitions, and the most repeated clauses are those which concern obedience to the *Rule* itself. In this sense, the nuns become irrelevant: their bodies, enclosed and defined, are a figure for the body of the text, which is the real object of Caesarius' ascetic attention.

We may now appreciate the full force for Caesarius of the injunc-

[83] *Caes.Serm.* 234. 4, CCSL 104, 938; 237. 2, CCSL 104, 945, recalling *Conl.* 4. 19, 183.
[84] *VCaes.* I. 62, MGH SRM 3, 483; modelled on Possidius' description of Augustine's household at *VAug.* 22, Pellegrino, 118–22. Here, as elsewhere, Caesarius can appear in an augustinian light while drawing ascetic inspiration from Cassian.
[85] *RV* 2–3, SC 345, 182.
[86] *RV* 9. 3, 13. 1, 17. 2, 19. 2, 26. 1; SC 345, 188, 190, 192, 194, 204.
[87] *RV* 18. 2–4, 20. 1–2, 66. 12–17, SC 345, 192, 194, 256. For a more detailed consideration of the liturgy, see SC 345, 114–28 (comparing *Inst.* 2. 2. 2, SC 109, 58–60).
[88] *RV* 63. 1–2, SC 345, 246.
[89] *RV* 48. 4, 64, SC 345, 234, 250.

tion of Isaiah, 'Cry out, without ceasing' (Isa. 58: 1). This was the imperative for the watchman, he insisted in his encyclical letter to his fellow bishops.[90] Keep talking, he was saying, keep filling your mouth and the ears and minds of your hearers with words; otherwise the devil will invade these boundaries and occupy these spaces. 'Cry aloud, without ceasing' becomes the poignant refrain of the bishop's *Life*. Bereft of their master's voice, his supporters and disciples sought to commemorate and to reproduce its power. They quoted and echoed the sermons,[91] praised Caesarius as a preacher,[92] told their particular stories. The deacon Stephen recalls the bishop talking in his sleep: when he awoke, Stephen said to him, 'It is your way always to cry out without ceasing.'[93] But Caesarius could not continue to speak from the grave. 'Although his sermons are recited, the voice that cried without ceasing has now ceased to cry.'[94] The *Life* becomes a desperate attempt to amplify a voice that has irrevocably stilled.

The plight of Caesarius' biographers arose, not only from the bishop's death, but from the ambivalent rhetorical legacy he had left them. In one sense, Caesarius' mission as a preacher had been to secure the assimilation by his hearers of an inherited language— the words of Scripture and the texts of the Fathers. In devoting his prodigious energies to the fulfilment of this vocation, however, Caesarius had left his successors with an indelible sense of his own voice. His claim simply to represent an established tradition jarred with the palpable force of his intervention. Caesarius' very rhetorical charisma undermined his own attempts to routinize the spiritual purification of his flock—a paradox his biographers were unable to resolve.

This tension between the language of tradition and the voice of the individual speaker was inherent in the asceticism of 'pure speech' as promulgated by Cassian. As we shall see in the following chapter, Caesarius' contemporaries in Italy—ascetic leaders such as Eugippius of Lucullanum and Benedict of Nursia—dealt with this ambiguity by seeking to bury their own rhetorical identities beneath the authority of a patristic consensus they had themselves constructed. Using the fiction of an anonymous master passing on the precepts of ascetic

---

[90] *Caes.Serm.* I. 10, CCSL 103, 7. See above, p. 81.

[91] See e.g. *VCaes.* prol., I. 28, I. 54, I. 61; MGH SRM 3, 458, 478, 482, quoting *Caes.Serm.* I. 3, I. 10, I. 15, 13. 4, CCSL 103, 2, 7, 11–13, 67.

[92] Ibid. I. 54–5, MGH SRM 3, 478–9.

[93] Ibid. II. 6, MGH SRM 3, 486.

[94] Ibid. II. 32, MGH SRM 3, 496.

wisdom, they established the ground rules for the development of the genre of the *Rule*, and the regular cenobitic tradition. Such a cancellation of authority of the individual speaker was not, however, a step all ascetics in power were prepared to take—Caesarius for one, and for another, Gregory the Great.

5

The Anonymity of The Rule of St Benedict

There can be few more vivid illustrations of the moral power of humility than that afforded by the *Rule of St Benedict*. 'Keep this little rule that we have written for beginners. After that you may set out for the loftier summits', closes the text.[1] The consequence, of course, is that the *Rule* for beginners acquires monumental status, being hailed for over a thousand years as the definitive formulation of the monastic life. Its appeal is readily ascribed precisely to its winning lack of self-importance.[2] While the *Rule*'s humanity speaks directly to many of its modern readers, this ought not to prevent recognition of the histori-cally specific intervention made by this mid-sixth-century text in the ascetic tradition thus far considered. The author of the *Rule*'s determination to write for beginners, we shall argue, represented not merely a generalized modesty, but a particular resolve to establish a monastic community and a language of authority which did not presume a high, or even a uniform, level of ascetic competence among its members. The *Rule* solves the problem of asceticism and commu-nity that had specifically defeated John Cassian: how experts and beginners could live together in a monastery.

A sense of tradition, of participation in a long-established culture, is fundamental to the self-understanding of the author of the *Rule*. Like a grammarian or a doctor, what he composed was a handbook, designed to summarize and to pass on existing lore, adapted as neces-sary to meet the practical needs of his audience as he assessed them. Clarity and accessibility were his primary rhetorical goals, not origi-nality or the establishment of his own literary persona.[3] Although the manuscript tradition is unanimous in ascribing the text to

---

[1] *RB* 73. 8–9, SC 182, 674; tr. *RB 1980: The Rule of St Benedict in Latin and English*, ed. T. Fry (Collegeville, Minn., 1981), 297. See de Vogüé, 'Introduction', SC 181, 40, caution-ing readers not to dismiss the *Rule*'s humility as a mere topos.

[2] See e.g. *RB* 18. 25, SC 182, 534: the spiritual master whose precepts the *Rule* embodies speaks of 'we feeble-minded ones'—which makes the more confident perspective of the *Rule of the Master* seem positively boastful. Cf. e.g. *RM* 28. 3, SC 106, 150: 'we, who are spiritual'. For a recent example of *RB*'s continuing appeal to a modern, lay audience, see E. De Waal, *Seeking God: The Way of St Benedict* (London, 1984).

[3] K. Zelzer, 'Benedikt von Nursia als Bewahrer und Erneurer der monastischen Tradi-tion der Suburbicaria', *RBS* 18 (1994), 203–19, esp. 204–5.

'Benedictus',[4] and although we possess a portrait of this Benedict from the hand of Pope Gregory the Great, composed with the help of the holy man's disciples, the text of the *Rule* itself is presented anonymously as the precepts of an unnamed teacher.[5] Gregory's account of Benedict in the *Dialogues* has become as definitive a portrait of its subject as is the *Rule* an encapsulation of the monastic life; since the eighth century at least, *Life* and *Rule* have been fused to make a 'benedictine' tradition.[6] While the *Life* is indeed a blessing for the study of the reception of the *Rule* in the generations after its composition, it does not always aid the attempt to reconstruct the tradition to which the author of the *Rule* belonged. Gregory's very admiration for Benedict and his *Rule* led him, as we shall see, to endow Benedict with the authority of an eschatological prophet, so abstracting this monastic teacher from the immediate cultural context in which he was formed.[7]

The author of the *Rule* himself, while he names the distant patristic authorities whom he regarded as the founding fathers of his tradition, does not trouble to identify for his readers his closest source of inspiration—assuming, perhaps, that they will already know. Only in the second half of this century have the *Rule of St Benedict*'s modern readers come to share in this knowledge.[8] It is now all but universally

---

[4] See de Vogüé, SC 181, 149–50.

[5] *RB* prol. 1, SC 181, 412, for the *praecepta magistri*. At *Dial.* II pref., SC 260, 128, Gregory lists his sources for his account of Benedict as Constantinus and Simplicius, who succeeded Benedict as abbot (at Montecassino), Valentinianus, 'for many years in charge at the Lateran', and Honoratus, a recluse at Subiaco. These men are not otherwise attested. At *Dial.* II. 1. 3–8, SC 260, 130–6, Gregory dramatizes the issue of the holy man's (frustrated) desire to avoid publicity: Benedict's secret retreat at Subiaco is discovered by a priest on Easter Sunday.

[6] On the benedictine tradition, see J. Leclercq, *L'Amour des lettres et le désir de Dieu: initiation aux auteurs monastique du moyen âge* (Paris, 1957); tr. K. Misrahi, *The Love of Letters and the Desire for God* (New York, 1963), 11. P. Meyvaert, 'Problems concerning the "Autograph" Manuscript of Saint Benedict's Rule', *RBen* 69 (1959), 3–21, broaches the topic of Paul the Deacon's assimilation of the *Dialogues* and the *Rule*. See *Dial.* II. 36, SC 260, 242, for Gregory's recommendation of the *Rule* as a source for anyone wishing to know more of Benedict's life, 'quia sanctus vir nullo modo potuit aliter docere quam vixit'.

[7] In seeking to compensate for this abstraction, A. de Vogüé, 'La Règle du Maître et les Dialogues de s. Grégoire', *RHE* 61 (1966), 44–76, compares the monastic regime of Subiaco as described by Gregory with the *Rules* of the Master and Benedict; while G. Cracco, 'Gregorio Magno interprete di Benedetto' in *S. Benedetto e otto secoli (XII–XIX) di vita monastica nel Padovano*, Coll. *Miscellanea erudita*, 33 (Padua, 1980), 7–36, endorses Gregory's view of Benedict's development from cloistered cenobite to apostle of the countryside.

[8] D. Knowles, 'The *Regula Magistri* and the *Rule* of St Benedict', in his *Great Historical Enterprises* (Oxford, 1963), 139–95, remains the classic account of the controversy. B. Jaspert, *Die RM–RB Kontroverse*, *RBS Supplementa* 2 (Hildesheim, 1975; 2nd edn. 1977) is

accepted that the *Rule of St Benedict*, in its structure and much of its content, is drawn directly from the earlier, longer *Rule of the Master*, whose author has proved more successful than Benedict in avoiding subsequent identification.[9] Intense debate and exhaustive research over the past fifty years have resulted in the consensus that the *Rule of the Master* was composed south-east of Rome in the first three decades of the sixth century.[10] To the author of the *Rule of St Benedict* then, writing himself in the same milieu in the period 530–560, the Master was the pre-eminent ascetic teacher of the previous generation, whose precepts he sought to pass on to present and future monastic communities.

Our appreciation of the reputation and influence of the Master has been further enhanced by the identification of another sixth-century reader and adapter of his *Rule*. Most scholars now believe Eugippius, abbot of a monastic community at Castellum Lucullanum near Naples 511–*c*.535, to have been the compiler of a cento *Rule* which draws as heavily as does the *Rule of St Benedict* on the *Rule of the Master*.[11] The one surviving manuscript of the florilegium, a late sixth-century copy, is in fact closely related in script and origin to our earliest copy of *Rule of the Master*.[12] As we shall see below, Eugippius is a much less elusive

the definitive bibliographic guide. For sage comment on the continuing research and debate in this area, see S. Pricoco, 'Il monachesimo in Italia dalle origini alla Regola di san Benedetto', in *La cultura in Italia fra tardo antico e alto medioevo: Atti del convegno tenuto a Roma, dal 12 al 16 Novembre 1979*, Consiglio nazionale delle ricerche (Rome, 1981), 621–41; id., 'Il primo monachesimo in Occidente: Alcune considerazioni su un dibattito attuale', *Studi e ricerche sull'oriente cristiano* XV (1992), 25–37; id., ed., *La Regola di San Benedetto e le Regole dei Padri* (Verona, 1995), pp. ix–lxiv; id. 'Il monachesimo occidentale dalle origine al maestro: Lineamenti storici e percorsi storiografici', in *Il monachesimo occidentale dalle origini alla Regola Magistri*, *Studia Ephemeridis Augustinianum* 62 (1998), 7–22.

[9] De Vogüé, SC 181, 173–314, gives a synoptic table of the relation between *RM* and *RB*, and a meticulous statement of the case for the priority of *RM*. The shared material between the two *Rules* is principally constituted by the following sections: the types of monks (*RM* 1, *RB* 1), the abbot (*RM* 2, *RB* 2), and the grades of humility (*RM* 10, *RB* 7).

[10] De Vogüé, SC 105, 221–3. However, the doubts expressed by P. Meyvaert, 'Towards a History of the Textual Transmission of the *Regula S. Benedicti*', *Scriptorium* 17 (1963), 83–110, remain pertinent; and a forthright dissenting note has been expressed by M. Dunn, 'Mastering Benedict: Monastic Rules and their Authors in the Early Medieval West', *EHR* 416 (1990), 567–94. (For the ensuing debate between de Vogüé and Dunn, see *EHR* 418 (1992), 95–111).

[11] *Eugippii Regula*, ed. F. Villegas and A. de Vogüé, *CSEL* 87 (1976). The material shared with *RM* and *RB* is as follows: on the types of monks (*REug* 27), on the abbot (*REug* 2), and on the grades of humility (*REug* 28).

[12] Par. Lat. 12634 (containing the *Rule of Eugippius*) and Par. Lat. 12205 (containing the *Rule of the Master*): see below for further references concerning the attribution of the *Rule* and on the manuscript tradition.

figure in the historical record than either the Master or Benedict, and he allows us to envisage, independently of the testimony of Gregory in the *Dialogues,* what these *Rule* writers may have been like, and in what kind of circles they may have moved. Although the state of the manuscript tradition of all three *Rules* is likely to continue to frustrate the best scholarly efforts to determine the precise development of the regular cenobitic tradition, the overall impression is clear. In the Latin West in the first half of the sixth century, while ascetic leaders in southern Gaul were seeking to mobilize the resources of the ascetic tradition to support the exercise of episcopal authority, successive generations of Italian ascetics were attempting to define, on the basis of their acute learning in the tradition, how monastic community could be constituted through the authority of a *Rule*, and, as we shall see, of an abbot.[13]

The continuing effort to place the *Rule of St Benedict* in its historical context serves to make more, rather than less, urgent the question of its perennial appeal. Since the late sixth century, two kinds of answer have been given to this question. For Gregory, the first recorded reader of the *Rule*, its merits are intrinsic to its author: it is a work 'radiant in its language, outstanding in its discretion', whose teaching directly reveals the life of the teacher.[14] Gregory's point was not necessarily to deny the existence of the Master: at least one scholar has suggested that, in isolating *discretio* as the *Rule*'s hallmark, Gregory may have had in mind precisely Benedict's achievement in rendering the fundamentals of the Master's teaching in a text three times as short, and immeasurably more memorable.[15] None the less, Gregory's emphasis on the *Rule*'s rhetorical brilliance contrasts with the assessment delivered three hundred years later by the Carolingian reformer Benedict of Aniane. In promulgating the *Rule* throughout the Empire, this Benedict explicitly presented his namesake not as an individual, but as a workman in the field of the ascetic tradition 'culling his own rule from others, and contracting into a single sheaf the sheaves of his

---

[13] A theme broached in the classic study of A. de Vogüé, *La communauté et l'abbé dans la règle de s. Benôit* (Paris/Brussels, 1961); tr. C. Philippi and E. Perkins, *Community and Abbot in the Rule of St Benedict,* 2 vols. (Kalamazoo, Mich., 1979, 1988).

[14] *Dial.* II. 36, SC 260, 242. The much-discussed citation of *RB* in *InlReg* 4. 70, CCSL 154, 330, cannot now be relied upon as evidence of Gregory's views of *RB*, given the grave doubts about the authenticity of this work voiced by A. de Vogüé, 'L'Auteur du Commentaire des Rois attribué à saint Grégoire le Grand: un moine de Cava?', *RBen* 106 (1996), 319–31. See below, Ch. 6, for further discussion.

[15] Knowles, *Great Historical Enterprises*, 191.

predecessors'.[16] A crude balance sheet would suggest that Benedict of Aniane's view carried more weight in the early Middle Ages. His towering role in the diffusion of the *Rule* needs no rehearsal here, whereas Gregory's praise for the *Rule* entailed neither his observance nor promulgation of it—he may even have contributed, unwittingly, to the *Rule*'s lack of impact in Rome until the tenth century, so hostile were the Roman clergy to Gregory and his disciples.[17]

Although the 'gregorian' and the Carolingian assessments of the merits of the *Rule* can readily be seen to complement each other, their differing accents are still visible in modern analyses of the *Rule*. For some, the *Rule* is a timeless classic, a product of the genius of its author, whose literary and spiritual gifts are only thrown into relief when comparison is made with the *Rule of the Master* or other contemporary texts.[18] In his famous comparison between the *Rule of St Benedict* and the *Institutes* of Cassiodorus, Jean Leclercq took it as a sign and reason for the *Rule*'s greatness that its author erased specific markers of time and place.[19] While Cassiodorus' concern for details, in particular concerning monastic education, ensured his long-term (relative) oblivion, Benedict's capacity in his *Rule* to screen out the

---

[16] *Concordia Regularum*, pref., PL 103, and 15A. For Benedict of Aniane, see J. Semmler, 'Benedictus II: una regula – una consuetudo', in W. Lourdaux and D. Verhelst (eds.), *Benedictine Culture 750–1050*, Medievalia Lovaniensia Series I/Studia (Louvain, 1983), 1–49. For the wider Carolingian reception of *RB*, see K. Zelzer, 'Von Benedikt zu Hildemar: Zu Textgestalt und Textgeschichte der Regula Benedicti auf ihrem Weg zur Alleingeltung', *Frühmittelalterliche Studien* 23 (1989), 112–30; M. de Jong, *In Samuel's Image: Child Oblation in the Early Medieval West* (Leiden, 1995).

[17] See the debate between O. Porcel, *La doctrina monastica di san Gregorio Magno y la 'Regula Monachorum'* (Madrid, 1951) who argued for a 'benedictine' Gregory, and K. Hallinger, 'Papst Gregor der Grosse und der Hl. Benedikt', *StAns* 42 (1957), 231–319; see also the reply of O. Porcel, 'San Gregorio y el monacato: Cuestiones controverdidas', *Monastica* 1, *Scripta et Documenta* 12 (Abadia di Montserrat, 1960), 1–95, and the brief notice by P. Verbraken, *StudMon* 2 (1960), 438–40. Meanwhile, G. Ferrari, *Early Roman Monasteries: Notes for the History of the Monasteries and Convents at Rome from the V through the X century* (Rome, 1957) demonstrated that the *Rule* was not predominantly observed in Roman monasteries until the 10th cent.: see 379–402.

[18] See e.g. R. W. Southern, *Western Society and the Church in the Middle Ages* (Harmondsworth, 1970), 218–23: 'We can read the mind of Benedict in his silences, omissions, alterations, and additions, as well as the material he was content to take without alteration from the Master' (222).

[19] See Leclercq, *Love of Letters*, 21: 'Vivarium is a "monastery school"; St Benedict's monastery is exclusively a monastery; it does possess a school, but it is never spoken of and in no way modifies the monastic ideal. . . . Cassiodorus enters into details on the organization of studies as well as of everything else in the life of his monastery. St Benedict gives directives which will retain their value regardless of time and place, in the realm of culture as well as in others, and within which great variations remain possible.'

damaging effects of social class, to transcend the love of letters, and to focus undividedly on the desire for God ensured that his text would endure in western monastic tradition.[20]

However, the principal authority in this field over the past generation, Adalbert de Vogüé, has explicitly sought to foster a more Carolingian approach to the *Rule*.[21] Its character as a text must be explained without reference to Benedict's 'personal experience or supposed psychology', argues de Vogüé, both of which lie beyond critical reconstruction. If the *Rule* appears more universal, or more compassionate for human weakness, than that of the Master, this is not to be ascribed to Benedict's individuality, but to his readiness to speak with the voice of Augustine.[22] For de Vogüé, the *Rule of Benedict* remains fundamentally in the Egyptian tradition of the cenobitic life of obedience to abbatial command, but its defining achievement is to have incorporated an augustinian vision of community of charity, a 'horizontal' perspective, to complement the 'vertical' emphasis on obedience drawn from Cassian, and pervasive in the *Rule of the Master*.[23] The *Rule*'s greatness inheres, then, not in the impress of a particular 'spiritual physiognomy', but in its 'representation of the whole tradition'.[24]

The interpretation of the *Rule* and of its teachings on moral authority presented here shares in the premiss that we should proceed by attention to the ascetic tradition in which the *Rule*'s author positioned himself. I seek only to clarify the following point. From de Vogüé's account, despite its careful nuancing, readers could be forgiven if they gained the overall impression that the secret of the *Rule of St Benedict* is that, of all monastic *Rules*, it is the least 'monastic': by its use of Augustine, the *Rule* goes beyond what is perceived to be the more specialized perspective of the desert represented by Cassian. As we have seen, however, this is not the only way to read these fifth-century authorities. Augustine's commitment to the monastery as an institution was in many ways greater than that of

---

[20] See, in particular, H. M. R. E. Mayr-Harting, 'The Venerable Bede, the Rule of St Benedict, and Social Class' (Jarrow Lecture, 1976).

[21] De Vogüé, *Community and Abbot*, 18–19. Striving to resist the tendency to psychologize the author of the *Rule*, in this, his first major work, de Vogüé refers throughout not to 'Benedict' but to the '*RB* redactor' (although the bracing astringency of this nomenclature is softened in his subsequent edition of the *Rule*: here its author is simply 'Benedict').

[22] See e.g. A. de Vogüé, 'Saint Benoît en son temps: règles italiennes et règles provençales au VIe siècle', *RBS* 1 (1972), 169–93; repr. in id., 450–514.

[23] See de Vogüé, *Community and Abbot*, 458–82; id., 'Introduction', SC 181, 33–79.

[24] De Vogüé, *Community and Abbot*, 18–19.

Cassian, who was ambivalent about the moral benefits of cenobitic life, and who built into his analysis of ascetic virtue a measure of institutional flexibility. This basic feature of his approach is well understood by the *Rule of St Benedict*. What accounts for the universalism of the *Rule* is not so much its author's augustinianism as the depth of his assimilation of the universalist in Cassian. His augustinianism, conversely, is what allows him so lucidly to outline a monastic context for the implementation of the spiritual technique of the *Institutes* and *Conferences*. While preserving the spirit of Cassian's widely applicable science of moral perfection, the *Rule* solved Cassian's ambivalence about cenobitism—his reluctance to allow ascetic experts to cohabit with their more naïve brethren—by appealing to Augustine's vision of the monastery as a community where differences between inmates would be resolved, if necessary through the exercise of authority. The result is a brilliantly realized account of the monastery as a community and an institution, which was, indeed, to carry all before it in subsequent centuries.

In the sixth century, however, the author of the *Rule* was one monastic legislator among many, and regular cenobitism was only one mode of participation in the ascetic tradition.[25] As compared to the *Rule of the Master*, what marks out the *Rule of St Benedict* may be its use of Augustine: in the wider context of sixth-century ascetic writing, however, what distinguishes the Italian cenobitic *Rules* from the texts of their gallic contemporaries Pomerius and Caesarius is their unswerving and explicit commitment to Cassian's analysis of moral purification. Few other writers in this period, whatever their debts to Cassian, saw fit openly to acknowledge these. Only in the *Rule of St Benedict* do we find open homage to Cassian, and silence on the authority of Augustine.[26] As its author was doubtless aware, his *Rule* offered a solution to the unresolved problem of cenobitism in Cassian's work, but the 'loftier heights' to which, at the conclusion of his *Rule*, he directed his monastic beginners, were none other than those of the *Institutes* and the *Conferences*.

[25] For an overview and guide, see A. de Vogüé, *Les Règles Monastiques Anciennes 400–700*, Typologie des Sources du Moyen Age Occidental 46 (Turnhout, 1985).

[26] See *RB* 42. 5, 73. 5, SC 182, 584, 672, for references to Cassian; and A. de Vogüé, 'Les Mentions des oeuvres de Cassien chez Benoît et ses contemporains', *StudMon* 20 (1978), 275–85, repr. in id., *Recueil*, 562–72; for comparative discussion, see A. de Vogüé, 'Cassien, le Maître, et Benoît', in J. Gribomont (ed.), *Commandements du Seigneur et libération évangélique: Études monastiques proposées et discutées à Saint-Anselme, 15–17 février 1976* (Rome: Editrice Anselmiana, 1977), 223–35 (repr. in *Recueil*, 545–57).

THE LOVE OF LETTERS AND THE MAKING OF RULES

At the climactic moment of Gregory's *Life* of Benedict, the holy man, now abbot of Montecassino, witnesses the soul of Germanus of Capua ascending into heaven, born aloft by angels.[27] The story, as we shall see, encapsulates Gregory's vision of Benedict;[28] it also tantalizes modern scholars with its prosopographical indices. The first person to whom Benedict recounts his experience is a visitor to his community, the deacon Servandus, abbot of the monastery founded in Campania by the patrician Liberius. As we have seen, Liberius was an important lay patron of Caesarius of Arles, and one of the few known intermediaries between the well-documented ascetic culture of Provence and that, more inchoate in the sources, of central Italy. The deceased bishop of Capua himself represents a trail back to Rome: later in the *Dialogues*, it is he who lays to rest the ghost of the deacon Pascasius, condemned to haunt a bath-house for his support of the schismatic Laurence, defeated by Symmachus in the violent feud over papal office at the start of the sixth century.[29] Pascasius, however, was also the author of a treatise on the holy spirit much admired by Gregory, and we know him to be the sponsor of Abbot Eugippius' *Life of Severinus*.[30] Gregory's account of Benedict's vision therefore places him at the confluence of several worlds—Gallic asceticism, the Laurentian schism, Roman literary culture—without specifying exactly how he relates to any single one. The *Dialogues* never bring us closer than this to the historical Benedict.

If we wish to go further, it is to Eugippius that we may turn in seeking to imagine what kind of figure the author of the *Rule of St Benedict* may have cut. Their likeness is suggested by the epithets accorded them by their admirers: Gregory's famous description of Benedict as *scienter nescius et sapienter indoctus*[31] is matched, and perhaps glossed, by the notice accorded to Eugippius by Cassiodorus in the *Institutes*, where he remembers his friend as more learned in divine than human letters—a compliment, intended to indicate that Eugippius was a

[27] *Dial.* II. 35, SC 260, 236–42.
[28] See below, Ch. 7.
[29] *Dial.* IV. 42. 1–4, SC 265, 150–2.
[30] For Pascasius' *libri* on the holy spirit, now lost, see *Dial.* IV. 42. 1, SC 265, 150, where they are regarded as *rectissimi et luculenti* by Gregory, despite Pascasius' dubious political choices. This is the only other use of the unusual adjective *luculentus* in the *Dialogues*—besides the description of *RB*. It is tempting to suppose this is more than a coincidence, and that Gregory wanted to signal some kind of kinship between Pascasius and Benedict.
[31] *Dial.* II. 3. 14, SC 260, 150.

highly learned man who eschewed verse composition for works of moral instruction.[32] Of Eugippius' intellectual interests, it is his augustinianism, in particular, which supplies a suggestive context for the *Rule of St Benedict*, given its distinctive inclusion of Augustine alongside Cassian as a source.[33] Eugippius' social world is no less illuminating for our purposes. Like Benedict, he was an 'out-of-town' ascetic, much of whose career none the less revolved around Rome. His situation, like that of Pomerius, was characterized by a tension between his command of his subject and his need for patronage.[34] The search for a resolution of this tension between moral authority and social dependency, we suggest, underlies Eugippius' work as a Christian pedagogue, and specifically as a monastic legislator: the same may well have been true of Benedict.

Eugippius was, however, dependent on the comfort of strangers in a way that Benedict may never have experienced. According to his own account, Eugippius was a refugee from the Danube frontier, the Roman population having been ordered to evacuate the province of Noricum by the Gothic general Odoacer in the early 480s.[35] With his companions, Eugippius made the journey south bearing the body of their spiritual master Severinus, who had laboured heroically for twenty years to sustain peace and order in the province, as Eugippius was to relate in his memoir of the holy man. In Italy, Severinus' disciples seem to have been well received. The matron Barbaria invited them to resettle as a monastic community at Castellum Lucullanum.[36] As abbot of the community there from 511 until his death *c*.536, Eugippius fostered links with aristocratic circles in Rome; we find him in the number of spiritual advisors grouped around the Anicii.[37] Using the library of the virgin Proba, daughter of the consul Symmachus (and associated with Galla whose story Gregory told in the *Dialogues*),[38] Eugippius compiled a collection of *Excerpts* of Augustine, which he dedicated to Proba.[39] He enjoyed a measure of

[32] Cassiodorus, *Institutiones* 23, 'De Abba Eugippio et Abba Dionisio', ed. R. Mynors (Oxford, 1937), 61–3.
[33] On Eugippius' augustinian scholarship, see, above all, the work of M. M. Gorman listed below in the Bibliography.
[34] See above, p. 67.
[35] Eugippius, *Vita sancti Severini* 44–6, ed. P. Régerat, SC 374, 286–96.
[36] Ibid. 46. 1, ed. Régerat, 292.
[37] For a fuller characterization of this circle, see C. Pietri, 'Aristocratie et société cléricale dans l'Italie chrétienne au temps d'Odoacre et de Théodoric', *MEFR* 93 (1981), 417–67.
[38] *Dial.* 4. 42, SC 165, 150–4.
[39] *Eugippii epistula ad Probam virginem*, CSEL 9. i, 1.

scholarly autonomy, building up a large library and an extremely productive scriptorium at Lucullanum. Another advisor to Proba and
Galla, and a keen augustinian, the African bishop and abbot
Fulgentius of Ruspe, asked Eugippius to have copied some books from
the library at Lucullanum.[40]

Contact with the libraries and salons of Rome brought exposure to
Roman civic politics. In sending his *Life of Severinus* to the Laurentian
Pascasius and the *Excerpta* to the Symmachan Proba, Eugippius seems
to have been careful to distribute his attentions evenly between the two
sides of the papal schism. There were other feuds to negotiate, such as
the brief but noisy revival of the 'semi-Pelagian' controversy in the
early 520s.[41] The perils of landing on the wrong side in a political or
doctrinal conflict in Rome were offset by the moral dangers of safety
within the enclosure at Lucullanum. How was Eugippius to make sure
that the body of Severinus did not become simply the patrimony of
wealthy patrons? The rumour that a high-ranking layman was plan-
ning to write an account of Severinus filled him with alarm and
prompted his own *Commemoratorium*.[42] His narrative pointedly
dramatizes the issue of frank speech to those in power. Time and
again, Severinus is fearless in his willingness to rebuke worldly poten-
tates.[43] Lucullanum, in short, was no safe haven: it was, after all, the
residence of the last Western Emperor Romulus Augustulus, himself
displaced, like Eugippius, by Odoacer.[44]

As a writer, Eugippius seems to have negotiated the delicacies of his
situation through the medium of compilation. The florilegium was a
very flexible medium: the *Excerpta Augustini* and the *Rule* could serve

---

[40] Fulgentius of Ruspe, *Epp.* 2 (to Galla), 3 and 4 (to Proba), 5 (to Eugippius), CCSL 91,
197–240. Note also the two letters to Eugippius from Fulgentius' biographer, the deacon
Ferrandus, PLS 4, 22–38. For Fulgentius' loyalty to Augustine, see Ferrandus, *Vita
Fulgentii* 2. 5–10, ed. G. Lapeyre (Paris, 1929), 19. For his contacts, see S. T. Stevens, 'The
Circle of Bishop Fulgentius', *Traditio* 38 (1982), 327–40.

[41] On this, see C. Tibiletti, 'Fausto di Riez nei giudizi della critica', *Augustinianum* 21
(1981), 567–87, and 'Polemiche in Africa contro I teologi provenzali', *Augustinianum* 26
(1986), 499–517.

[42] Eugippius, *Epistula ad Pascasium* 1–2, ed. Régerat, 146–8.

[43] See e.g. Eugippius, *Vita Severini* 5. 1–4, 40. 1–6, ed. Régerat, 190–4, 274–6.

[44] T. Hodgkin, *Italy and her Invaders*, 6 vols. (2nd edn., Oxford, 1896), ii. 523; iii. 172–3,
for the identification of Barbaria as Romulus' mother. The suggestion continues to meet with
approval, if not universal acceptance: cf. e.g. R. A. Markus, 'The End of the Roman Empire:
A Note on Eugippius, *Vita sancti Severini* 20', *Nottingham Medieval Studies* 26 (1982), 1–7,
at 1 and n. 3; Régerat, SC 374, 292–3 n. 1. For a broader discussion of the *Life of Severinus*
and the figure of the female patron in this context, see K. Cooper, 'The Martyr, the *matrona*,
and the Bishop: Networks of Allegiance in Early Sixth-Century Rome', *Early Medieval
Europe* (forthcoming).

as vehicles both of consensus, and of the determined assertion of moral autonomy. The extracting of textual nectar, flitting from text to text like the bee, was a standard ancient classical literary practice.[45] It was entirely natural for the literati of the Christian empire to begin to excerpt from the growing body of Christian texts in circulation around the Mediterranean. These compilations were neither an otiose nor a neutral display of erudition: florilegia could serve a rhetorical purpose. In early fifth-century Gaul, as we have seen, ascetic disciples of Cassian and their augustinian critics sought to summon and array the authority of these masters by compiling extracts from their work.[46] Eugippius had no need to engage in polemic: it was rather the apparent neutrality of the compiler's stance which met his needs. It was difficult to accuse the maker of the *Excerpts of Augustine* of flattering rich virgins—the issue that had proved so volatile in Jerome's day.[47] Both in the *Excerpts* and still more in the *Rule*, Eugippius articulated an enduring, incorruptible moral voice, precisely through the adoption of a low profile. The *Rule* was his last will and testament. While the memoir of Severinus had sought to render vivid the memory of a specific, idiosyncratic figure, in the *Rule* Eugippius sought to disengage himself from worldly ties, and to submerge his voice beneath the blended voices of existing tradition.

Eugippius' *Rule*, known to exist from a notice in Isidore of Seville, was long presumed lost.[48] Eugippius' name makes no appearance in Benedict of Aniane's meticulous codification of Latin monastic *Rules*.[49] In the 1960s, however, the suspicion grew that it had, after all, survived in the shape of a monastic florilegium in a late sixth/early seventh century Italian manuscript (Par. Lat. MS 12634).[50] This text

---

[45] H. Chadwick, art. 'Florilegium', *Reallexicon für Antike und Christentum*, 7 (1966), 1131–60.   [46] See above, Ch. 2.

[47] Jacques Fontaine, 'Un Sobriquet perfide de Damase: matronarum auriscalpius', in D. Porte and J.-P. Néraudau (eds.), *Hommages à Henri le Bonniec: Res sacrae* (Brussels, 1988), 177–92.

[48] For the existence of the *Rule*, see Isidore, *De viris illustribus* 26, PL 83, 1097A. Eugippius is said here to have composed a *regula* on his death-bed to bequeath to the monks remaining in the monastery of S. Severinus. His composition of the *vita sancti Severini* is also noted by Isidore. Whether or not the attribution is correct, however, the *Rule* is, none the less, a reliable index of the kind of text Eugippius could have produced, and, as we shall see, the codex in which it is found constitutes a valuable witness to the culture of compilation in which he operated.

[49] For the Carolingian career of Par. Lat. 12634, and the cognate Par. Lat. 12205, see D. Ganz, *Corbie in the Carolingian Renaissance* (Sigmaringen, 1990), 38, 65, 72–3, 76–7.

[50] L. Verheijen, *Règ.Aug.*, 2 vols. (Paris, 1967), i. 111–17, first suggests the Eugippian attribution. For a date of *c*.600, with references to the vacillating opinions on this point, ibid. i. 112–13.

was well known, especially to scholars of Augustine. The florilegium opens, indeed, with a version of the *Rule of Augustine*,[51] which is then followed by forty-five extracts from a number of other texts, including the *Rule of the Master*, Cassian's *Institutes* and *Conferences*, and the *Rule of Basil* in the Latin translation of Rufinus of Aquileia.[52] To substantiate the suggestion of Eugippian authorship, Adalbert de Vogüé undertook a close comparison of the editorial techniques of the florilegium with those of the *Excerpta Augustini*.[53] He was led to argue that the same hand, with a direct, even clumsy, approach to chipping out segments from other texts, was at work in both compilations. In 1976, together with Fernand Villegas, he published a critical edition of the florilegium in Par. Lat. 12634 as the *Rule of Eugippius* in the Corpus Scriptorum Ecclesiasticorum Latinorum.[54] The attribution and the edition have been almost unanimously accepted.[55]

The florilegium itself contains the very passages that are held in common by the *Rules* of the Master and of Benedict; and like the *Rule of St Benedict*, albeit without the same elegance, what the *Rule of Eugippius* offers is an augustinian vision of monastic community to counterbalance the more hierarchical approach of his principal source, the Master.[56] The extraordinarily compelling synthesis of tradition effected by Benedict is here sketched through the blunt power of juxtaposition of extracts from inherited texts.

Of the greatest intellectual interest, the manuscript witness of the *Rule of Eugippius* is also highly relevant to an elucidation of the context for the *Rule of St Benedict*. The one manuscript copy of the *Rule of Eugippius*, known as codex E, is very closely related to the earliest copy of the *Rule of the Master*, a late sixth-century/early seventh-century manuscript (Par. Lat. 12205) known as codex P.[57] So long as the

---

[51] At fo 20ʳ, an *explicit* names the body of text just cited as the *Regula sancti Augustini episcopi*. In the parlance adopted by modern scholars, what the *Rule of Eugippius* cites is the *Ordo monasterii* followed by the *Praeceptum*: these terms were coined by Verheijen in *Règ.Aug.*

[52] A. de Vogüé, 'Nouveaux aperçus sur une règle monastique du VIe siècle', *Revue d'Ascétique et de Mystique* 41 (1965) 233–65 (*Recueil*, 337–72), assesses the contents of the florilegium.

[53] A. de Vogüé, 'La Règle d'Eugippe retrouvée?', *RAM* 47 (1971), 233–65 (*Recueil*, 373–405).

[54] As above, n. 11.

[55] See, again, the dissent of Dunn, 'Mastering Benedict', at 572–3.

[56] De Vogüé, 'Saint Benoît en son temps', 188–93.

[57] See Augustin Genestout, 'Le Plus ancien témoin manuscrit de la Règle du Maître, le Parisinus lat. 12634', *Scriptorium* 1 (1946–7), 129–42, and *Regula Magistri: Édition diplomatique des manuscrits latins 12205 et 12634 de Paris*, ed. François Masai and Hubert

Master was thought of as postdating Benedict, little effort was devoted to clarifying the relationship between the P and E texts of the Master's *Rule*. Once the priority of the Master was admitted, however, it became a matter of paramount importance to determine which version Benedict had known and used.[58] Some scholars, in particular François Masai, persisted in regarding the 'shorter version' transmitted by the florilegium as a better witness to the earlier state of the *Rule of the Master*, and one closer to the version drawn on by Benedict. The more obvious alternative, asserted by de Vogüé, was that the compiler of the florilegium had made a selection from the 'longer version'—an editorial task very similar to that undertaken by Benedict. This solution, despite commanding wide assent, does not resolve all the textual irregularities between the three *Rules*, and discussion continues.[59]

Establishing the precise relationship between the three *Rules* may be less important and, in fact, less revealing of the wider cultural context in which the Italian *Rules* for cenobites emerged: attention to the codices P and E themselves may be more productive. These books seem to have been produced and to have circulated within a specific network of ascetic literary exchange operating in Italy over the fifth and sixth centuries. The work of Caroline Bammel has made it possible to trace with some accuracy the reading and publishing circle of Rufinus of Aquileia—and it is here that we may plausibly locate the production of the *Rule* manuscripts.[60] Bammel identified distinctive copying conventions used by Rufinus and his circle, and then by his

Vanderhoven (Brussels/Paris, 1953). For a critical edition of the 'long version' of the Rule of the Master, see A. de Vogüé, *La Règle du Maître*, 3 vols., SC 105–7 (1964).

[58] The debate is most easily accessed through A. de Vogüé, 'Les Recherches de François Masai sur le Maître et saint Benoît, I: Inventaire et analyse, II: Essai de synthèse et de bilan', *Studia Monastica* 24 (1982), 7–42, 271–309. See also the incisive intervention of Klaus Zelzer, 'Nochmals "À propos de la tradition manuscrite de la Règle bénédictine"', *RBS* 12 (1983), 203–7.

[59] P. Meyvaert, 'Problems concerning the "Autograph" Manuscript of St Benedict's Rule', *RBen* 69 (1959), 3–21; and 'Towards a History of the Textual Transmission of *Regula S. Benedicti*', *Scriptorium* 17 (1963), 83–110; both repr. in id., *Benedict, Gregory, Bede*, chs. III, IV; F. Masai, 'L'Edition de Vogüé et les editions antiques de la Règle du Maître', *Latomus* 26 (1967), 506–17; and K. Zelzer, 'Zur Stellung des Textes receptus und des interpolierten Textes in der Textgeschichte der Regula s. Benedicti', *RBen* 88 (1978), 205–46; and id., 'L'Histoire du texte des Règles de Saint Basile et de Saint Benoît à la lumière de la tradition gallo-franque', *RBS* 13 (1984), 75–89.

[60] C. P. Hammond Bammel, 'Products of Fifth-century Scriptoria Preserving Conventions Used by Rufinus of Aquileia', *JTS* NS 29 (1978), 366–91; 30 (1979), 430–62; 35 (1984), 347–93. For the immediate context of Rufinus' literary production, see ead., 'The Last Ten Years of Rufinus' Life and the Date of his Move South from Aquileia', *JTS* NS 28 (1977), 372–429.

disciples in succeeding generations right into the sixth century. The primary interests of the Rufinians seem to have been the translations of Rufinus and the works of Augustine.[61] For example, the earliest known copy of Eugippius' *Excerpts of Augustine*, a sixth-century half-uncial manuscript, bears the paleographical 'signature' of the Rufinian copying circle.[62] This manuscript is in turn associated with a copy of Rufinus' translation of Origen's *Peri Archon*, which bears the inscription of its owner, a deacon Donatus at the oratory of St Peter's at Lucullanum in 562.[63] While it may be too much to assume that Eugippius himself was heir to the manuscripts used by Rufinus and his disciples in the fifth century, this does not diminish the relevance of the network of connections at work here in establishing a context for the production of monastic *Rules*.[64]

A glance at the contents of the two Paris manuscripts containing the *Rule of the Master* (codex P) and the *Rule of Eugippius* (codex E) suggests that they, too, belong within a Rufinian milieu.[65] Both codices are composite volumes, binding together a number of independently composed manuscripts, not all of which have survived.[66] Codex P, according to a Carolingian inscription on its flyleaf, used to contain the *Inchiridion Rufini Praesbyteri*: this may safely be identified as the *Sentences of Sextus* (a pagan philosophical text, attributed to the

---

[61] Bammel, 'Products' (1978), 366–76, points out that, after Rufinus' death *c*.412 in Sicily, his companions Pinian and Melania continued their journey to North Africa, to found a monastery at Thagaste: from here, they may well have assisted in the diffusion of Augustine's works among Rufinian circles in Italy.

[62] Vat.Lat. 3375, *CLA* 16; see Bammel, 'Products' (1979), 436.

[63] The connection between the copy of Eugippius' *Excerpta Augustini* and that of Rufinus' translation of Origen's *Peri Archon* is indirect. Vat.Lat. 3375 (the *Excerpta Augustini*) is closely associated via script and provenance with Monte Cassino 150, a copy of the Ambrosiaster's *Commentary on Romans*. The Ambrosiaster manuscript bears an inscription that it was owned and read by a priest Donatus at Lucullanum in 569/70—almost certainly the same as the deacon Donatus who inscribed his copy of Rufinus' translation of Origen's *Peri Archon* (Metz 225). For the paleographical relation between Vat.Lat. 3375 and Montecassino 150, see E. A. Lowe, 'A List of the Oldest Extant Manuscripts of St Augustine, with a Note on the Codex Bambergensis', *Miscellanea Agostiniana*, ii. 235–51, at 246–51 (repr. in id., *Paleographical Papers 1907–1965*, ed. L. Bieler, 2 vols. (Oxford, 1972), i. 301–14, at 311–14).

[64] Bammel drew the conclusion that Eugippius himself took over a convention he found in the 'Rufinian' Augustine manuscripts he was using: 'Products' (1979), 436. Gorman has cautioned, however, that Vat.Lat. 3375 is far from the autograph and can therefore tell us little about the scribal conventions of Eugippius' monastery at Lucullanum: 'The Manuscript Tradition of Eugippius' *Excerpta Augustini*', *RBen* 92 (1982), 242–4.

[65] See Bammel, 'Products' (1979), 451 n. 3.

[66] For a full description of these codices, see Masai and Vanderhoven, *La Règle du Maître*, 13–26 (codex P), 26–42 (codex E).

martyr Pope Sextus) translated by Rufinus, and quoted in all three *Rules*.[67] Appended to the *Sentences* may have been another text of Rufinus' transmitted in Basil's name, the *Admonition to a Spiritual Son*, the interest of which we shall see shortly. Codex E contains Rufinus' translation of Evagrius' *Sentences to Monks*, and some sermons attributed (falsely) to Augustine. The *Rule of Eugippius* itself opens, as we have seen, with the full text of the *Regulations for a Monastery* transmitted in Augustine's name, followed by Augustine's *Praeceptum*.[68] In the collection of excerpts, Basil's *Rule for Monks*, again translated by Rufinus, features prominently. Both manuscripts also contain copies of other monastic rules.[69] In other words, the *Rules* known to us as the *Rule of the Master* and the *Rule of Eugippius* have been bound by their early medieval copyists and readers in books together with the texts and authors on which they draw. These codices evoke the long arc of Christian literary production and exchange from the age of Rufinus to that of Gregory the Great.

The literary culture of Eugippius and Benedict is still misapprehended. The concern on the part of the *Rule of St Benedict* to speak to beginners is often interpreted as a sign of declining cultural standards in sixth-century Italy.[70] On this view, Christian scholars such as Cassiodorus experienced a lowering of the cultural horizon in the course of their lifetime. As he finished his days writing a treatise on spelling to his disciples in the monastery of Vivarium in southern Italy, we are encouraged to imagine his wistful nostalgia for the Christian university he had planned to found at Rome before the violence and attrition of the Gothic Wars.[71] Viewed without prejudice, however, the production of Boethius' translations of Plato and

[67] For the text inscription on the flyleaf, see Masai and Vanderhoven, *La Règle du Maître*, 25 and Pl. Ia. For Rufinus' translation, see H. Chadwick (ed.), *The Sentences of Sextus*, Texts and Studies NS 5 (Cambridge, 1959). It is cited by *RM* 9. 31, 10. 31, SC 105, 412, 436; by *REug* 28. 76, CSEL 87, 58; and by *RB* 7. 61, SC 181, 488.

[68] These texts are explicitly attributed to Augustine, with the note: 'Explicit regula sancti Augustini episcopi'. This has been crucial in the discussion of the 'Rule of Augustine', and no less important for de Vogüé in establishing the thesis of an 'augustinian wave' descending on Italy in the 530s. See *Règ.Aug.*, i. 111–17; de Vogüé, 'Nouveaux aperçus sur une règle monastique du VIe siècle', and 'La Règle d' Eugippe retrouvée?', and below for further discussion of the uses of Augustine's authority by the florilegium.

[69] These texts are most conveniently edited and discussed by A. de Vogüé, *Les Règles des saints Pères*, SC 197, 198; and in turn by Pricoco, *La Regola di san Benedetto e le Regole dei Padri*.

[70] The fact that *RM*, unlike *RB*, is not presented as a *Rule* for beginners has been taken as a measure of such decline: see de Vogüé's comment, SC 181, 39–44.

[71] See H.-I. Marrou, 'Autour de la bibliothèque du pape Agapit', *MEFR* 48 (1931), 124–69.

Aristotle, Eugippius' *Excerpta Augustini*, and Cassiodorus' treatise *On Spelling* all provide evidence not of cultural decline, but rather of the burgeoning literary interests of the Roman and Campanian élite.

Monastic *Rules* were a further manifestation of the culture of scholarly transmission, which sought to impart received wisdom as efficiently as possible to an audience eager for spiritual instruction. The problem faced by their authors was not the waning level of literary competence, but the unchecked vitality of the tradition of lay literary patronage, both a blessing and a curse for a moral teacher. A monastic *Rule* was an opportunity to imagine a community which was not beholden to the generosity of a donor, nor vulnerable to the instability of urban politics. It was a place where a Christian pedagogue could teach and expect to be heard.

The most vivid illustration of the search for a moral voice through regular cenobitism, and the most intriguing example of the Rufinian context for the *Rule of St Benedict*, is afforded by one of the lost texts in codex P, pseudo-Basil's *Admonition to a Spiritual Son*. This is an obscure work, which Rufinus may have appended to his translation of the *Sentences of Sextus*.[72] It seems, however, to have been close to the heart of the author of the *Rule*. Pseudo-Basil begins:

Listen, my son, to the lessons of your father, and lend your ear to my words, and freely lend me your ears, paying attention with a faithful heart to everything that I shall say to you.[73]

This is, almost verbatim, the opening of the *Rule of St Benedict*. (The opening of the *Rule of the Master*, although not exactly the same, is couched in similar terms.). Coupled with the injunction at the close of the *Rule* to read Basil's texts, it suggests that Benedict was addressing an audience of Italian ascetics whose reading and writing habits are still visible in some of our earliest Latin manuscripts. These habits, we

---

[72] The flyleaf in codex P refers to a *Monita cuiusdam parentis ad filium* appended to the *Inchiridion Rufini Praesbyteri* (i.e. the *Sentences of Sextus*). In the preface to this work, Rufinus says that he has appended *quaedam religiosi parentis ad filium*. For the suggestion that this appended text is the 4th-cent. *Admonitio S. Basilii ad filium spiritualem*, and that Rufinus is its most likely author see P.-M. Bogaert, 'La Préface de Rufin aux Sentences de Sexte et à un oeuvre inconnue', *RBen* 82 (1972), 26–46, at 43–4. See also E. Manning, 'L'Admonitio S. Basilii ad filium spiritualem et la Règle de saint Benoît', *RAM* 42 (1966), 475–9; A. de Vogüé, 'Entre Basile et Benoît: l'*Admonitio ad filium spiritualem* du pseudo-Basile', *RBS* 10/11 (1981), 19–34. For the text itself, see P. Lehmann, ed., *Die Admonitio S. Basilii ad filium spiritualem*, *Sitzungsberichte der Bayerischen Akademie der Wissenschaften* Ph.-H. Kl., 1955, Heft 7 (Munich, 1955); also PL 103, 683–700.

[73] Pseudo-Basil, *Admonitio*, Lehmann, 30; PL 103, 684D. Cf. *RB* prol. 1–3, SC 181, 412; *RM* prol. 1–21, SC 105, 288–92.

now suggest, were formed not only by the generalized set of expecta-tions of the literate élite: the *Rules* appeal specifically to the inherited teachings of Cassian to provide a fully coherent programme of how and why to read as an ascetic.

THE OBEDIENCE OF THE CENOBITE

Everyone knows that a benedictine monk takes vows of poverty, chastity, and obedience. Of poverty, however, the *Rule* says very little, of chastity nothing at all, and its notion of obedience is far more precise than we might expect. The *Rule* opens with the injunction of a spiritual teacher:

> Listen carefully, my son, to the master's instructions, and attend to them with the ear of your heart. This is advice from a father who loves you: welcome it, and faith-fully put it into practice. The labour of obedience will bring you back to him from whom you had drifted through the sloth of disobedience.[74]

Benedict here speaks also for the Master and Eugippius: all three *Rules* are presented as the teaching of an unnamed master, who demands of his pupil a distinctive mode of obedience.[75] Obedience in these *regulae magistri* is a quality of attention (the literal meaning of *ob-audientia*). The kinds of obedience we might expect to see discussed—the prompt execution of commands, the internalized subjugation of the will of the spiritual son to the divine will—are both seen to follow from his taking to heart the words of his master.

The anonymity of the *magister* who speaks in these *Rules* is central to the notion of obedience they project. This teacher is not a particular individual, but a personification of the *magisterium* of tradition. The instruction he dispenses is not the idiosyncratic or untutored insight of the maverick—rather the accumulated wisdom of an unbroken tradi-tion of spiritual expertise. The fact that the three *Rules* are all *regulae magistri* holding long sections of text in common suggests a concerted effort to construct such a magisterial tradition in sixth-century Italy. If we wish to understand the identity of 'the Master', we need, not to comb the prosopographical records, but to examine the derivation and composition of the core of material shared by the three *Rules*.

---

[74] *RB* prol. 1–2, SC 181, 412.
[75] *RM* prol. 1, Thema 23–4, SC 105, 288, 300; *REug* 18, CSEL 87, 29–34. For compara-tive commentary on *RM* and *RB* on obedience, see de Vogüé, *Community and Abbot*, 179–251.

The scene of instruction framing the *Rules* recalls, not coinciden-
tally, the *Conferences* of John Cassian. The *magister* who issues these
Rules embodies Cassian's notion of spiritual expertise, and the aural
obedience of his pupil harks back explicitly to Cassian's understanding
of the getting of ascetic wisdom through the occupation of the mind
with sacred texts. The achievement of the *Rules* was to call upon
Cassian's notion of *occupatio mentis* as the key to reading the material
they have excerpted and synthesized. To literate groups already
habituated to the collection of extracts, the *Rules* supplied the extra
rationale of Cassian. If what the mind needed for its purification was
sacred reading material, then what better way to provide it than to
sample from the canon of venerated Christian writers, and of course
from Scripture? When the disciples ask a question, it is the Lord who
speaks through the *magister*.

The Master, Eugippius, and Benedict achieve a graphic realization
of the abstract logic of Cassian's analysis. In his final set of *Conferences*,
as we have seen, Cassian developed a discussion of types of monks: the
cenobites, direct descendants of the first Christian community
Jerusalem, and the anchorites who develop from the cenobites. He
had been unable to decide, however, which kind of life was best,
and he was uncertain about the terms on which cenobitic life was
actually possible. The *Rules* have no such equivocation. 'There are
clearly four kinds of monks', opens chapter one of the *Rule of St
Benedict*:

First there are the cenobites, that is to say, those who belong to a monastery, where
they serve under a rule and an abbot. Second there are the anchorites or hermits,
who have come through the test of living in a monastery for a long time, and have
passed beyond the first fervor of monastic life.[76]

Cutting through Cassian's vacillations, the *Rules* assert that those
who achieve purity of heart as cenobites may go on to lead lives of
anchoritic perfection—but extreme care was needed before permitting
this to happen.[77]

Then there were two kinds of false monks, summoned by the *Rules*
from the pages of Cassian in order to render vivid through contrast
the virtues of cenobitism. Cassian had described in some detail the
error of the sarabaites, men who did not adhere to the authority of a

[76] *RB* 1. 1–3, SC 181, 436, tr. *RB 1980*, 169. Cf. *RM* 1. 1, 1. 75, SC 105, 328, 346; *REug*
27. 1, 27. 19, CSEL 87, 47, 49.
[77] *RB* 1. 4–5, SC 181, 436–8; *RM* 1. 4–5, SC 105, 328–30; *REug* 27. 4–5, CSEL 87, 47.

rule or spiritual guide, and he had briefly referred to a fourth kind
of inauthentic monk: seizing the rhetorical moment, the Italian
Rules, having already brought into being the *magister*, achieve another
unforgettable personification. They create the figure of the gyrovague,
the deliriously misguided monk who embodies *evagatio mentis*, the
wandering state of attention that results from failure to observe a
proper *occupatio mentis*. Noting Cassian's sarabaites in passing—they
live in random groups of two or three, following their own whims—
the *Rules* evoke the spectre of monks who are entirely unstable,
actually moving from place to place every three or four days.[78]
Benedict and Eugippius find the gyrovagues to be almost unspeakable:
not so the Master, who, in an appropriately circuitous digression,
describes the incessant wanderings of these monks, for whom even
the wide deserts of Egypt were not big enough.[79] Without fixity of
spiritual purpose, the Master observes, the gyrovagues are prey to all
the vices. They are driven on from place to place by their stomachs:
enslaved by gluttony, they will go to almost any lengths to obtain a free
meal.[80] Their relentless eating and wandering must needs be accompanied by a constant stream of specious self-justification. They arrive
at a place with their heads bowed in humility; once their pretences are
exposed, 'they leave in two or three days all proud and ungrateful'.[81]
'Wandering incessantly from place to place', the Master concluded
poignantly, 'they do not even know where to establish their place of
burial.'[82] This so-called 'satire of the gyrovagues' may be a comment
on monastic life in sixth-century Campania,[83] but it is more certainly
to be interpreted as an essay about cenobitism. Its purpose is to

---

[78] On sarabaites: *RB* 1. 6–11, SC 181, 438–40; *RM* 1. 61–2, SC 105, 330–2; *REug* 27. 6–
12, CSEL 87. 48. On gyrovagues: *RB* 1. 10–11, SC 181, 438–40; *RM* 1. 13–74, SC 105, 332–
46; *REug* 27. 13–18, CSEL 87, 48–9.

[79] The digressiveness of *RM* on the gyrovagues is crucial for Masai's view of the relation
between *RM* and *REug* (or, in his terms, the 'longer' and the 'shorter' version of *RM*). Masai
argued that *REug* is prior, because *RM*'s digression is inserted into a phrase which runs
without interruption in *REug*: see *Settimane* IV, 447.

[80] In Cassian's classification of the vices, as seen above, gluttony was the first adversary of
the monk: the gyrovagues as 'anti-monks' are thus pitiably unable to surmount the first
hurdle. The priority of gluttony may explain also why *REug* gives early attention (*REug* 2)
to the office of cellarer in the monastery.

[81] *RM* 1. 72, SC 105, 344.

[82] *RM* 1. 74, SC 105, 346. Cf. the nuns at Arles, whose burial place is defined the moment
they enter the convent. *RV* 73. 1–2, SC 345, 272.

[83] Cf. Gregory, *Ep.* I. 40 (CCSL 140, 46) to Anthemius, Gregory's *rector* in Campania.
The letter reads like the realization of the *Rules*' collective nightmare: monks are wandering
around from monastery to monastery, submitting to no abbot or *Rule*; they own property;
some even cohabit with women, or publicly display their wives.

contrast the errant body of the gyrovague with the stability of the obedient cenobite.[84]

Having conjured up the gyrovague, the Master and Benedict then delineate the figure of the abbot (the sequence of Eugippius is different: the abbot precedes the types of monks).[85] The abbot is entrusted with fostering the aural virtue of the monks. He is the living mediator of the word of God to the monks, as the Rule is the textual mediator. But he himself must remain obedient to the *Rule*. The abbot, in other words, is subordinate to the *magister*, and many of his utterances are actually scripted for him (although we shall see that the three *Rules* propose different roles for the abbot within this general framework).

What the *Rules* then set out is a spiritual, devotional, and practical programme of verbal purity drawn from Cassian's technology of mental preoccupation.[86] Every waking and sleeping hour demands control of language and of silence. A form of continence, silence is a figurative cloister keeping the ears and mouth inviolate to all speech save God's.[87] When monks do speak, they should do so with the greatest caution, ever wary of sins of the mouth. 'Let us follow the Prophet's counsel: I said, I have resolved to keep watch over my ways that I may never sin with my tongue. I have put a guard on my mouth.'
[88] Monks shall not burst out into laughter or shouting, they shall speak few words, and those quietly and with *gravitas*. These prohibitions are repeated three times in the early chapters, being then established as the ninth, tenth and eleventh grades of humility.[89] The twelfth grade insists that the monk keeps his head bowed in humility (literally— towards the ground) on a permanent basis.[90]

[84] See *REug* 28, CSEL 87, 91: the conclusion to the floriliegium is an extract drawn from Jerome's letter to Rusticus of Narbonne (*Ep.* 105. 9), which recommends the cenobitic life over the eremitic life of solitude, where it is easy to forget oneself: 'Intus corpore lingua foris vagatur.'   [85] *REug* 25 on the abbot, 28 on the types of monks.
[86] See e.g. *RM* 50. 3, SC 106, 222: 'Nam cum frater aliquid operatur, dum oculum in laboris opere figit, inde sensum occupat, de quod facit, et cogitare aliqua non vacat et desideriorum non mergitur fluctibus.' Cf. *RM* 8. 10, 11. 3, 11. 97, 82. 11; SC 105, 400, SC 106, 8, 28, 338 (and for further references, see de Vogüé's index, SC 107, 306–7). Cf. de Vogüé, 'Les deux fonctions de la méditation dans les Règles monastiques anciennes', *RHS* 51 (1975), 3–16 (repr. in *Recueil*, 807–20) arguing for a shift from manual labour to *lectio divina* as the focus for *meditatio* across the 5th and 6th cents.: both contexts for *meditatio* are, however, directed towards the same goal of *occupatio mentis*.
[87] *RM* 7. 18, 9. 29, SC 105, 384, 412.
[88] *RB* 6. 1, SC 181, 471; *RM* 8. 31, 105, 404, citing Ps. 38: 2–3.
[89] For the threefold repetition: *RM* 3. 57–60, 8. 33–4, 10. 75–81, SC 105, 368–70, 406, 434–6; echoed in *REug* 16. 1–3, 28. 70–5, 29. 1–5, CSEL 87, 27–8, 58, 61, and *RB* 4. 52–4, 6. 3–8, 7. 56–61; SC 181, 460, 470–2, 486–8.
[90] *RM* 10. 82–6, SC 105, 436–8; *REug* 28. 77–81, CSEL 87, 58–9; *RB* 7. 65–6, SC 181,

The liturgy is the area most evocative of the concern to regulate speech. What came out of the monks' mouths and at what time of day could be precisely, and self-consciously, prescribed.[91] One brief example must suffice, concerning the arrangements for night-time. All the Rules prescribe that at night, between compline and nocturns, complete silence is to fall on the community. This silence is dramatized in all the Rules (although not to quite the same extent in Benedict as in the Master and Eugippius). Starting the description of the liturgy with compline, the Master and Eugippius prescribe that the monks' last words be 'Set a watch, O Lord, before my mouth: keep the door of my lips' (Ps. 140: 3). Silence is then to fall, 'a silence so great that you would not think that there was a single brother there'.[92] Nocturns then begins in the Master with 'O Lord, open thou my lips and my mouth shall be full of praise' (Ps. 50: 17). To assemble the monks to break the silence of the night, two monks are entrusted with the task of waking the community. When they awake, they must say together quietly 'O Lord, open thou my lips and my mouth shall show forth thy praise'.[93] There is to be no chink in the armour of holy speech.

Outside church, the *Rules* are no less concerned to maintain control of speech. At mealtimes and in the summer evenings, Benedict commands readings of the *Rule*, Cassian's *Conferences*, or some other suitable text (not the Heptateuch or the Books of Kings).[94] The dangers of verbal pollution were constantly present, warns the *Rule*. A slothful brother might stop himself and others from reading with stories and idle talk.[95] At the beginning of the night office, monks might wait outside the oratory, so leaving themselves open to stories and chat.[96] On journeys (undertaken only on monastery business),

---

488. On the grades of humility and Cassian, see Masai, 'Recherches sur le texte originel du De humilitate de Cassien'; A. de Vogüé, 'De Cassien au Maître et à Eugippe: le titre du chapitre de l'humilité', *StMon* 23 (1981), 247–61. On the liturgical future of humility in these physiological terms, see the Lenten *oratio super populo*, 'Humiliate capita vestra Deo' introduced into the Roman sacramentary in the late 6th or early 7th cent.: J. A. Jungmann, *The Mass of the Roman Rite: Its Origins and Development* (New York, 1955), 429, 431. I owe this reference to Henry Mayr-Harting.

[91] *RM* 33–49, SC 106, 176–222; *RB* 8–19, SC 182, 508–38.

[92] *RM* 30. 13, SC 106, 164.

[93] *RM* 30. 8–16, 31. 10–32, SC 105, 164, 170–2; *REug* 22, CSEL 87, 74–5; *RB* 9. 1, 22, SC 182, 510, 542, is less concerned with specifying the terms for the purification of speech than the other *Rules*: see below, n. 106.

[94] *RM* 24, SC 106, 122–32; *RB* 38, SC 182, 572–6. For evening readings, see *RB* 42. 1–4, SC 182, 584. There are no similar readings prescribed in *RM* or *REug*.

[95] *RB* 48. 18, SC 182, 602.

[96] *RB* 43. 8, SC 182, 588.

monks were especially vulnerable to exposure to unclean speech.[97] Mindful perhaps of the impossibility of sustaining a fully pure regime, Benedict signals that Lent was the time, and the monastic oratory was the place, where monks should make a special effort to avoid rhetorical temptation.[98] In the Master, almost all verbal exchanges are prescribed in detail. Installation of the weekly servers, punishment of offenders, admission of postulants, and the election of the new abbot—all these occasions are 'liturgified' with the lines of the participants precisely scripted.[99] Private prayer and private reading were in the same way activities designed to promote holy learning and holy speech. The prayer that was heard of God did not involve an out-pouring of many words; it was (in Benedict) the 'short and pure prayer'.[100] The Italian *magistri*, in short, sought to realize to an unprecedented degree Cassian's vision of an ascetic community of perfected discourse.

MONASTIC COMMUNITY AND ABBATIAL AUTHORITY

The Italian *Rules* aspire to the anonymity of a unified tradition—but the *magister* who speaks in all of them teaches a different lesson in each. Within their shared frame of reference as rules for cenobites, the Master, Eugippius, and Benedict each project differing visions of how the cenobitic community will be organized, and how the authority of the abbot will function therein. These differences, and especially the distinctiveness of the *Rule of St Benedict* have been the subject of microscopic analysis: our goal here is not to emulate these, but to show how these differences relate to the differing approaches to the moral authority of the speaker and his relation to his listener(s) with which we have been concerned throughout this book.[101]

Having committed themselves to the *coenobium* as the venue for the

---

[97] *RB* 67. 4–5, SC 182, 662.

[98] *RB* 45, 49, 52, SC 182, 604–06, 611.

[99] *Septimanarii*: *RM* 19, SC 106, 90–8; punishment of offenders: *RM* 13–14, SC 106, 34–62; *REug* 40, CSEL 87, 81–5; postulants: *RM* 89, SC 106, 370–8; abbatial election: *RM* 92–3, SC 106, 410–40.

[100] *RB* 48. 4–5, SC 182, 600 on private reading. *RB* 20. 3–4, SC 182, 536–8, on private prayer. *RB* here adds, in a characteristic saving clause, that prayers should be short, 'nisi forte ex affectu inspirationis divinae gratiae protendatur'. For comment, see A. de Vogüé, 'La Règle de saint Benoît et la vie contemplative', *CollCist* 27 (1965), 89–107.

[101] This is to venture on ground already definitively charted by de Vogüé, *Community and Abbot*, and in his two SC editions of *RM* and *RB*.

ascetic arts as Cassian had adumbrated them, the Italian *magistri* must all confront the issues that had made Cassian hesitate to give the *cenobium* his full endorsement. The main problem for communal ascetic living, as we have seen, lay in Cassian's own axiom that the ascetically expert could not easily live under the same roof as their more naïve brethren, because the latter would not be able to tolerate the correction of their more advanced colleagues. Conversely, Cassian had been reluctant to endorse the authority of any ageing ascetic, conscious as he was of the possibilities that charisma could be deceptive, unfounded on true expertise. The realization both of monastic community and of abbatial authority was inhibited by Cassian's analysis, and the Italian *magistri* seek to overcome these inhibitions.

Eugippius, whose intentions can only be guessed at from the selection and juxtaposition of texts, affords a view of the competing visions of monastic community embedded in the traditions with which he is familiar. The florilegium starts with the full text of Augustine's *Praeceptum* (preceded by the *Ordo monasterii*), solemnly closing with the notice: 'Here ends the Rule of the holy bishop Augustine.' For some commentators, this demonstrates the unwavering augustinian sympathies of the compiler, and the shorter extracts that follow are to be understood as a gloss on Augustine's vision of the monastery.[102] It may be, however, that here, as elsewhere, the authority of Augustine is being invoked to lend credence to an entirely different vision of monastic community. There follows, as we have seen, a series of extracts drawn principally from Cassian's *Institutes* and *Conferences*, and sharing material with the Master. No overt attempt is made to reconcile the augustinian community of charity with Cassian's description of the community of pure speech; a 'third party' is introduced, however, in the person of Basil of Caesarea, whose monastic teachings are excerpted in the translation made by Rufinus, and his role may be to strike a point of balance between Augustine and Cassian. Like the latter, Basil/Rufinus uses the terminology of the desert—the eremitic and cenobitic lives—but he is no less emphatic than Augustine in advocating the communal life of charity on the model of the Jerusalem community. No explicit gloss as to the arbitrating role of Basil's view of the monastery is provided, however: the overall strategy of the compilation is to preserve without compromise the anonymity of the Master in his transmission of tradition. The *Rule*

---

[102] See *Règ.Aug.* i. 115–16; de Vogüé, 'Nouveaux aperçus sur une règle monastique du VIe siècle', and 'La Règle d' Eugippe retrouvée?'

of Eugippius defines a field of possible communities, but cedes to the community of its readers the final decision as to how to identify themselves as a group.

Such diffidence was not for the Master. His approach to the problem of community held firm to Cassian's central contention about the impossibility of maintaining different levels of ascetic achievement in the community. He was certain, however, that the regime he sought to put in place would ensure parity of standards. Placing confidence, like Caesarius of Arles, in the control of detail, the Master aspired to an exhaustive accuracy of moral prescription and surveillance. He envisages a community divided into two groups of ten, whose every word or gesture is subject to scrutiny from a prior.[103] Those who visit the community are no more exempt from this regime: lodged apart, in quarters with no monastery tools or utensils, they are to be accompanied by two monks on a twenty-four hour basis. *Custodia, custodire, cautela custodiendi*: these are the watchwords of the text.[104]

Prescriptive in the last degree, the Master spells out the rewards that inmates of the community can expect to attain: drawing on the *passiones* of the Roman martyrs, he describes the heavenly destination of the pure in speech and heart. Having ascended the ladder of humility, and having left this life, the Master's disciples can expect to inhabit a land of unbounded joy, a world where night never falls— there are not even any shadows—in a territory saturated with light and sound, taste, and smell. The relentless preoccupation of the senses with holy discourse in the monastery now gives way to a life lived under a cloudless sky, in meadows full of flowers, irrigated by rivers flowing with milk and honey, where angels and archangels sing on the banks. Trees bear fruit one need only look at to have tasted.[105]

Although reproduced in Eugippius, none of this material appears in the *Rule of St Benedict*. For all that he owed to the Master, Benedict

---

[103] *RM* 11. 35–6, SC 106, 14–16.

[104] See e.g. *RM* 11, SC 106, 6, announcing the programme for the rest of the *Rule*: 'Incipit ordo monasterii: modus, observatio, gradus, continentia, custodia et mensura . . .'.

[105] *RM* 10. 92–122, SC 105, 438–44 and *REug* 27, CSEL 87, 59–61, both drawing on *Passio Sebastiani* 13, PL 17, 1117–19. See also *RM* 3. 83–94, SC 105, 372–94, drawing on the 5th-cent. apocryphal *Visio Pauli*. Both *passio* and *visio* number among the texts condemned by the Pseudo-Gelasian decree (*Decretum Gelasianum de libris recipiendis et non recipiendis*, ed. E. Dobschütz, TU 38, 4 (Leipzig, 1912), 1–13, at 12). The decree, although uncertainly dated itself, has been used to establish a chronology for the composition of *RM*, *REug*, and *RB* (see de Vogüé, SC 105, 221–30, with the criticism of Dunn, 'Mastering Benedict'). For a broader discussion of the *rules* and the Roman martyr tradition, see Cooper, 'The Martyr, the matrona, and the Bishop'.

moved in a different direction in his elucidation of the terms of community, both worldly and otherworldly. His *Rule* is premised on a determination to devise a community in which the weak and the strong can coexist—to start with the lowest common denominator, without sacrificing the essentials of the ascetic art. The control of detail is immediately relinquished. Not all occasions are liturgified: when monks rouse each other for nocturns they should do so not with Ps. 50: 17, as in the Master and Eugippius, but with 'quiet encouragement, for the sleepy like to make excuses'.[106] Temperate in his imagination of the daily routine of the monks, Benedict is equally restrained in the promises he makes to those who follow him. No vistas of a sensory Paradise are opened to the spiritual sons of this Master, who is content simply to invoke Paul's assurance to the Corinthians, 'Eye hath not seen, nor ear heard, what the Lord is preparing for those who love him' (1 Cor. 2: 29).[107]

The elimination of prescriptive detail in his *Rule* allowed Benedict to take advantage of the flexibility of Cassian's analysis of moral purity—even beginners would be able to master the spiritual arts as here defined—and at the same time to focus with an uncluttered mind on the problem that had defeated Cassian of differing spiritual abilities in the community. It is at this point that Benedict turned (like Eugippius) to Augustine: the notions of monastic community and abbatial authority articulated in Augustine's *Rule* showed that it was, after all, possible to construct a 'mixed' *cenobium*. It was not only that Augustine insisted on the primacy of charity, regardless of different levels of ascetic competence: it was also that he reminded readers of Cassian of the other differences that obtained in the community besides that between 'experts and ingénus', above all, that of social class. The issue of class was a welcome source of diversion, as it were, from the otherwise intractable problem of relations between the spiritually weak and the strong.

Half-way through his *Rule*, Benedict turns, in unmistakably augustinian language, to the question of private property:

Above all, this evil practice must be uprooted and removed from the monastery. . . . No one should presume to give, receive, or retain anything of his own, nothing at all—not a book, writing tablets, or stylus—in short not a single item . . . For their needs, they are to look to the father of the monastery, and are not allowed

---

[106] *RB* 9. 1, 22, SC 182, 510, 542. See de Vogüé's comment, SC 184, 227–80.
[107] *RB* 4. 77, SC 181, 464. See also prol. 49, SC 105, 424: 'inenarrabile dilectionis dulcedine'.

anything which the abbot has not given or permitted. 'All things should be the common possession of all', as it is written, so that no one presumes to call anything his own.[108]

Although the *Rule* does not reproduce Augustine's exact observations about the difficulty of getting rich and poor to cohabit, it is almost as determined to insulate the community from the damaging effects of snobbery or class resentment.[109] The masterstroke in this programme is the principle of superiority instituted by Benedict: he who arrives at the first hour to join the community is senior to the man who comes at the second.[110] This simple measure not only neutralized the memory of worldly differences, it also stemmed the invidious likelihood that an unauthorized hierarchy of ascetic ability would recrudesce in the space left by the forbidden element of class or worldly status.[111]

Differences in the community could not be entirely eradicated, of course: the Jerusalem community provided for Benedict, as for Augustine, a model of how they could be accommodated:

It is written: 'Distribution was made to each as he had need'. By this we do not mean to imply that there should be favouritism—God forbid—but rather consideration for weaknesses. Whoever needs less should thank God and not feel distressed, but whoever needs more should feel humble because of his weakness and not self-important because of the kindness shown him. In this way all members will be at peace.[112]

The *Rule* insists that the simple and the expert can live together, across their differences, and without murmuring.[113]

As in Augustine's *Praeceptum*, the burden of distribution according to need must fall on a particular set of shoulders. While in Benedict, as in the other *Rules*, it is the *magister* who holds overall sway, and whose teachings apply universally to all inmates of the community, the abbot in Benedict is delegated with greater powers and responsibilities to minister to individual need:

He must know what a difficult and demanding burden he has undertaken: directing souls and serving a variety of temperaments, coaxing, reproving, and

---

[108] *RB* 33. 1–6, SC 182, tr. *RB 1980*, 231; recalling Augustine, *Praec.* 1, misquoting Acts 4: 32.
[109] See Mayr-Harting, 'The Venerable Bede, the Rule of St Benedict, and Social Class'.
[110] *RB* 63. 1–8, SC 182, 642–4.
[111] It was the abbot's prerogative to establish a ranking according to virtue: *RB* 63. 1, SC 182, 644.
[112] *RB* 34. 1–5, SC 182, 564, tr. *RB 1980*, 231–2.
[113] *RB* 34. 6–7, SC 182, 564. Cf. *Praec.* 2. 4, *Règ.Aug.* i. 422.

encouraging them as appropriate. He must so accommodate and adapt himself to each other's character and intelligence that he will not only keep the flock entrusted to his care from dwindling, but will rejoice in the increase of a good flock.[114]

The abbot, in other words, must experience the anxiety of authority— the strain of constantly calculating what he will say to each of his flock, and the possibility that his insight might one day fail him. Benedict is well aware of the extra burden of accountability that this imposes on the abbot, and the danger to all that the abbot will use excess force in correction. In response, he eschews the mania of supervision advo- cated by the Master: 'Excitable, anxious, extreme, obstinate, jealous, or over-suspicious he [the abbot] must not be. Such a man is never at rest.' Mindful of his own fragility, the abbot should bear in mind Jacob's discretion:

'If I drive my flocks too hard, they will all die in a single day.' Therefore, drawing on discretion, the mother of all virtues, he must so arrange everything that the strong have something to yearn for and the weak have something from which to run.[115]

Benedict was able, explicitly, to resolve the problem of communal living that had defeated Cassian—but only at the cost of admitting a degree of irresolution with regard to the question of authority. No abbot, however graced with discretion, could hope to avoid all error in his direction of souls.

Mindful of the intricate politics of correction, Benedict returns towards the end of his *Rule* to the theme of what sort of person the abbot should be—'Let him strive to be loved rather than feared'[116]— and on what a monk should do when given an impossible abbatial command. Benedict was, tentatively, prepared to envisage the possi- bility that monastic obedience did not preclude the possibility of reasoning with abbatial authority:

Should he [the monk] see that the burden is altogether too much for his strength, then he should choose the appropriate moment and explain patiently to his

---

[114] *RB* 2. 31–2, SC 181, 448–50, material not present in *RM*, although the theme is not entirely absent there. Both *RM* and *RB* cite 2 Tim. 4: 2 on the different modes of admoni- tion (*RM* 2. 23–5, *RB* 2. 23–5; also *REug* 25. *RB* omits *RM* 2. 26–31 on the abbot as child, father, and mother. See de Vogüé, *Community and Abbot*, 65–96, for a full discussion of the 'directories of the abbot'.

[115] *RB* 64. 18–19, SC 182, 652.

[116] *RB* 64. 15, SC 182, 650; and K. Gross, '*Plus amari quam timeri*: Eine antike politische Maxime in der Benediktinerregel', *VigChr* 27 (1973), 218–29.

superior the reasons why he cannot perform the task. This he ought to do without pride, obstinacy, or refusal. If, after the explanation, the superior is still determined to hold to his original order, then the junior must recognize that this is best for him.[117]

In his focus on the obedience of those under command, Benedict forgoes the opportunity to follow Augustine in imagining what it might be like to be the figure in authority issuing a command he finds to be impossible, or a rebuke he knows to be too harsh. The abbot does not have to stand alone in Benedict's *Rule*, as he does in that of Augustine. His isolation is countered, in the *Rule*'s closing section, by a call to obedience of all to all, according to rank.[118] All juniors must pay to their seniors the attentiveness they owed to the precepts of the *magister* and to the directives of the abbot. It was, in the final analysis, through a thickened regime of *obaudientia* rather than a luminous appeal to Jerusalem *communitas* that the monastery in the *Rule* would express itself as a community.

In observing the distinctive augustinianism of the *Rule of St Benedict*, then, we should not lose sight of the fact that his is a rule for cenobites in the matrix defined by the work of Cassian. The effect of Benedict's use of Augustine is not so much to balance out a reliance on Cassian, as to conscript augustinian authority and perspective to support a cenobitic interpretation of Cassian. Augustine's emphasis on the monastery as an apostolic, ecclesial community could be used to strengthen the language and practice of a cenobitism to which Cassian had given only partial support: this was Benedict's insight, as he sought to secure the vision of the *coenobium* already articulated by the Master. Further than this Benedict did not go: he did not seek to define the place of the monastery in the Church, nor within salvation history. These concerns, however, and specifically the question 'Could abbatial authority of the sort described in the *Rule* be exercised in the wider society of the faithful?' were precisely those which preoccupied the earliest documented reader of Benedict's *Rule*, Pope Gregory the Great.

---

[117] *RB* 68. 2–4, SC 182, 664, tr. *RB 1980*, 291. Cf. *RB* 64. 3–6 on the possibility that the local bishop will be brought in to depose an abbot who is complicit with the vices of his community (also *RB* 62. 8–11 on dealing with troublesome priests who join the community).

[118] *RB* 71. 1–9, SC 182, 668.

PART III

The Gregorian Synthesis

6

The Weakness of Gregory

In 577 the Lombards sacked the monastery of Montecassino, founded by Benedict some forty or fifty years previously. Some of the monks seem to have sought refuge in the city of Rome, installing themselves in a monastery near the Lateran palace.[1] Although safe, at least for the moment, and although no strangers to the city, we may imagine their discomfort.[2] The *Rule of St Benedict* did little to prepare its adherents for life in Rome at the end of the sixth century. Benedict had presumed a rural community with fields and a millpond, materially and liturgically self-sufficient—although not necessarily closed to the benign generosity of a patron like Barbaria, the imperial matron who seems to have provided for Severinus' disciples at Lucullanum. Benedict's disciples now found themselves back in a city, serving the liturgical needs of a major basilica, and dependent, along with the rest of the populace, on the organized largesse of the papal administration—for grain, and for blankets in winter.[3]

Not so far away, on the Caelian Hill, stood the monastery of St Andrew's, recently established in his family mansion by Gregory, the former prefect of the city, now a convert to the ascetic life. The inmates of the community were a group of like-minded aristocrats some of whom Gregory had known since childhood; in the course of the next twenty years, many were to leave the city as abbots, bishops, and missionaries to the edges of the known world.[4] There can have been no more intellectually earnest, socially confident circle of young men in the late ancient Mediterranean world. Sympathy for the plight of the Montecassino refugees, and a measure of fascination, perhaps,

---

[1] *Dial*. II, prol. 2 on Benedict's disciple Valentinianus, 'who for many years was in charge of the Lateran monastery'; II. 17 on the destruction of Montecassino. However, it is only the much later account of Paul the Deacon (*History of the Lombards* IV. 17) that actually attests the flight of monks from Montecassino to Rome, with a copy of Benedict's *Rule*: for critical discussion of this much debated problem, see Ferrari, *Early Roman Monasteries*, 242–50, and Meyvaert, 'Problems concerning the "Autograph" Manuscript of Saint Benedict's Rule'.

[2] *Dial*. II. 3. 14, SC 260, 150, on the sons of Roman noblemen flocking to Benedict.

[3] On blankets for ascetics in winter, see *Ep*. VII. 23, CCSL 140, 477.

[4] e.g. Peter, appointed in *Ep*. I. 1 to oversee papal lands in Sicily; Maximian, future bishop of Syracuse; Marinianus, archbishop of Ravenna; Claudius, abbot of St Apollinaire, Ravenna; Augustine and Mellitus, sent to England as missionaries.

led Gregory to befriend Valentinianus, the leader of the group. Over
fifteen years later, Gregory, now occupying the Lateran palace as
bishop of the city—the first monk, indeed, ever to hold this office—
described his conversations with Benedict's disciples, and the fruit
they bore: the *Life* of Benedict in the *Dialogues*.

No other historical figure attracted Gregory's attention in the same
way as did Benedict.[5] Through his account of the holy man's life,
Gregory took the measure of the distance between his own universe
and that of the ascetic culture he had inherited. If the *Rule of St
Benedict* did not speak so clearly to the changed needs of his displaced
monks, the memories they carried of their teacher became, in
Gregory's hands, a new language of identity, more suited to the times.
The Benedict of the *Dialogues* presents a very different figure from the
wisdom teacher of the *Rule*, and the contrast is not merely a function
of the generic difference between *Life* and *Rule*. Gregory, whose
admiration for the *Rule* we need not doubt, offered to his immediate
circle and to Benedict's disciples a narrative of their mentor as a moral
giant, exorcising the countryside, lifted up to the heavens in the
company of angels.[6] This was a Benedict for the last days—an eschatological appropriation of the moral voice that speaks in the *Rule*. It is
tempting, perhaps overly so, to regard the encounter between
Benedict's monks and Gregory as a meeting at the frontier between
emissaries from different worlds.[7]

In the modern era, Gregory is often depicted as a man at the border,
poised between between the the Roman and the Germanic worlds,
between East and West, and above all, perhaps, between the ancient
and medieval epochs—a characterization that does not necessarily
serve him well.[8] Certainly, in stationing Gregory at the frontier, we
begin to acknowledge the immense future influence of his account of
Benedict, as of all his writings, in the medieval Church and beyond.
However, this acknowledgement is frequently based on the assump-

   [5] In *Dialogues* I, Gregory and his interlocutor Peter discuss the miracles and virtues of
twelve different figures; in III there are thirty-six bishops and abbots. IV moves into the
present and contains a whole series of visions from men and women at Rome.
   [6] See below, Ch. 7.
   [7] *Mutatis mutandis*, see Southern, *Western Society and the Church*, 217, on the contrast in
universes evoked by the *Rule of St Benedict* and Felix's *Life of Guthlac*: 'The lonely and
superhuman struggles with demons, the hand-to-hand combats, the duckings, the beatings,
the draggings through bog and fen. . . . For such experiences as these, the *Rule of St Benedict*
offered little opportunity.'
   [8] E. Caspar, *Geschichte des Papsttums*, 2 vols. (Tübingen, 1933), ii. 408, cited by R.
Markus, *Gregory the Great and his World* (Cambridge, 1983), p. xii.

tion that Gregory, as a hinge figure engaged in cultural transmission, has no original point of view. Installed in the patristic canon as the fourth Latin Father, Gregory tends to be typecast as a 'moral' thinker, whose assimilation of the texts of Augustine and Cassian was of critical import—but who was himself less capable of analytical or innovative thought, and who therefore concentrated his energies on reducing the complexities of earlier patristic writings for consumption by a future medieval audience.[9] Gregory's Edwardian biographer, an avowed admirer of his subject, in whose debt modern scholars still stand, exemplifies this approach:

> Growing up amid the relics of a greatness that had passed, daily reminded by the beautiful broken marbles of the vanity of things, he [Gregory] was accustomed to look on the world with sorrowful eyes. The thrill, the vigour, the joy of life were not for him. . . . He never attained a perfect sanity of view. From his birth he was sick—a victim of the malady of the Middle Ages.[10]

At the start of the account, the reader meets the young Gregory cast, ironically, in the mould of Gibbon, surveying the dilapidation of Rome.

The premises on which these verdicts are based are open to question. An involvement in cultural transmission need impose no constraint on originality; a spiritually driven lack of interest in institutions or political theory need entail no lack of interest in power. It is suggested here that Gregory was committed above all else to a meditation on power and its uses deliberately divorced from an institutional or a 'high' theoretical context. Over nearly two centuries, successive generations in the ascetic movement had confronted, explored, and argued over the multifarious social consequences of their own profuse claims to otherworldliness. Now, for the first time, a monk was bishop of Rome. Acutely conscious of the exalted character of his station, and hugely learned in the vast body of patristic literature already in existence, Gregory determined, with astonishing single-mindedness, to answer one question: how to harness the full force of ascetic detachment to the exercise of power in this world.[11] His

---

[9] See the verdicts of Caspar, *Geschichte des Papsttums*, ii. 514, and J. M. Wallace-Hadrill, *The Frankish Church* (Oxford, 1983), 118, both cited by Markus, *Gregory*, 203. C. Dagens, *Saint Grégoire le Grand: culture et expérience chrétiennes* (Paris, 1977), 18–28, 439, mounts a defence of Gregory against his detractors, while none the less conceding that originality is not a quality displayed by him.

[10] F. Homes Dudden, *Gregory the Great: His Place in History and Thought*, 2 vols. (London, 1905), i. 15.

[11] On Gregory and his sense of office, see R. A. Markus, 'Papal Primacy: Light from the

response is irreducible to any single formulation, theory, or institutional practice. What Gregory offers is a language—a discourse of moral authority, at once fierce and infinitely malleable. It is not too much to say that Gregory's intervention permanently raised the ceiling of expectation of those in public office, in the medieval West and beyond. For better or for worse, the gregorian sense of the moral possibility attendant on the exercise of power has proved unforgettable.[12]

An understanding of the language Gregory devised—how he honed his 'voice'—requires that we look not to his medieval future, but at his past. Gregory identified instinctively with very ancient traditions of moral reflection and instruction. When he seems most 'personal' to us, as he does in the preface to the *Dialogues*, lamenting the burdens of office, depicting himself in secluded conversation with a spiritual companion, to his readers Gregory would have seemed an instantly recognizable participant in the broad tradition represented in the sixth century by Boethius' *Consolations of Philosophy* and Pomerius' *On the Contemplative Life*, looking back to Cassian's *Conferences* and to Augustine's Cassiciacum dialogues, and behind all these, to the dialogues of ancient philosophy.[13] It remains for Gregory's modern audience to trace the specific ways in which Gregory's discussion of power and detachment resulted from his potent assimilation of earlier ascetic writers on this theme in the Latin West.

Profoundly traditional as were Gregory's intellectual instincts, what animated Gregory's thinking was his sense of the immediate future. The *Dialogues*, for all their fascination with Benedict, are concerned with the quickening of historical time. The narratives of past holy men and women of Italy give place to stories set in the present, in Rome. The ruin of the senate and the imperial palace were but two of Gregory's witnesses. Everywhere, he saw signs of the impending cataclysm. Storms came unexpectedly in the summer time;[14] a sinner's corpse was expelled from its place of burial in anticipation of the final

---

Early Middle Ages', in id., *From Augustine to Gregory the Great: History and Christianity in Late Antiquity* (London, 1983), ch. XVI. On Gregory's consciousness of patristic literature, in particular the work of Ambrose and Augustine, see esp. *HEz.* I, pref., CCSL 142, 4.

[12] As seen by Leclercq, *Love of Letters*, 26. 'Without knowing it, we are living, in great measure, on his modes of expression and on his thoughts, and for that very reason, they no longer seem new to us.'

[13] For a brief comparison between Gregory and Boethius, see O'Donnell, 'The Holiness of Gregory', 69–70.

[14] *HEv.* II. 35. 1, PL 76, 1260C. See also *HEv.* I. 10. 2, PL 76, 1111.

reckoning.[15] In the death-bed visions of teenage girls, as in the celebration of the Mass, the nearness of Judgement is palpable and eerie,
like the tricks of the light in the breaking of dawn.[16] What Gregory
offered the exiles from Montecassino was a way of making sense of the
loss of their original home, as yet another sign of the home-coming
that all were about to experience. No Christian writer since Paul of
Tarsus, perhaps, had as vivid a sense of the nearness of the end times
as did Gregory.

AUTHENTICATING GREGORY

'Who is Gregory the Great?', one scholar has asked, so forcing the
issue of Gregory's unresolved identity in modern scholarship.[17] This
irresolution is nowhere more clearly indexed than in the continuing
debates about the authenticity of the works commonly included in the
gregorian corpus.[18] Characteristic of these discussions is a tendency to
invoke notions of an 'essential' Gregory— whether defined through an
evocation of his spirituality or the scanning of his clausulae endings—
by which the attribution of particular works may be confirmed or
denied. The possibility that Gregory could have encompassed contra-
dictions as a thinker and a writer is, perhaps, too rarely admitted (in
contrast to the ample room for complexity and development afforded
Augustine of Hippo).[19]

At the centre of the debate over authentication are the *Dialogues*. In
his preface, Gregory was nothing if not programmatic in his intentions
for the work, explaining why he has turned aside from his usual business of scriptural exegesis to the narration of miracle stories. This was
not a fundamental change of course, he maintains. The histories of his
own day were no less revealing of the presence of God in the world
than those recounted in Scripture. To some hearers, indeed, *exempla*
were more effective than *praedicamenta*: not so, however, to some later
readers of the *Dialogues*, who have been unable to reconcile the stories
of holy men, devils and, for example, the theft of monastic lettuces

[15] *Dial.* II. 55, SC 265, 183.
[16] e.g. *Dial.* IV. 18, SC 265, 70: the Virgin appears to Musa, sister of the Roman monk
Probus, surrounded by girls of Musa's age.
[17] O'Donnell, 'The Holiness of Gregory', 62.
[18] For a short guide to Gregory's life and his works, with accompanying bibliography, see
C. Straw, *Gregory the Great*, Authors of the Middle Ages IV, nos. 12–13 (London, 1996).
[19] An exception being S. Boesch Gajano, 'La proposta agiographica dei "Dialoghi" di
Gregorio Magno', *Studi Medievali* 3rd ser., 21 (1980), 623–64.

with the searching deeps of Gregory's biblical homilies.[20] Since the early modern period, indeed, the *Dialogues* have been something of a test case in the critical reception of medieval hagiography. For Reformation and Enlightenment scholars they illustrate the credulity of even the most advanced of medieval intellects, or at least their readiness to pander to popular superstition.[21] To this day, indeed, attempts continue to be made to 'save' the greatness of Gregory from the perceived idiocy of the *Dialogues* by arguing that these are a pseudonymous work.[22]

The overall trend of scholarship on hagiography in the past generation, however, has obviated the need for such a case, in its demonstration that it was the élite, not the masses, in the late Roman world who were responsible for the creation of the cult of the saints, and who did so for anything but superstitious reasons.[23] As regards the *Dialogues* in particular, from the mid-1970s a series of studies from Italian scholars,[24] and a new edition,[25] established a fresh critical context for

[20] On exemplarity, see B. Bremond *et al.* (eds.), *L'"exemplum"*, Typologie des sources du moyen âge occidental 40 (Turnhout, 1982); M. Van Uytfanghe, 'Modèles bibliques dans l'hagiographie', in P. Riché and G. Lobrichon (eds.), *Le Moyen Age et la Bible*, Bible de tous le temps 4 (Paris, 1984), 449–88; J. Le Goff, 'Les exempla chez Grégoire le Grand', *Hagiographies, Cultures, Sociétés*, 103–17 (with discussion, 117–20). Recent discussion of the literary form of the *Dialogues* owes much to A. Vitale-Brovarone, 'La forma narrativa dei *Dialoghi* di Gregorio Magno: problemi storico-letterari', and 'Forma narrativa dei *Dialoghi* di Gregorio Magno: prospettiva di struttura', *Atti dell'Accademia delle scienze di Torino*, II, *Classe di scienze morali, storiche e filologiche*, 108 (1974), 95–173; 109 (1975), 117–85.

[21] To von Harnack, *History of Dogma*, v. 262, famously, Gregory is the inventor of 'Vulgarkatholicism'.

[22] See F. Clark, *The Pseudo-Gregorian Dialogues*, 2 vols. (Leiden, 1987). The response has consisted largely, and (to my mind) persuasively of a rebuttal of Clark's arguments. See R. Godding, 'Les Dialogues de Grégoire le Grand: À propos d'un livre récent', *AB* 106 (1988), 201–29; Meyvaert, 'Enigma of Gregory the Great's Dialogues'; A. de Vogüé, 'Grégoire le Grand et ses "Dialogues" d'après deux ouvrages récents', *RHE* 83 (1988), 281–348; id., 'Les Dialogues, oeuvre authentique et publiée par Grégoire lui-même', in *Gregorio Magno*, ii. 27–40.

[23] P. R. L. Brown, *The Cult of the Saints: Its Rise and Function in Latin Christianity* (Chicago, 1981); R. Van Dam, *Leadership and Community in Late Antique Gaul* (Berkeley/Los Angeles, 1985), and id., *Saints and their Miracles in Late Antique Gaul* (Princeton, 1993). This is not to say that there was no discussion or dissension about the miraculous in this period; see e.g. M. Van Uytfanghe, 'La controverse biblique et patristique autour du miracle et ses repercussions dans l'Antiquité tardive et le haut Moyen Age latin', *Hagiographie, cultures, sociétés*, 205–32, with discussion at 232–3; id., 'Scepticisme doctrinal au seuil du Moyen Age? Les objections du diacre Pierre dans les *Dialogues* de Grégoire le Grand', in *Grégoire le Grand*, 315–24, with discussion, 324–6.

[24] See A. Vitale-Brovarone, 'La forma narrativa dei *Dialoghi* di Gregorio Magno'; S. Boesch Gajano, 'Dislivelli culturali e mediazioni ecclesiastiche nei *Dialoghi* di Gregorio Magno', in C. Ginzburg (ed.), *Religioni delle classi popolari*, *Quaderni storici* 41 (1979), 398–415; ead., '"Narratio" e "espositio" nei Dialoghi di Gregorio Magno', *Bulletino dell'Istituto*

the discussion of the text, in which the issue of Gregory's 'credulity' disappeared, and discussion could begin anew of the *Dialogues* in relation to Gregory's other writings and, more broadly, Latin hagiography.[26] Future research is likely to focus, in particular, on the suggestion that the *Dialogues* represent Gregory's response to the Roman *gesta martyrum*, a rapidly expanding literature in the fifth and sixth centuries, offering tales of pre-Constantinian heroism in the arena. These are almost uniformly fictional, but closely connected with the contemporary growth of cult sites around the city under aristocratic patronage. The stress laid by Gregory in the *Dialogues* on the ascetic life as a 'peace-time martyrdom', and on the correct, ethically driven interpretation of miraculous power, may represent a critique of the florid, fiercely competitive devotional culture associated with martyrs of the *gesta* and their lay patrons. In ways that are still obscure to us, because work on the *gesta* is still in its early stages, the *Dialogues* may therefore form part of the story of Gregory's uneasy relationship with sections of the Roman clergy and their patrons.[27]

As the preface to the *Dialogues* makes clear, by 593 Gregory had established a literary identity as an exegete; his preference was to expound difficult books of the Old Testament to a relatively small audience,[28] often extempore efforts which he later wrote up for official circulation.[29] The exegetical corpus transmitted under his name is not,

storico italiano per il medio evo e Archivio Muratoriano 88 (1979), 1–33; ead., 'La proposta agiographica dei "Dialoghi" di Gregorio Magno', *Studi Medievali* 3rd ser., 21 (1980), 623–64; ead., 'Demoni e miracoli nei "Dialoghi" di Gregorio Magno', *Hagiographie, cultures, sociétés*, 263–80, with discussion 280–1. G. Cracco, 'Uomini di Dio e uomini di chiesa nell'alto medioevo (per una reinterpretazione dei "Dialoghi" di Gregorio Magno', *Ricerche di storia sociale e religiosa* NS 12 (1977), 163–202; id., 'Ascesa e ruolo dei "viri dei" nell'Italia di Gregorio Magno', in *Hagiographie, cultures, sociétés*, 283–96, with discussion, 296–7.

[25] A. de Vogüé (ed.), *Grégoire le Grand: Dialogues*, 3 vols., SC 251, 260, 265 (Paris 1978–80); reviewed by S. Pricoco, *Orpheus* NS 2 (1981), 434–42.

[26] See e.g. J. Petersen, *The 'Dialogues' of Gregory the Great in their Late Antique Cultural Background* (Toronto: Pontifical Institute of Medieval Studies, 1984); W. McCready, *Signs of Sanctity: Miracles in the Thought of Gregory the Great* (Toronto: Pontifical Institute of Medieval Studies, 1989).

[27] See Boesch Gajano, 'La proposta agiographica dei "Dialoghi" di Gregorio Magno', 649–64.

[28] Gregory's audience has been much discussed. J. McClure, 'Gregory the Great: Exegesis and Audience' (Oxford Univ. D. Phil. thesis, 1979) argues that Gregory spoke always to the monks of St Andrews. I follow P. Meyvaert, 'The Date of Gregory the Great's Commentaries on the Canticle of Canticles and on 1 Kings', *Sacris Erudiri* 23 (1979), 191–216, in envisaging a less institutionally restricted group (although any reliance on the Commentary on 1 Kings by any party in this discussion is now vitiated by doubts on the authenticity of that work).

[29] P. Meyvaert, 'The Enigma of Gregory the Great's Dialogues: A Response to Francis

however, unproblematic. No one disputes that Gregory's first and longest work was his *Moralia in Job*, thirty-five books of commentary on the book of Job begun in Constantinople in the late 570s and finished in Rome in 591. For the next two years, he expounded the book of Ezekiel, although it was a further eight years before he finalized the editing of twenty-two homilies in two books.[30] The difficulty comes in determining the extent of his activities after 593. In a letter of 602, Gregory reveals that he had also worked on Proverbs, the prophets (unnamed), the Song of Songs, the Books of Kings, and the Heptateuch.[31] What has survived under Gregory's name is a fragment of the Song of Songs[32] and a long commentary on the First Book of Kings. While the authenticity of the former does not seem to be in question, that of the latter has been under debate for centuries. Many have observed that its language is often untypical of Gregory. One explanation is that this reflects the role of one of Gregory's disciples, Claudius of Ravenna, in writing up Gregory's sermons—editorial work with which Gregory was distinctly unhappy. It has recently been pointed out, however, that the earliest manuscript of the Commentary on 1 Kings is twelfth-century, from the monastery of Cava. We know the abbot of the community, Peter, to have been a keen gregorian, and to have written a Commentary on 1 Kings, the scope of which matches exactly that transmitted under Gregory's name. It seems highly likely that Peter, knowing that Gregory had commented on the Book of Kings, presented his own exegesis as the work of his revered master. For the present, therefore, it is safest to exclude the Commentary on 1 Kings as we have it from the authentic gregorian canon.[33]

   To one side of the *Moralia* and the *Homilies on Ezekiel* stand the

---

Clark', *JEH* 39 (1988), 335–81 at 348 ff. offers a clear discussion of Gregory's mode of composition.

[30] Gregory seems to have worked continuously on the opening chapters of the prophet for two years, before moving on to the vision of the Temple in Ezek. 40. See *HEz.* I, pref., CCSL 142, 3, for the eight-year gap between the time of delivery (most likely in 593) and the finished edition (601). It is difficult to date with certainty these stages of the work's composition: see P. Meyvaert, 'The Date', 201–2 n. 25.

[31] *Ep.* XII. 6, CCSL 140A, 975.

[32] For the composition of the Commentary on the Song of Songs, see P. Meyvaert, 'The Date'; R. Bélanger, *Commentaire sur le Cantique des Cantiques*, SC 314 (1984), 22–8. Markus, *Gregory*, 16 and n. 72.

[33] See A. de Vogüé, 'L'Auteur du Commentaire des Rois attribué à saint Grégoire: un moine de Cava', *RBen* 106 (1996), 319–31; id. 'Le *Glossa Ordinaria* et le Commentaire des Rois attribué à saint Grégoire le Grand', *RBen* 108 (1998), 58–60. Discussion of de Vogüé's find has already begun: F. Clark, 'The Authorship of the Commentary in I Regum: Implications of Adalbert de Vogüé's Discovery', *RBen* 108 (1998), 61–79.

Homilies on the Gospels.[34] These Gregory delivered in the first two years of his papacy, at St Peters and the major cult sites of the city. Unlike his Old Testament exegesis, then, these sermons were composed for specific liturgical occasions and for a broad audience. The change of context, it has been observed, does not seem to have suited him. Certainly the *Homilies* are authentic, but Gregory is seen to have given a somewhat fitful performance. He was not a pulpit orator, being physically too weak to perform regularly before large audiences, and temperamentally unsuited to keeping his teaching simple and clear for the benefit of the people.[35] A measure of his discomfort as a popular preacher is the number of the stories recounted in the *Homilies* which then reappear in the *Dialogues*, where they are expounded at greater length and moral subtlety. On other occasions in the *Homilies*, Gregory seems to have decided to abandon the attempt to keep his teaching simple.[36] One scholar comments: 'The *Homilies on the Gospels* mark a decline in the popular homiletic tradition which was one of the most important features of Western exegesis in the fourth and fifth centuries.' [37] A less dismissive approach is possible, however, if we regard the *Homilies* in the same light as the *Dialogues*, as a source for Gregory's complicated relationship with the clerical and cultic life of Rome, in particular martyr piety.[38]

For Gregory's involvement in ecclesiastical and worldly business scholars turn immediately to the over 800 letters preserved in his *Register*, where we may read of his administrative dealings and political negotiations in Rome and Italy, and across the known world, Syria, North Africa, Asia Minor, and the West.[39] These are not, however, a

---

[34] Cited here after the edition in PL 76, 1075–1312: the new edition in CCSL 141 (Turnhout, 1999) appeared too late for me to take account of it. See also the translation, introduction, and commentary given by M. Fiedrowicz, *Gregor der Grosse: Homiliae in Evangelia*, 2 vols., *Fontes Christiani* 28 (Freiburg im Breisgau, 1997).

[35] For a critique in these terms, see McClure, 'Gregory the Great', ch. 4, esp. 157, 164.

[36] *HEv.* II. 34. 12, PL 76, 1254B, drawing on pseudo-Dionysius, *De caelesti hierarchia*. See C. Micaelli, 'Riflessioni su alcuni aspetti dell'angelologia di Gregorio Magno', *Gregorio Magno*, ii. 301–14.

[37] McClure, 'Gregory the Great', 157. Or again: 'Gregory was not especially concerned with one of the most important facets of the antique rhetorical tradition, one which had been carefully utilized by such great popular preachers as Augustine and Caesarius: the immediate personal contact of speaker and audience' (164).

[38] See e.g. J. F. Baldovin, *The Urban Character of Christian Worship: The Origins, Development and Meaning of Stational Liturgy*, *Orientalia Christiana Analecta* 228 (Rome, 1987), 105–66; A. Chavasse, 'Aménagements liturgiques à Rome, au VIIe et VIIIe siècles', *RBen* 99 (1989), 75–102; C. Leyser, 'The Temptations of Cult: Roman Martyr Piety in the Age of Gregory the Great', *Early Medieval Europe*, forthcoming.

[39] See F. Homes Dudden, *Gregory the Great: His Place in History and Thought*, 2 vols.

transparent record. They represent a collection made by Gregory himself from a much larger original number. One scholar calculates that the letters in the *Register* represent barely a twentieth of those composed by Gregory and by the papal chancery. Exacting philological work confirms the common-sense suspicion that Gregory composed only those letters which required his specific attention, while leaving the management of routine transactions to his notaries. The selection criteria used, and the overall purpose of the collection, remain as yet beyond our view.

A rallying-point for all readers of Gregory is the *Pastoral Rule*, the only systematic treatise from his pen. In four books, Gregory discusses what sort of person should assume power, what the proper response to the assumption of power was, how moral authority should be exercised over those for whom one is responsible, and how the ruler should always return to himself to monitor his own conduct. Composed in the months immediately after his consecration as Pope in 590, the *Pastoral Rule* is as close as we may come to Gregory's centre of gravity as a writer and thinker: in the closing books of the *Moralia*, we can see the text of the *Rule* taking shape in Gregory's mind. In the letters Gregory composed at his accession, and in the *Homilies on Ezekiel*, we see Gregory repeating and redeploying sections of the work.[40] This was as definitive a formulation as he could manage of his teaching on authority—a point clearly appreciated by Gregory's definitive early medieval biographer. John the Deacon, writing in the late ninth century, structured the four sections of his *Life of Gregory* on the pattern of the four books of the *Pastoral Rule*.[41]

John the Deacon's approach has had few modern exponents. Twentieth-century interpreters of Gregory have been reluctant in the

(London, 1905); see also H. H. Howarth, *Saint Gregory the Great* (London, 1912), and J. Richards, *Consul of God: The Life and Times of Pope Gregory the Great* (London, 1980). On the *Register*, see D. Norberg, *In Registrum Gregorii Magni studia critica* (Uppsala Universiteits Arsskrift, 1937/4; 1939/7; id., 'Style personnel et style administratif dans le Registrum epistolarum de S. Grégoire le Grand', in J. Fontaine *et al.* (eds.), *Grégoire le Grand* (Paris, 1986), 489–97; and E. Pitz, *Papstreskripte im frühen Mittelalter. Diplomatische und rechtsgeschichtliche Studien zum Brief-Corpus Gregors den Großen* (Sigmaringen, 1990), for an estimate of some 20, 000. For discussion (with a more cautious estimate), see Markus, *Gregory*, 206–8.

[40] *Mor.* XXX. 3. 13, CCSL 143B, 1500, sets out the programme of *RP* III, and announces the composition of the work. See B. Judic (ed.), *Grégoire le Grand: Règle Pastorale*, 2 vols. SC 381–2 (1992), 17–21, 74–6.

[41] See W. Berschin, *Biografie und Epochenstil im Lateinischen Mittelalter*, 3 vols. (Stuttgart, 1986), ii. 372–87.

extreme to offer an integrated account of their subject.[42] Most scholarship adopts a 'localized' approach to Gregory, concentrating on one or other aspect of his life and works. In the British scholarly tradition, based on a reading of the *Register*, Gregory has most often appeared as a practical man of business. This archive supplies a roll-call of Gregory's achievements: he saved Rome from destruction at the hands of the Lombards, he reorganized the administration of the papal states, he maintained papal authority in the face of encroachments from the Patriarch of Constantinople, he established links with the Frankish Kingdoms, and most importantly (for these English writers), he sent a party of monks, led by Augustine, to convert the Anglo-Saxons. About Gregory himself as a monk there is very little: his monastic conversion and his biblical exegesis are regarded, essentially, as private matters, with little to illuminate his public career.[43] These are, by contrast, the very texts which hold the attention of continental and, more recently, American scholars. From this perspective, Gregory appears as a spiritual writer immersed in the texts of Scripture and of the earlier Church Fathers.[44] Even in acknowledging his long-term significance, however, this kind of work on Gregory threatens to abstract his moral thinking from its specific context in the world of the late sixth century. The 'secularized' and 'spiritualized' approaches agree in dividing Gregory's exterior life from his interior thought, his active from his contemplative life. Only in 1997 did a biography of Gregory appear as firmly based in the complexities of the letters as of his exegesis.[45]

[42] For an overview of modern scholarship, see R. Godding, 'Cento anni di ricerche su Gregorio Magno: A proposito di una bibliografia', in *Gregorio Magno*, i. 293–304. The reference work announced here—the same author's *Bibliographia di Gregorio Magno (1890/1989)* (Rome, 1990)—is indispensable.

[43] See e.g. Homes Dudden, *Gregory*, ii. 285–6; Richards, *Consul*, 263–5.

[44] Among the best examples: R. Gillet, 'Grégoire le Grand', art. *DSp* 6: 872–910; C. Dagens, *Saint Grégoire le Grand: culture et expérience chrétiennes* (Paris, 1977); M. Frickel, *Deus totus ubique simul: Untersuchungen zur allgemeinen Gottgegenwart im Rahmen des Gotteslehre Gregors des Grossen*, Freiburger theologische Studien 69 (Freiburg im Breisgau, 1956); and now M. Fiedrowicz, *Das Kirchenverständnis Gregors des Grossen: Eine Untersuchung seiner exegetischen und homiletischen Werke*, Römische Quartalschrift für Christliche Altertumskunde und Kirchengeschichte 50 (Freiburg im Breisgau, 1995); C. Straw, *Gregory the Great: Perfection in Imperfection* (Berkeley/Los Angeles, 1988). The major international conferences on Gregory in the past two decades have begun to witness scholars forsaking these local traditions, but the basic division between the 'historical' Gregory and the 'spiritual/literary' Gregory has remained in place. See *Grégoire le Grand* (Paris, 1986), *Gregorio Magno e il suo Tempo* (Rome, 1991), and Cavadini (ed.), *Gregory the Great* (Notre Dame, 1995).

[45] Markus, *Gregory*.

It is possible to look to Gregory himself for a ratification of these divisions. His representation of his career seems to support just such a division, turning as it does on his election to the papacy in 590. In a flurry of letters at his election, and then repeatedly throughout his sermons, he presents the assumption of office as an almost unendurable burden.[46] As a monk, he says, he had achieved a modicum of contemplative equilibrium: now he is a bishop, it is dissipated in any number of trivial concerns. These laments continue long into Gregory's papacy; conjoined with complaints about his illness (he had gout), they make up a picture of unrelieved suffering in papal office, set against the nostalgia for the haven of the cloister that he enjoyed before consecration.

These protestations of reluctance and of suffering must feature in any account of Gregory, but their interpretation has been constrained, not abetted, by the divided state of gregorian historiography. The secularist tradition understands Gregory's plaints as an extended *nolo episcopari*, a ritual gesture of good faith offered up by all civic magistrates in the ancient world. In the spiritualized perspective, the suffering of Gregory seems no 'mere' topos, but the genuine expression of an ascetic man who took office in spite of himself.[47] More recent work, in particular an approach to Gregory as a writer and thinker who positively thrives on paradox and antithesis, suggests that neither dismissal of his words as topos, nor defence of their sincerity accurately represents the understanding shared by Gregory and his audience of the conditions of public utterance by men in power.[48] These declarations, I have suggested, constitute a 'rhetoric of vulnerability' central to Gregory's continuing exercise of moral authority. Abdication, or the suggestion of it, was far from his mind. This is not to say that Gregory's suffering in office was fabricated: only that the import of his words will be misconstrued until we appreciate the rhetorical conventions in which he spoke.[49]

Gregory, whose sense of ironic self-deprecation is among the least studied phenomena of Late Antiquity, was far from incapable of the

---

[46] See e.g. *Mor. Epistula ad Leandrum* I, CCSL 143, 1–2; *Epp.* I. 5–7, CCSL 140, 5–10; *Dial.* prol. 3–6, SC 260, 12–14.

[47] See e.g. Gillet, 'Grégoire le Grand', *DSp* 6: 875–6; Dagens, *Grégoire*, 84, 140.

[48] Straw, *Gregory*, passim. See also ead., 'Adversitas et Prosperitas': une illustration du motif structurel de la complementarite', *Grégoire le Grand*, 277–88, and 'Gregory's Politics: Theory and Practice', in *Gregorio Magno*, i. 47–63.

[49] C. Leyser, '"Let Me Speak, Let Me Speak": Vulnerability and Authority in Gregory the Great's *Homilies on Ezekiel*', in *Gregorio Magno*, ii. 169–82.

rhetorically light touch.[50] 'There are two things that are bothering me in this matter', he confides in his hearers, as he prepares to explain to them the vision of the Temple of the Prophet Ezekiel:

One is that this vision is shrouded in such thick obscurity that it seems difficult to throw any light on it. The other is that I have learnt that the Lombard King Agilulph has crossed the Po and is moving at top speed to besiege us.[51]

At the time, this display of intellectual *sang froid* in the face of impending military disaster was doubtless intended to steady the morale of his entourage. The fact that, eight years later when he came to edit the *Homilies*, Gregory thought this remark worth preserving suggests it was not mere bravado that led him to make it. He was a man who inhabited the world of Old Testament exegesis and the world of barbarian invasion with equal aplomb.

AUTHORITY AND ISOLATION IN ROME

Whatever we think of Gregory, we might pause at least to consider what he and his circle looked like from the outside. A person of apparently relentless 'moral seriousness', surrounded by a coterie of like-minded ascetics, Gregory was, to many, an infuriating and a divisive figure.[52] No sooner had he died than his enemies built a huge fire to burn all his books.[53] This is a ninth-century story—but there is good contemporary evidence for the enmities that Gregory inspired wherever he went, both in Rome and in Constantinople.[54] Like the Caesarii in Arles, Gregory and his circle were evidently regarded as a serious nuisance, especially by the Roman clerics they displaced in the Lateran palace. Equally apparent is Gregory's own readiness to sense that his friends and disciples had betrayed, or at best, misunderstood him. This fraught political context inside the city of Rome, and inside the circle of the gregorians, holds a key to understanding the rhetorical effort Gregory had to make to present himself as an unimpeachable ruler, and his insistent meditation on the isolation of those in power.

[50] As observed by Caspar, *Geschichte des Papsttums*, ii. 431 n. 5, in connection with Gregory's letter (*Reg.* II. 44) to Natalis of Salona, a letter also picked out for comment by H. Mayr-Harting, 'Perspectives on St Augustine of Canterbury', paper delivered at Winchester College, 1997; see further below, Ch. 7.

[51] Gregory, *HEz.* II pref., CCSL 142, 205.

[52] Markus, *Gregory*, 204.

[53] John the Deacon, *Vita Gregorii*, IV. 69, PL 75, 221–2.

[54] Llewellyn, 'Roman Church: Legacy of Gregory I'.

Gregory was rarely out of the limelight. Born into a prominent Roman family,[55] classically educated, and politically ambitious, we encounter him first in the historical record in 574, as Prefect of the City of Rome.[56] Two years later, he decided to give up his civic office, and to live as a monk in the family home on the Caelian hill (he founded six other monasteries on the family estates in Sicily).[57] Gregory was later to present this development in his career as a dramatic conversion, a flight from the storm-tossed world into the safe haven of the cloister.[58] We ought to remember, however, that such a gesture of retirement from public life was a profoundly traditional one, its association with Christian monasticism notwithstanding.[59] From the days of the Republic, Romans in public office had been wont to seek out the life of leisured philosophical reflection, far from the din and intrigue of the Senate. It was understood that, whatever the attractions of *otium*, a return to the original *negotium* was never far away for such men.[60]

It is unlikely, then, to have surprised Gregory when, within three years of his monastic conversion, he was sent as papal envoy to the imperial court at Constantinople. It was here that he began to expound the Book of Job to a small, Latin-speaking circle of ascetics and lay-people from the West and Constantinople.[61] Gregory also embroiled himself in a protracted debate with the patriarch Eutychius about the resurrection of the body, which left him physically exhausted, and his opponent on his death-bed.[62] After five years, he was recalled to Rome, and put to work as a deacon in the papal administration. (One of the

[55] See Markus, *Gregory*, 8, and the references there given.

[56] See *Ep* IV. 2, CCSL 140, 218–19 (although the witness of the manuscript tradition of this letter is not without ambiguity: see Markus, *Gregory*, 8 and n. 35).

[57] See Gregory of Tours, *LH* X. 1, MGH SRM 3, 4–6, the source for Paul the Deacon, *Vita Gregorii*, I. 4, PL 75, 43B, and also John the Deacon, *Vita Gregorii*, I. 5–6, PL 75, 65A.

[58] *Epistula ad Leandrum* 1, CCSL 143, 1–2.

[59] See e.g. G. D. Gordini, 'Origini e sviluppo del monacesimo a Roma', *Gregorianum* 37 (1956), 220–60. G. Ferrari, *Early Roman Monasteries*, inventories what we know from documentary sources about what monasteries there are.

[60] See Matthews, *Western Aristocracies*, 1–12; André, *L'otium*.

[61] *Ad Leandr.* 1, as above, n. 58. On Latin-speaking at Constantinople, see A. Cameron, 'A Nativity Poem of the Sixth-Century A.D.', *Classical Philology* 74 (1979), 222–32; ead., 'Images of Authority: Élites and Icons in Sixth-century Byzantium', *P&P* 84 (1979), 3–25.

[62] See *Mor.* XIV. 56. 72–4, CCSL 143A, 743–5, for Gregory's account of the debate. Cf. the opposing perspective of Eustrates, a disciple of Eutychius who composed a panegyric one year after his master's death: here Gregory appears as an 'ignoramus'. See *Vita Eutychii* 9. 89, PG 86, 2373D–2376A. See Y.-M. Duval, 'La Discussion entre l'apocrisiaire Grégoire et le patriarche Eutychios au sujet de la résurrection de la chair: L'arrière plan doctrinal oriental et occidental', in *Grégoire le Grand*, 347–66.

letters that he drafted for his master Pope Pelagius has recently been discovered.[63]) In the winter of 590, when Pelagius died of the plague, Gregory was the obvious candidate to replace him. He reportedly tried to flee the city in an effort to avoid election; the rumour only served to confirm his eminent suitability.[64] Gregory was to hold office for fourteen years, until, enfeebled by gout, he died in 604.[65]

To the natural rhythms of a public career in the ancient Mediterranean were added the extraordinary strains of the late sixth century. In the course of Gregory's adult lifetime, there were visible signs of a changing order. Peoples were on the move: from the Eurasian steppes onto the plains of Hungary rolled the Avars: as a consequence, the Lombards, the nomadic people who had been settled there, were forced westwards. In 568, desperate for food, they burst into Friuli. Their invasion marked the end of Roman Italy.[66] The armies of the Ostrogoths and the Eastern Roman Empire, having exhausted each other across three decades of conflict could offer no resistance to the newcomers. The Lombards did not sack Rome, but they did not need to: plague had already done far more damage than war.[67] The Senate had ceased to meet, many of its members having chosen to return to Constantinople with the defeated imperial troops. The Emperor still held Ravenna, and displayed such military and political presence as he was able in northern Italy, but Gregory and his peers knew that responsibility for defence and for feeding the citizens of Rome now lay not with the imperial bureaucracy, but with the Roman clergy, the only municipal administrative body still in operation. In Gregory's lifetime then, the importance of the clerical office in Rome, and of its bishopric in particular, underwent a transformation. The survival of the city now depended on St Peter's deputy on earth.

The year 590 in particular was a moment of civic crisis in Rome. The plague in which Pope Pelagius died carried off many of his fellow

---

[63] See P. Meyvaert, 'A Letter of Pelagius II composed by Gregory the Great', in Cavadini (ed.), *Gregory*, 94–116.

[64] See Gregory of Tours, *LH* X. 1, MGH SRM 3, 4–6.

[65] On Gregory's illness, see e.g. *Ep*. XI. 26, CCSL 140A, 899, to Rusticiana, discussed below (p. 172). See also *Ep*. XI. 21, CCSL 140A, 801–92.

[66] See C. J. Wickham, *Early Medieval Italy: Central Power and Local Society, 400–1000* (London, 1982); T. S. Brown, *Gentlemen and Officers: Imperial Administration and Aristocratic Power in Byzantine Italy, AD 554–800* (Rome, 1984); B. Ward-Perkins, *From Classical Antiquity to the Middle Ages: Urban Public Building in Northern and Central Italy, AD 300–800* (Oxford, 1984); H. Ashworth, 'The Influence of the Lombard Invasions on the Gregorian Sacramentary', *Bulletin of the John Rylands Library* 36 (1953–4), 305–27.

[67] See P. Allen, 'The "Justinianic" Plague', *Byzantion* 49 (1979), 5–20.

citizens. Depleted by famine and disease, and swollen with refugees, the population huddled into the bend of the River Tiber, turning their backs on the monumental classical centre, and looking towards the shrine of St Peter for protection.[68] It was these straitened circumstances that made clergy and people break with tradition in their choice of bishop. In choosing for the first time a monk, the Romans may have been reaching for the kind of moral leadership that a trained ascetic, rather than a careerist cleric, would provide. If so, then Gregory did not disappoint them: his immediate response to the plague was to institute a penitential procession around the city churches, inspiring a measure of solidarity among the citizen body.[69] It was, in a sense, in his interest to magnify rather than allay the sense of crisis that had brought him into power. Only an atmosphere of high moral tension and eschatological expectation would render plausible his claim to extraordinary spiritual authority that suspended normal operations of power in Rome.

News of Gregory's leadership travelled beyond Italy to the Loire valley.[70] In Rome, however, *communitas* in the face of plague soon dissolved into political rancour, at least in high clerical circles. The occupation of the Lateran palace by Gregory and his monastic associates was nothing less than a *coup d'état* as far as the Roman clergy were concerned. They were a close and jealous corporation, prone to feuding with each other and with their lay relatives and patrons.[71] The office of the papacy could easily become involved in these feuds, as demonstrated in the prolonged schism at the start of the sixth century between the supporters of Pope Symmachus and of Laurence, his (eventually defeated) opponent.[72] The conflict was conducted in all media, from street violence to the establishment of rival cult shrines around the city, and the composition of polemical tracts and martyr passions. Beneath the immediacy of factional strife, however, lay

[68] See Krautheimer, *Rome*, 59–87. Against this, however, must be set R. Coates-Stephens, 'Housing in Early Medieval Rome, 500–1000 AD', *Papers of the British School at Rome* 64, 239–59, which persuasively argues for a less pessimistic view of Dark-Age Rome. The particular circumstances of the 590s (and Gregory's highly charged description of them) should not be used to characterize the whole period.

[69] Gregory edited no text of the sermon, but a version was transmitted by a Frankish deacon present in Rome to Gregory of Tours: see *LH* X. 1, MGH SRM 3, 407–9 (and, in this century, A. Camus, *La Peste*).

[70] Gregory of Tours, *LH* X. 1, MGH SRM 3, 406–9. See H. Chadwick, 'Gregory of Tours and Gregory the Great', *JTS* 50 (1949), 38–49.

[71] See P. Llewellyn, *Rome in the Dark Ages* (London, 1970), chs. 4–5.

[72] For accounts of the schism, see Caspar, *Geschichte des Papsttums*, ii. 82–192; J. Moorhead, *Theodoric in Italy* (Oxford, 1992), 114–39.

systemic tensions between clergy and laity in the increasingly power-ful Roman Church. The schism was at heart a debate around the nature of gifts—the terms on which lay aristocrats acted as patrons to the Church, whether or not they had autonomy over ecclesiastical foundations.[73] The Laurentian schism, and the disputed issue of lay patronage, provides a context for the fractious relationship at the end of the century between the ascetic gregorians and their opponents in the Roman clergy—although precise parallels and connections remain, as yet, out of view. It is clear none the less that the struggle between Gregory's disciples and the Roman clergy was to continue for two generations into the seventh century.[74]

At no point did Gregory himself stand aloof from the tense and crowded devotional life of the city, with its barely-contained and long-remembered conflicts. His resignation of the office of urban prefect was no escape route: in choosing St Andrew as the patron for his own monastery, Gregory signalled, whether willingly or not, his affiliation with the Symmachan party, who had been assiduous in their pro-motion of the cult of Andrew.[75] As pope, it was incumbent on him to preach at all the major martyr shrines of the city, despite his deep and expressed reservations about the nakedly grasping and vindictive spirit in which the Romans solicited the aid of the saints.[76] Something of his sense of claustrophobia is evident in the *Dialogues*, where he did not hesitate to caricature the papal court as a den of flatterers, less worthy of respect than the dishevilled charismatics roaming the countryside.[77] If this was a critique of the Roman clergy, it was, by the same token, a lonely self-portrait of a man who dared not place his trust in those around him.

Unafraid of confrontation, Gregory did what he could to shape his immediate environment. At the shrine of St Pancras, he replaced an

---

[73] For an account in these terms, see P. Llewellyn, 'The Roman Church during the Laurentian Schism: Priests and Senators', *Church History* 45 (1976), 417–27; id., 'The Roman Clergy during the Laurentian Schism: A Preliminary Analysis', *Ancient Society* 8 (1979), 245–75; C. Pietri, 'Donateurs et pieux établissements d'après le légendier romain (Ve–VIIe s.)', in *Hagiographie, cultures et sociétés*, 435–53; 'Evergétisme et richesses ecclésias-tiques dans l'Italie du IVe à la fin du Ve s.: l'exemple romain', *Ktema* 3 (1984), 317–37; and now Cooper, 'The Martyr, the *matrona*, and the Bishop'.

[74] Llewellyn, 'Roman Church: Legacy of Gregory I'.

[75] As discussed by J. Alchermes, '*Cura pro mortuis* and *cultus martyrum*: Commemoration in Rome from the Second through the Sixth Century' (New York University PhD thesis, 1989).

[76] *HEv*. II. 27. 7, PL 76, 1208C–1209A.

[77] See esp. *Dial*. I. 4. 10–11, SC 260, 46–8, on Equitius of Valeria. I owe to Hannah Jones the idea that Gregory here describes his own situation.

apparently indolent group of priests with a monastic community to ensure that the crowds of the faithful who flocked there were given some liturgical guidance.[78] In the Lateran, he expelled the boy acolytes from the papal chamber—this being where a clerical career started in Rome—and sacked the highest-ranking clerical officials.[79] He made his palace a site of earnest discussion, expounding difficult books of the Old Testament to his small circle of intimates. At the heart of the stories of Job and Ezekiel, Gregory believed, lay a resolution of the question of moral authority, and it was this theme that he wished to pursue.

Gregory's followers themselves did not always read his intentions clearly. Marinianus of Ravenna, a former colleague of Gregory's in St Andrews, read out sections of the *Moralia in Job* in church, and was roundly rebuked by Gregory for so doing: 'This is not a work for popular diffusion.'[80] Claudius of Ravenna, another close associate, was scolded in the same letter for his 'useless' attempt to write up his notes on Gregory's homilies on the Book of Kings. Gregory was concerned enough about the conditions under which his texts circulated to send out a notice of a single error in the text of his forty *Homilies on the Gospels*;[81] and when his notary began to keep a commonplace book of Gregory's exegetical asides, Gregory intervened to make sure the book was properly organized in the canonical order of scripture.[82] We can frequently see his mind at work, and nowhere more so than in the English mission, when he changed his mind about the best missionary strategy, as he struggled to 'get it right'.[83] Gregory's willingness to admit his own errors and change course we find highly appealing—but we might spare a thought for those who had to follow his directives. For all his care in thinking on authority, Gregory was not always an easy master to serve.

Gregory himself sensed that authority involved abandonment: friends became enemies, lost touch. He could only watch in frustration

---

[78] *Reg.* IV. 18, CCSL 140, 237.

[79] See App. 3, CCSL 140A, 1095, for the replacement of Archdeacon Laurentius by Honoratus. *Ep* V. 57a, MGH Epp. 1, 362, for the expulsion of boys from the chamber.

[80] *Ep.* XII. 6, CCSL 140A, 974–7.

[81] See *HEv.* pref., PL 76, 1075–8, enjoining the dedicatee of the Homilies, Secundinus of Tauromenium, to emend the text in one particular, and to prevent the circulation of any defective copies. On the non-circulation of the *Dialogues*, see Meyvaert, 'The Enigma', 381.

[82] See Paterius, *Liber Testimoniorum*, PL 79, 683A–684A, and Meyvaert, 'The Enigma', 352–61.

[83] See R. Markus, 'Gregory the Great and the Origins of a Papal Missionary Strategy', in *Studies in Church History* 6 (1970), 29–38.

as a feud developed in Ravenna between his two protégés, Marinianus and Claudius: he could see 'stupid people' gathering around Marinianus, drawing him into a local world of petty enmities, away from all the values Gregory had attempted to inculcate.[84] It was the same in the case of another of his closest friends, Venantius of Syracuse. In the year that Gregory ascended to the papal throne, Venantius left his monastic vows to marry a rich noblewoman—a poignant parting of the ways.

Many foolish people thought that once raised to the heights of episcopal office, I would refuse to speak to you. That is not the situation: quite the contrary. The logic of my position compels me to speak; I may not keep silence.[85]

From here Gregory launches into a prophetic denunciation of his friend's apostasy: as the watchman of the house of Israel, he must declare the shortcomings of those in his charge.[86] His friend ignored him, led astray by the gaggle of flatterers Gregory knew to be surrounding him. Venantius' transformation from monastic brother to boorish lay *seigneur* seemed to be complete, when, two years later, his henchmen broke into the episcopal palace at Syracuse and man-handled the bishop, with whom Venantius was in dispute.

Gregory knew well the resentment that any man in power was likely to encounter, even or especially from those closest to him—but he was determined to surmount the obstacle so posed. His handling of Venantius through the course of the 590s is a case in point. To some commentators Gregory has given the impression that, in a wholly uncharacteristic moment of favouritism, he acquiesced in his former colleague's intimidation of the bishop.[87] If we follow the course of his correspondence with Venantius and his family, however, it is clear that no such surrender has taken place.[88] When Venantius and his wife fell ill, Gregory was on hand to advise them how to meet the moral challenge of sickness. After their deaths, in 602, we find Venantius'

---

[84] See Markus, *Gregory*, 152–3. Cf. for similar conflicts five centuries later in the circle of Gregory VII: I. Robinson, 'The Friendship Network of Gregory VII', *History* 63 (1978), 1–22.

[85] *Ep.* I. 33, CC 140, 39. My translation.

[86] This letter is the first recorded instance of Gregory's use of Ezekiel 3 on the *speculator*. For further discussion, see Leyser, '"Let Me Speak"'.

[87] F. Homes Dudden, *Gregory the Great* (London, 1905), ii. 194–9, regarded Gregory's relationship with Venantius as 'a problem not easy of solution', where the usually impeccable pope seems to have colluded in the scandal of Venantius' breaking into the palace of John of Syracuse.

[88] See *Epp.* I. 33, CCSL 140, 39–41; III. 57, 205–6; VI. 42–3, 425–6; IX. 32, CCSL 140A, 592–3; XI. 18, 23, 25, 59, at 887–8, 893–4, 895–7, 965–6 respectively.

two daughters hurrying to Rome in answer to Gregory's summons, eager to receive instruction on marriage and the reading of scripture. Far from being a 'scandal not easy of resolution', the case of Venantius illustrates Gregory's refusal to fall silent, or to allow those beneath him to turn their backs on him, and his persistence seems, in fact, to have been rewarded. Acutely conscious of the isolation imposed by authority, Gregory was resolved to find a moral language that would allow those in power to sustain and be sustained by the community for which they were responsible.

MONASTERY AND CHURCH IN THE LAST DAYS

Gregory was a man who lived his life in public, urban institutions, in the company of other, institutional men. He knew the spiritual cost of this way of life, but he also knew the lure of physical escape to be illusory. The true ascetic would find his own, interior detachment:

What avails the solitude of the body, if the solitude of the heart be wanting? For they who live bodily removed from the world, but yet plunge deep into the tumults of human conversation with the thoughts of worldly desires are not in solitude. But if anyone is bodily oppressed with crowds of people, and yet suffers from no tumults of worldly cares in his heart, he is not in a city.[89]

The otherworldly landscape of interior solitude extends throughout Gregory's exegetical writings.[90] The institutional culture of the Church, on the other hand, which constituted his daily context, melts away here, more dramatically so than in the biblical sermons of Augustine or Caesarius. Gregory simply offers no discussion of secular, monastic, or ecclesiastical office-holding: all such particulars have been been removed in the attempt to analyse the moral core of the experience of authority. Gregory had a boundless capacity imaginatively to detach himself from institutional culture while operating directly in it—but we should never mistake this for a lack of interest in the moral questions posed by power and social organization.

Gregory's sense of detachment drew on the resources of philosophical tradition concerning the active and contemplative lives, reaching back to Plato. The philosopher is never disturbed by the crowd or by the presence of power. He can move and speak freely at

---

[89] *Mor.* XXXI. 38. 72, CCSL 143B, 1603–4.
[90] See e.g. P. Aubin, 'Intériorité et extériorité dans les Moralia in Job de saint Grégoire le Grand', *RSR* 62 (1974), 117–66.

court, without being of the court. As mediated to Christian intellectuals by Origen, this tradition was bound in with an approach to
Scripture. Beneath the letter of the word lay its true inner meaning, as
beyond the physical, institutional carapace of earthly existence lay the
realm of the spirit. Origen's teachings were mediated in turn for
western ascetics by Ambrose and Augustine, and their influence on
Gregory is acknowledged by him in a rare moment of explicitness. He
offers his readers 'the mean trickle' of the *Homilies on Ezekiel* in contrast to the deep, crystal fountains they can drink from in the writings
of these two holy fathers.[91]

It was not only the Origenist inheritance, however, which allowed
Gregory to use allegorical exegesis as a vehicle for detachment from
earthly existence. He deployed also a reading of contemporary history
in which he constantly mapped his experience and that of others onto
the eschatological dimension. It was the nearness of the end that made
institutions seem irrelevant to this deeply traditional, institutional
man. At the same time it was this eschatological mapping that drove
him from the terrain of interior contemplation back into the world of
civic action.

This leads us to one of the great paradoxes of Gregory as an ascetic
writer and thinker. The first monk to be Pope showed himself relatively uninterested in monastic institutions or in traditional ideas of
monastic community. The point bears some emphasis. Although it is
now accepted that Gregory neither observed nor systematically sought
to promote the *Rule of St Benedict*, the assumption lingers that he must
instinctively have favoured the monastic cause. After all, this seems to
have been the ground of objection to him of the Roman clergy. As far
as Gregory was concerned, however, to call for an ascetic understanding of clerical office, was not the same as 'promoting monasticism'. He
made almost no effort to advertise his own monastery, he propounded
no consistent practice nor general theory of the monastic life. We look
in vain for any discussion of the relative merits of the eremitic and
cenobitic paths. The question of monastic community that had, in
varying degrees, preoccupied writers from Augustine to Benedict
receives little or no attention from Gregory. The great antitheses of
Latin monasticism—Desert and City, Monastery and Church—and
its single most potent motif—the Jerusalem community—are muted if
not entirely absent here. In leaving aside these themes, Gregory had in

---

[91] *HEz*. pref., CCSL 142, 3.

a sense turned the ascetic tradition in which he was schooled against itself.

This was a considerable feat of detachment. Monastic affairs were a constant feature of his episcopal duties. Well over 200 letters in the *Register* deal with monasteries in some form or other, the vast majority of these concerning Italy, especially Campania and Sicily. Gregory's commitment to dealing with this round of business is not in question, whether it be in making sure monks or nuns behave, or in protecting them from bishops and laymen. But as a recent, exhaustive study of the *Register* concludes, 'Despite Gregory's deep preoccupation with ascetics and ascetic communities, there can be no real justification of talk of a "monastic policy"'.[92] His dealings with monasteries never rose above the level of the traditional and the pragmatic. He was concerned to enforce guidelines and practice established in western monastic lore and in imperial legislation from Chalcedon onwards.

There was doubtless much that Gregory could take for granted, and that did not require extensive further comment. Augustine and others had spoken of the Jerusalem community, and this obviated the need for further comment from Gregory. When Augustine of Canterbury asked, for example, how should he organize his new episcopal household, Gregory issued this brisk reply:

> Brother, as you should know from your study of monastic tradition, bishops should not live apart from their clergy in the English Church, which thanks to God has recently been brought to the faith. You should therefore institute the way of life which our fathers followed at the beginning of the Church, in which no one said that anything belonged to him, but they held all things in common.[93]

Even as a summary, however, this was somewhat terse, and it stands alone in the gregorian exegetical corpus. This is only one of a handful of cases where Gregory even refers to the verses from Acts, prompting the suspicion that his interests as an ascetic lay elsewhere.[94]

---

[92] G. Jenal, *Italia Ascetica atque Monastica*, ii. 830.

[93] Gregory, *Libellus Responsionum*, cited in Bede, *Ecclesiastical History* I. 27. On the *Libellus*, see P. Meyvaert, 'Le libellus responsionum à Augustin de Cantobéry: une oeuvre authentique de saint Grégoire le Grand' in *Grégoire le Grand*, 543–50. On Bede and Acts 4, see G. Olsen, 'Bede as Historian: The Evidence from his Observations on the First Christian Community at Jerusalem', *JEH* 33 (1982), 519–30.

[94] See *Mor.* XXX. 6. 2–3, CCSL 143B, 1506–7, cited below, n. 113 and Ch. 7 n. 76; *Mor.* XXIX. 3. 5, 1438, is a slight verbal echo. *Ep.* III. 65, CCSL 140, 215–16, to Theotimus, a doctor in Constantinople, represents a standard epistolary use of Acts 4: 32 to avow friendship: see e.g. Ruricius of Limoges, *Ep.* II. 10 (to Pomerius), CSEL 6, 385. The references at *InIReg* I. 61, and *InIReg* V. 14 can no longer be regarded as securely gregorian. (For discussion of the former passage see A. de Vogüé, 'Renoncement et désir: La Définition du

The *Dialogues*, of course, abound in monasteries, but they present no more coherent a picture of the monastic life than do the letters.[95] Indeed, frustratingly for the institutional historian, the *Dialogues* and the *Register* cannot be made to corroborate each other's accounts of monastic topography or culture in sixth-century Italy.[96] In part this is unsurprising. The *Dialogues* are 'ascetic pastorale' for cityfolk, not a survey of monastic Italy.[97] In collecting these stories of usually rural holy men and women Gregory sought, at least in part, to sustain the discussion of the monastic wilderness flourishing in ascetic circles in sixth-century Rome.[98] However, as Gregory's contemporary Gregory of Tours demonstrated, stories about local charismatics could have a bearing on how bishops and holy men were to relate to each other. His best-known vignette of the encounter between priest and prophet is that concerning the Lombard stylite Wulfoliac, who was asked to descend from his pillar at Trier by a group of (unnecessarily in Gregory of Tours's mind) sceptical bishops.[99] The *Dialogues*, by contrast, sought less to reflect upon relations between stylites and bishops than to argue that all alike found themselves in a new, eschatological landscape. Juridical discussion of relations between monasteries and bishops, or even rhetorical invocation of the contrast between desert and city, was no longer relevant: all earthly communities were withering away as the moment of the heavenly citadel drew nearer.

One incident in the *Dialogues* illustrates Gregory's eschatological view of monastic community. In the year of his accession to the papacy, he recounts, he discovered that a monk of St Andrew's had

moine dans le Commentaire de Grégoire le Grand sur le Premier Livre des Rois', *CollCist* 48 (1986), 54–70.)

[95] Markus, *Gregory*, 66.

[96] Jenal, *Italia Ascetica atque Monastica*, i. 266–303.

[97] Revealing of the urban perspective of the *Dialogues* are *Dial.* 3. 14. 4, SC 260, 306, and 4. 37. 3, SC 265, 126. In these passages, the wilderness (*eremus*) is presumed to lie outside the city walls, quite distinct from the monastery (*monasterium*) inside.

[98] For example, the *Sayings of the Desert Fathers* were translated into Latin as the *Vitae patrum* by the future popes Pelagius I (555–61) and John III (561–75); see A. Mundò, 'L'Authenticité de la Regula S. Benedicti', *StAns* 42 (1957), 105–58, at 129–36. Cf. M.-E. Brunert, *Das Ideal der Wüstenaskese und seine Rezeption in Gallien bis zum Ende des 6. Jahrhunderts* (Münster, 1994); and H. I. Jones, 'The Desert and Desire: Virginity, City, and Family in the Roman Martyr Legends of Agnes and Eugenia' (Univ. of Manchester MA thesis, 1998).

[99] For the column occupied by the Lombard holy man Wulfoliac, see Gregory of Tours, *LH* VIII. 15–16, MGH SRM 3, 333–6. Desert living in the Touraine is discussed in C. Leyser, '"Divine Power Flowed from this Book": Ascetic Language and Episcopal Authority in Gregory of Tours' *Life of the Fathers*', in K. Mitchell and I. Wood (eds.), *The World of Gregory of Tours* (Leiden, forthcoming).

secreted some private property.[100] This breach of trust recalls the
scandal of Januarius in the household of Augustine of Hippo, some
170 years previously, although in comparing the two incidents, we
should bear in mind the palpable differences between the two contexts.
St Andrew's was not the episcopal household, and the precise terms of
Gregory's jurisdiction over the house are unclear.[101] As a small group
of like-minded aristocrats, the inmates of St Andrews could afford to
remain innocent—in their monastery at least—of the electric charge of
social tension familiar to the more socially mixed group of ascetics in
Hippo. But if Gregory's monks had no need to contend with issues of
class resentment or disdain, this left them all the more sensitive to
moral duties and tensions. Gregory's actions and his subsequent
description of the affair reveal all the more clearly the shared assumptions and the basic contrasts between Augustine of Hippo's vision of
the monastery and his own.

The subject of Gregory's story was his own doctor, a man named
Justus. As he lay on his death-bed (possibly from the plague), Justus
confided to his brother Copiosus, also a doctor (but not a monk), that
he had three gold coins hidden in his medicine chest. This information, once divulged, 'could not easily be hidden from the brethren'.
When Gregory found out, he took it ill 'that a brother who had lived in
the community with us' should have committed so grave a fault. 'For
it had always been the custom of our monastery that all the brothers
should live as a community—and that no one was allowed to own anything for himself.'[102] Gregory's concerns were to punish the fault in
Justus, in order to purify his soul, and by making an example of his
case, to prevent any of the brethren from following him into his
avarice.

Community of property, and the unity of hearts and minds as
articulated in Acts 4, was not, however, the only point of the story.
Gregory's concern was to emphasize his own strategies of correction,
not so much in the context of the monastery, as of the wider community of the living and the dead, and the modes of communication

---

[100] *Dial.* IV. 57, SC 265, 184–94.

[101] Gregory was not the abbot of St Andrews (see Markus, *Gregory*, 10 and n. 44). De
Vogüé suggests that this incident there might have taken place during an interregnum: see
SC 265, 191, n. 11.

[102] *Dial.* IV. 57. 10, SC 265, 188: '. . . quippe quia eiusdem monasterii nostri semper
regula fuerat, ut cuncti fratres ita communiter viverent, quatenus eis singulis nullo habere
propria liceret.' It is unclear whether Gregory has a written *Rule* in mind here, or simply a
binding norm taken as read by all members of the community.

between them. He summoned the prior, named Pretiosus (!) and ordered that Justus be deprived of the company of all, without any explanation. Only at the point of death was his brother Copiosus to tell him why he had been shunned by the community, so as to induce a purifying compunction. *Pour encourager les autres*, his corpse was then to be cast in a hole with his three pieces of gold.[103] So intimidated were the brethren by these measures that, like the clergy in Hippo inventoried by Augustine, they brought out for Gregory's scrutiny all their belongings, however trivial or innocuous. Gregory recalls: 'They were terrified, lest they do anything worthy of rebuke.'

After thirty days, Gregory relented on both the living and the dead. He instructed Prior Pretiosus to organize mass for Justus' soul for the next thirty days—without, however, telling Copiosus of his decision. At the end of this period, Justus appeared to his brother in a vision, and told him of his reception back into communion. When Copiosus went to St Andrews to tell the monks of his vision, they in turn revealed to him their daily sacrifice for Justus, which had clearly proved efficacious.[104] 'Vision and sacrifice chimed in together.'[105] This is the triumphant moment of the story. The moral of Justus' transgression and purgation was eschatological, giving yet another sign of the merging of the old world with the world to come. In this context, while common ownership of property remained a defining feature of the monastic life, it was not the only means by which community could be expressed.[106]

In the world of Gregory's exegesis, monasteries have all but disappeared. There are no *monachi*, or cenobites, or hermits.[107] From the outset of his work as an exegete, Gregory eschewed any of the technical language commonplace in the monastic tradition. A standard explanation for this is that, even if the majority of his audience were monks, he did not wish to confine himself to a monastic perspective,

---

[103] *Dial.* IV. 57. 11, SC 265, 190.

[104] Ibid. IV. 57, 13–16.

[105] Ibid. IV. 57, 16: 'concordante simul visione et sacrificio'.

[106] A. de Vogüé suggests that the story of Justus and his brother may bear some relation to the narrative of the brothers Cosmas and Damian, also doctors, but who spurn money (SC 265, 188–9 n. 8). Gregory's ancestor Felix founded the church of Cosmas and Damian in the monumental centre of Rome. If so, this would represent another point of contact (or competition) between the *Dialogues* and the *gesta* of the Roman martyrs, as discussed by S. Boesch Gajano, 'La proposta agiographica dei "Dialoghi"', 649–64.

[107] See Gillet, 'Spiritualité et place du moine', 325–8, noting *InIReg* as the great exception to this rule, and casting prescient doubts on its full authenticity. Contrast the importance bestowed on *monachi* by the *Rule of St Benedict*; see SC 181, 32–3.

but to rise to a broader ecclesial, Christian and human frame of reference.[108] We might regard him as a bishop like Caesarius who transferred monastic ideals into the wider theatre of the Church— were it not for the fact that, in his exegesis, his ecclesial language is as detached from institutional markers as is his monastic.

As an exegete, Gregory reached for vocabulary and schemata that would draw attention away from monastic or ecclesiastical institutions, towards the whole body of the faithful conceived of as a moral community. In this perspective, there were three orders of the faithful, signified by Noah, Daniel, and Job, whom the prophet Ezekiel had seen spared from the divine punishment of Israel:

What does Noah, who guided the ark through the waves, represent if not the order of rulers, who, while they govern the people to shape their lives, steer holy Church through the waves of temptation? What does Daniel represent if not the order of the continent who rule with devoted minds over Babylon which lies beneath them? And what Job if not the order of the married who advance to the heavenly country by the paths of earth?[109]

This is a hierarchy—but the three orders are united by one faith.[110]

Gregory here made his own the augustinian taxonomy of the three orders of the faithful—the married, the continent, and the rulers of the Church—in order to destroy it.[111] Augustine had used this scheme in his *Enarrationes in Psalmos* to demonstrate that, although there were false Christians among all three orders, none the less the order of the continent had a special role to play in uniting the whole body of the faithful.[112] Gregory moved away from the theology of Monastery and Church that Augustine had thereby constructed. He had little interest in the *continentes*; here and elsewhere, the *continentes* and *coniugati* as it were cancel each other out and are merged, so leaving two orders of the faithful—the *ordo praedicantium*, and the *multitudo audientium*. Gregory suggested that 'preachers and hearers' had in fact been the apostolic constitution of the Church.[113] Where Augustine saw a 'multi-

---

[108] Gillet, 'Spiritualité et place du moine', 328; Judic, *Règle Pastorale*, 62.

[109] *Mor.* I. 14. 20, CCSL 143, 34; see also 32. 20. 35, CCSL 143B, 1656; *HEz.* II. 4. 5, CCSL 142, 261–2. In *HEz.* the scheme becomes commonplace, not needing introduction through a particular scriptural text or designation of the *ordines*: see e.g. II. 1. 7, II. 7. 3, II. 9. 12; CCSL 142, 213–14, 317, 366. See Fiedrowicz, *Kirchenverständnis*, 188–91.

[110] *HEz.* II. 4. 6, CCSL 142, 262.

[111] Folliet, 'Les Trois catégories des chrétiens, survie d'un thème augustinien', 81–9, was the first to establish Gregory's dependence on Augustine here.

[112] Above, Ch. 1.

[113] *Mor.* I. 14. 19–20, CCSL 143, 33–4. See also *Mor.* XXX. 6. 22–3, CCSL 143B, 1338–9.

tude of believers', Gregory saw instead an audience, a multitude of hearers.

Gregory's interest lay in the role of the *rectores*. Augustine seems to have meant by this office-holders in the Church, and in particular bishops. Using a wide variety of terms—*rectores, pastores, praepositi*, and above all, *praedicatores*—Gregory abandoned the institutional definition for a moral vision of the leaders of the Church. Any Christian could, in theory, become a 'preacher' in Gregory's sense. 'Preaching' connoted not only pulpit oratory, but more broadly *doctrina*, teaching by word and example, combining the active and contemplative lives.[114] It was 'preaching' in this sense, across the community of the faithful, that dominated Gregory's attention, not the silence of the monastery.[115]

The *praedicatores* embody Gregory's radically non-institutional vision of the Church in the last days. Nowhere is this more dramatically illustrated than in the *Homilies on the Gospels* that Gregory preached at the basilica of the martyred Felicity, martyred with her seven sons:

We read in the more reliable accounts of her deeds that she feared leaving her seven sons alive after her in the flesh, just as bodily parents fear that their children may die first. When caught up in the sufferings of the persecution, she strengthened her sons' hearts in love of their homeland above through preaching. She gave birth in the spirit to those to whom she had given physical birth, so that by preaching she might bring forth to God those whom in the flesh she had brought forth to the world. . . . Should I call this woman a martyr? She was more than a marytr![116]

As we shall see in the following chapter, the witness of the gregorian preacher was at least as demanding as that of the martyr.

---

[114] On the preachers, see R. Ladner, 'L'ordo praedicatorum avant l'ordre des prêcheurs', in P. Mandonnet (ed.), *Saint Dominique: L'idée, l'homme et l'oeuvre* (Paris, 1937), 51–5; Dagens, *Grégoire*, 312–19; V. Recchia, 'Il "Praedicator" nel pensiero e nell'azione di Gregorio Magno', *Salesianum* 41 (1979), 333–74; Straw, *Gregory*, 201–6; Fiedrowicz *Kirchenverständnis*, 134–7; R. A. Markus, 'Gregory the Great's "Rector" and his Genesis', in *Grégoire le Grand*, 137–46; id., *Gregory*, 26–33.

[115] See *HEz.* II. 4. 6, CCSL 142, 262: 'Cum enim longe sit a continentibus et tacentibus excellentia praedicatorum'.

[116] *HEv.* I. 3, PL 76, 1086, tr. Hurst, 6.

THE PLACE OF THE PREACHER

One reader of the *Pastoral Rule*, expressing a widely held frustration, has pointed out: 'Nowhere does Gregory provide a context for the extremely individual spiritual direction he advises.'[117] For Gregory, however, any precision would have represented a constraint. The question of the unity of the Church as Gregory posed it could not be solved by cordoning off a physical space: the preachers did not address the faithful in a cloister, or in any other particular location. No one venue was worthy of their attention: Gregory saw everywhere the luminous presence of the next world.

Gregory specifically did not seek to locate himself in the monastery. On the rare occasions when it appears in Gregory's spiritual writings, the monastery is the place he has lost, or cannot even remember. As a bishop, he writes, his experience is of distraction and wasted effort. He is a man swept out so far to sea that he no longer has sight of the shore.[118] These expressions of longing for the lost haven of the monastery constitute, certainly, an expansion of the rhetoric of reluctance to power, but this does not exhaust their meaning. Gregory was making a point about monasticism itself. The monastic past for which he mourned was not only his own: it was also the cultural tradition which he had inherited, but from which he radically departed. Gregory could no longer enjoy the monastery as a place of belonging not only because of the unremitting demands of his office, but also, and more importantly, because he himself had erased the monastery as a site of significance within the Church. He had decided that the eschatological future of the whole body of the faithful, soon to be realized, was of greater moment than the monastic past.[119]

Recreating the first community of Christians at Jerusalem, whether in the desert or the city, was thus no longer especially urgent as a goal of monastic endeavour for Gregory. Albeit with remorse, he broke uncompromisingly with the tradition of Augustine, Cassian (to the limited extent that he was invested in the Jerusalem community), Pomerius, Caesarius, and Benedict: all of these men had envisaged the monastery as a separate space in which to 'search for a new

[117] McClure, 'Gregory the Great', 120.
[118] See e.g. *Dial.* pref. 4–5, SC 260, 12.
[119] This is not to say that the monastery was not a suitable venue for preaching: see *HEz.* II. 11. 5–6, CCSL 142, 171–2, discussed below (p. 16 ff.). But it was not an especially privileged venue as far as Gregory was concerned.

society'.[120] In this 'other place', social relations, as they problematized them, could be dismantled and then reassembled on the model of the Jerusalem community. They hoped to offer the new pattern of social living to the rest of the faithful. Gregory could not pause to implement such an arrangement. The Jerusalem community could no longer serve as a model here, because the idea of monastic community itself buckled at the approach of the Last Days.

To jettison the monastery as an institution was not, however, to abandon the augustinian dream of community, nor to forget what the ascetic tradition, in particular Cassian, had to say about moral authority. Gregory's relative lack of interest in the theology of monastic community went hand in hand with the sense that it was his duty as an ascetic rather, and as a preacher, to outline how both the married and the continent should assume a new authority appropriate to the moment.[121] He wished to found not a discrete community as had his predecessors in the monastic tradition, but a language of authority to be used across the whole ecclesial community.

[120] See J. Séguy, 'Une Sociologie des sociétés imaginées: monachisme et utopie', *AESC* 26 (1971), 328–54.
[121] *HEz*. II. 9. 12, 366.

7

A Language of Power

In the world of Gregory's texts, the incandescent language of
authority, inspired by the word of God, brooks no argument: all issues
of the unity of the faithful are thereby resolved. This vision of moral
community evidently depended upon the skill of the teacher in dispensing correction according to all as they had need. Such a solution
placed an enormous burden upon the preachers, who could not always
take refuge in what Gregory called the 'forest of scripture'.[1] Preachers
had, themselves, to speak, and Gregory was under no illusions as to the
difficulty of the task. 'The government of souls is the skill compre-
hending all skills.'[2]

Fundamental to the skill of the preacher was his ability to negotiate
the obstacles to being heard, above all the suspicion that his claim to a
moral authority was bound to provoke among his hearers. This was the
importance to Gregory of the virtue of humility: it is everywhere
emphasized in his work, not as a generally desirable Christian virtue,
but as the quality without which those in power will not be able to
survive. If they did not exhibit humility, they could never expect to be
heard in the same spirit. A ruler of true expertise had, as a matter of
course, to go to extraordinary lengths to charm away the tensions
arising from his assumption of power to correct. Gregory led by
example here. In what has become a famous passage in his *Homilies on
Ezekiel*, Gregory interrupted the progress of his allegorical exegesis of
the text with an outburst of apparent self-disgust. When he came to
the Lord's designation of the prophet as the watchman of the house of
Israel he felt, he said, literally stricken—found wanting as a pastor, his
negligence condemned as it were out of his own mouth. While still in
the monastery, he had been able to sustain his concentration on sacred
matters; once elected as pope, he had become distracted by trivia,
unable to collect himself or to set an appropriate example to others.
But he had to continue none the less, compelled as he was by the word
of God about the duty of the watchman to speak out.[3] The figure of the

---

[1] *HEz.* I. 5. 1, CCSL 142, 57.
[2] *RP* I, PL 77, 13A.
[3] *HEz.* I. 11. 5–6, CCSL 142, 171.

watchman, used initially by Gregory in his letter to Venantius of Syracuse, became the emblem both for the vigilance and the disarming humility of the Gregorian preacher.

Gregory's humility entranced his ancient audience, well versed in the conventions of *captatio benevolentiae*, but it has confused his modern readers.[4] His invocation of the watchman is one of the the key witnesses for the view that he became pope 'in spite of himself', that he longed for a return to the quiet of the cloister[5]—although what Gregory actually laments is not or not only the loss of contemplative repose, but also the opportunity to 'preach'.[6] To insist, however, that Gregory's is a 'personal' outburst threatens to obscure the fact that it is also an outburst of dialogue with earlier tradition. In so declaring his humility in high office, Gregory appealed in general and doubtless instinctively, to the Platonic tradition of the philosopher–king, the man who could be trusted with power precisely because it was distasteful to him. But his purposes were also more specific: he surely aimed to identify himself as a moral ruler in the language of authority developed by ascetics in the Latin West in the previous century and a half—as a watchman in the mould of Augustine, Pomerius, and Caesarius, to name but three.[7] Gregory's lament over his failure as a watchman in the *Homilies on Ezekiel* is, in this sense, entirely unsurprising: only through attention to the rhetorical tradition in which he located himself with no little finesse will we able accurately to characterize what is distinctive about his approach.

Like those before him, Gregory describes the 'burden' he bears in terms of a dilemma about speech:

I cannot keep silent, and yet if I speak, I will condemn myself. Let me speak, let me speak, so that the word of God passes through me, lodging in the heart of my neighbour, even as it transfixes me. Let me speak, let me speak, let the word of God sound through me, even as it sounds against me.[8]

The danger of condemning himself out of his own mouth was twofold. Not only might Gregory find his life indicted by the scriptural texts

---

[4] Not so Y. Congar, 'Ordinations *invitus*, *coactus* de l'Église antique au canon 214', *Revue des Sciences Philosophiques et Théologiques* 50 (1966), 169–97.

[5] e.g. Dagens, *Grégoire*, 133–45.

[6] Markus, *Gregory*, 25.

[7] A further possible source would be Leo the Great: see Mohrmann, 'Episkopos-Speculator'. This passage in the *Homilies* had its own careful gregorian protocols, as a comparison with the similar passages in the *Pastoral Rule* and the *Register* makes clear: see, in particular, the letter to Venantius of Syracuse discussed above (pp. 149–50).

[8] *HEz*. I. 11. 5–6, CCSL 142, 171.

that he sought to expound to his hearers: his words themselves might further undermine his moral credibility, as he felt himself borne away in what he called the 'flux of speech'. Was there a language he could use to avoid 'sins of the mouth'? Here, as throughout, we see that Gregory participated as enthusiastically as did any other other sixth-century ascetic in the tradition of 'plain speech' initiated in the Latin West by John Cassian, and adapted by generations of ascetics since then. He followed others too in linking the claim to plain speech with the rhetoric of vulnerability—the forswearing of rhetoric with the disinterest in power.[9]

Above all, however, Gregory made his own the insight sketched by Pomerius in his handbook for bishops and developed by Benedict in a monastic context: that the speech of the ruler, when properly applied, can bind up all divisions within the body of the faithful. Gregory pursued a language of authority that would carry all before it with a degree of concentration undreamt of by earlier writers. Augustine of Hippo had denied that the quantification of the ways of power was possible; his subsequent readers had tentatively moved to reverse his verdict, but only with Gregory do we find a writer prepared to stake all on the performance of the moral ruler, and to enumerate in detail how this might be possible. Gregory was prepared to take the risk of claiming to be morally qualified to lead, to shoulder all the burdens of the faithful, to act as the servant of the servants of God.

Gregory made his own the tradition of the watchman of the house of Israel on which he drew. In the Latin West, as we have seen, the *speculator* of Ezekiel was identified with the *episcopus*. For Augustine, the authority of the bishop as watchman is a burden to be shared with those over whom he must exercise power;[10] in appropriating the authority of Augustine, Caesarius of Arles used the figure of the watchman to legitimate a regime of intimate episcopal supervision.[11] Gregory's watchman was not necessarily a bishop: his authority was grounded in exclusively moral terms. 'God calls the man he sends to preach a watchman . . . so that his soul should remain on high . . . as a result of the virtue of his actions'.[12] Unlike Augustine, Gregory was

---

[9] The much-discussed *loci classici* of Gregory's renunciation of rhetoric are his letter to Didier of Vienne (*Reg.* XI. 34, CCSL 140A, 922–3) and the preface to the *Moralia*. See Dagens, *Grégoire*, 31 ff., and L. Holtz, 'Le Contexte grammatical de défi à la grammaire: Grégoire et Cassiodore', in *Grégoire le Grand*, 531–9.

[10] See above, Ch. 1.

[11] Above, Ch. 4.

[12] *HEz.* I. 11. 4, CCSL 142, 170.

prepared to suggest that the watchman had a certifiable moral claim to be set on high—but he understood that such a claim must immediately be 'earthed', that the reavowal of the watchman's humility must accompany any declaration of his powers of surveillance. Where a pastor in the mould of Caesarius was committed to relentless scrutiny of the tiny sins of the people, Gregory must depict his own descent little by little into the ways of sin:

My tongue does not keep to preaching as it should, neither does my life follow my tongue, try as I might to make it. I am often drawn into useless chat; being lazy and negligent, I stop encouraging and edifying my neighbours . . . What kind of a watchman can I be, in that I do not stand on the mountain of good works, but I lie down low in the valley of weakness?[13]

Only in acting as his own sharpest critic could Gregory hope to continue to minister to those in his charge. The expression of suffering in office was of paramount importance to Gregory's tenure of power.

As is but rarely observed, Gregory's invocation of the watchman in his *Homilies on Ezekiel*, and, simultaneously, of his own failure as a preacher, leads into a discussion of strategies of correction of all sorts and conditions of the faithful—a reprise of material from the *Pastoral Rule*.[14] The dominant figure in this discussion of preaching strategy is not Ezekiel, but Paul. It is to Paul that Gregory refers again and again in illustrating how different sinners can be led to listen to moral rebuke and advice. Gregory's Paul is an expert doctor, described in the language of ascetic *peritia* drawn from Cassian and his subsequent Latin readers. He is also a contemplative, a man who has been to the third heaven. As Pomerius' treatise *On the Contemplative Life* had adumbrated, the watchman's gaze was directed at the heavens as well as over his flock. In Gregory's fully articulated vision, the humility of the preachers bespeaks their converse with angels.

ST PAUL'S ADMONITION

Two great lists dominate the closing books of the *Moralia In Job*, one of sinners, the other of sins.[15] The latter has become notorious. Here Gregory enumerates the massed ranks of the vices assailing humanity—the seven principal sins and their dependants—so giving

---

[13] *HEz*. I. 11. 6, CCSL 142, 172.

[14] *HEz*. I. 11. 12–25, CCSL 142, 174–81. Cf. *RP* III. 24, 32; SC 382, 418–26, 490–6.

[15] *Mor*. XXX. 3. 13, XXXI. 45. 87, CCSL 143B, 1499–1500, 1610.

canonical form to Cassian's typology of vice in the *Institutes*. In the former list, anticipating his own treatise, the *Pastoral Rule*, Gregory itemizes the contrasting remedies required by sinners of contrasting temperaments, 'for often the things which profit some are bad for others. Whence every teacher, to the end that they may edify all in the one virtue of charity, ought to touch the hearts of his hearers out of one system of teaching, but not with one and the same address.'[16] The juxtaposition of these two monumental inventories implies an attempt to entwine two ancient strands of moral and pedagogic theory: the one, mediated to Gregory by Cassian, proceeded by imagining the stages in the attainment of virtue by a single soul, on the understanding that this was the moral history of everyman. The other tradition, represented by Augustine, eschewed such generalization, and insisted that every condition required its own carefully measured response.[17] Gregory's achievement was to bring these traditions together to form a unified science of admonition.

This was a bold solution to the problem of moral community, of the sort that Augustine had refused and that Cassian had unsuccessfully attempted. The key lay in Gregory's use of Cassian's language of moral expertise. As we have seen, the *Institutes* and *Conferences* had set out a history of apostolic life since the first Christian community in Jerusalem as a frame for a lesson in the techniques of moral purity; but Cassian had arrived at the point at which he could only conceive of monastic community if he assumed the same level of technical competence on the part of all inmates, abandoning the possibilities both of supporting weaker brethren and of trusting charismatic authority. Gregory's use of the *Institutes* and *Conferences* went to the essential of what Cassian was trying to do—that is, to describe what made a man pure in heart—and left all else by the wayside. In simply not attempting to find a monastic setting for the technique of purification, Gregory resolved at a stroke many of the problems about the institutionalization of ascetic purity upon which Cassian's analysis had foundered. Unencumbered with the question of cenobitism, Gregory armed himself with Cassian's language of *peritia*: as an augustinian, and as an eschatological preacher, he assumed that a moral expert must be able to speak to all sorts and conditions of hearers.

Expert charity thus knew no limits, in Gregory's account.[18] He

---

[16] *RP* III prol., SC 382, 258–60.
[17] See e.g. *De cat. rud.* 15. 23, CCSL 46, 147–8.
[18] See above all P. Catry, 'Amour du monde at amour de Dieu chez S. Grégoire le Grand',

refused to countenance the kind of dual standard envisaged by Cassian, where expert ascetics could love only those who shared their level of proficiency. All were bound to obey the 'double precepts of charity',[19] the love of God and the love of neighbour; the expert was the person who had achieved a level of technical competence in the performance of these obligations. It was 'through the bond of his charity' that the apostle Paul had commerce with the angels and with sinners alike. 'He was swept up by the power of the spirit to contemplative heights, and without demurring, brought low by the duty of love for others'.[20] Instead, therefore, of using Cassian's moral language to produce an inflexible opposition between *ingénus* and experts, Gregory used it to detail a whole range of antithetical pairs differentiated along cultural, social, and psychological axes: the rich and the poor, the healthy and the sick, the quarrelsome and the peaceable, the impulsive and the cautious. There were thirty-six pairs in all. Possessed of the charism of discernment—figured early in the *Pastoral Rule* as 'the nose of discernment'[21]—the expert would accurately distinguish the virtues and deficiencies of those in his charge.[22] In his determination to legislate for the distribution of charity—his synthesis of *caritas* and *peritia*—Gregory struck a new point of balance between the authority of Augustine and that of Cassian.

At the same time, Gregory's achievement owed much to his sixth-century ascetic colleagues who had already worked to develop a moral language endowed with the *numen* of the fifth-century fathers, but free of some of the constraining precision of their arguments. Gregory, like Pomerius and Caesarius of Arles before him, was more committed to the rhetorical benefits of the denunciation of vice than to any consistent analyses of its operation. A cardinal example is the great catalogue of sins. Expounding 'the battle afar off, the thunder of the captains, and the shouting' (Job 39: 25), Gregory evokes the invisible war waged against a huge army of cunning and relentless foes. At their head stands pride, the queen of the sins.[23] When she has conquered the heart—

StMon 15 (1973), 253–75, and id., 'L'amour du prochain chez S. Grégoire le Grand', *StMon* 20 (1978), 287–344.

[19] *RP* II. 3, PL 77, 29B–30A.

[20] *RP* II. 5, PL 77, 32D–33A.

[21] *RP* I. 11, PL 77, 24B–C.

[22] *Mor.* XXVIII. 8. 10. 23, CCSL 143B, 1608–9; XXXI. 44. 85, 1413–14.

[23] For a general survey, see M. Baasten, *Pride according to Gregory the Great: A Study of the 'Moralia'* (Lewiston/Queenston, 1986).

She surrenders it immediately to seven principal sins, as if to some of her generals, to lay it waste. . . . For pride is the root of all evil, as Scripture bears witness . . . But seven principal vices spring doubtless from this poisonous root, as its first progeny, namely vainglory, envy, anger, melancholy, avarice, gluttony, lust.[24]

So definitive for the medieval Church, in the context of Gregory's works the catalogue of the seven principal sins was a moment of apparent clarity in an extremely fluid discussion of vice and its expurgation. In particular, in identifying pride as the root of all sin, Gregory aimed to signal his augustinian good faith without wholly accepting Augustine's view of pride as a flaw emanating from the will, so as to leave in place the possibility of an ascetic remedy for a humanity beset not only by pride, but also by desire. As he moves to assimilate pride with desire, Gregory's tactics and conclusions closely resemble those of earlier writers such as Pomerius and Caesarius. For example, in reading the description of Behemoth given by God to Job—'He sleeps under the shady trees, under cover of the tall reeds, in the marshes' (Job 40: 11, 16)—Gregory as it were instinctively finds a way to run together pride and desire. The tall reed signifies pride, and the marshes desire, specifically sexual desire.

We can recognize [these vices] in the first people, who covered their genitals in shame, clearly showing that in trying to reach the inner heights, they soon bore the outward marks of shame on their flesh . . . Behemoth, as he seeks to destroy the whole person at one fell swoop, now raises up the mind in pride, now corrupts the flesh with pleasure and with lust.[25]

With this evocation of human shame and diabolic vindictiveness, Gregory blurs Augustine's fundamental distinction between the original, spiritual crime and its subsequent, corporal punishment. He thereby retains the possibility and the value of the ascetic remedy for desire. In the sequel to this passage, he draws the contrast between the marshlands where the devil lives and the drylands, meaning the minds of the just, drained by ascetic labour of the brackish waters of carnal desire.[26]

'Desire' as a category was, however, no more clearly defined than

---

[24] *Mor.* XXXI. 45. 87, CCSL 143B, 1610. Gregory also substituted Latin terms for Cassian's Greek terms. (Thus *gastrimargia* became *ventris ingluvies, cenodoxia inanis gloria, filargyria avaritia*.) The lists of sins are compared and discussed by R. Gillet, ed., *Grégoire le Grand, Morales sur Job, Livres I–II*, SC 32bis, 89–102.

[25] *Mor.* XXXII. 14. 20–1, CCSL 143B, 1644–5, with the quotation at 1645.

[26] Ibid. XXXIII. 3. 5–9, CCSL 143B, 1673–8. For a very clear exposition of Gregory's reading of Augustine in this context, see Straw, *Gregory*, 90–127, esp. 112.

pride. As we have seen in the case of Pomerius, it was also the goal of sixth-century ascetics to treat Cassian in the same way as Augustine—to recall the mood of Cassian's analysis of temptation without its analytical rigour. Gregory can often be found assuming that moral purification begins with the fight against gluttony.[27] For Gregory, as for Cassian, the sacred history of gluttony ends with Christ's first temptation in the wilderness: the second Adam refuses the devil's offer of food, and so atones for the failure of the first to do so, and establishes a pattern for his followers to imitate.[28] Fasting is thus the *sine qua non* of any ascetic commitment, from which all else follows: 'everybody knows', affirms Gregory, that lust comes from gluttony: it is obvious from the proximity of the stomach to the genitals.[29] The next stage, according to Gregory's own classification, would be anger, and from there, despair. Identifying the consequences of gluttony in the *Pastoral Rule*, however, Gregory moves from lust to 'too much talking', and 'frivolous behaviour'.[30] In other words, he was even less prone to abide by his own schematizations than was Cassian.

In Gregory's work, an evocation of the power of desire erodes the physiological clarity of Cassian's analysis, and this development is brought to a logical conclusion in his discussion of nocturnal emission. For Cassian, there had been no clearer index of a man's moral purity than his control of his semen while he slept. Already in Pomerius, this great theme of the *Institutes* and *Conferences* had been reduced to a mere vignette—and we find Gregory engaged in a similar reduction. It is unlikely that he would have discussed nocturnal emission at all had he not been pressed by Augustine of Canterbury to pronounce on the issue. Augustine had asked whether a man who had experienced a nocturnal emission could receive the eucharist—or celebrate it in the event that he was a priest. Summarizing ascetic tradition here quite

[27] Cf. Esau, who, Gregory reminds his audience, lost his birthright because he wanted even simple food—lentils—'inflamed as he was with desire', *Mor.* XXX. 17. 60, CCSL 143B, 1532.

[28] Ibid. XXX. 17. 57–62; CCSL 143B, 1529–33. See also *HEv.* I. 16. 2–3; PL 76, 1136A-C. The parallel between Adam and Christ's temptations is Cassian's: see *Conl.* 5. 6, SC 42, 193.

[29] *Mor.* XXXI. 45. 89, CCSL 143B, 1611.

[30] *RP* III. 19, PL 77, 81A-C. Such superfluous talk Gregory takes to be a mark of heretics and of women. On the former, see e.g. *Mor.* III. 22. 42–4, V. 13. 30; CCSL 143B, 142–4, 239 (on Eliphaz the Temanite, whom Gregory understands to represent heretics). On the latter, see e.g. *Dial.* IV. 53. 1–2, SC 265, 178 (on a Sabine holy woman); *HEv.* II. 38. 15, PL 76, 1291–2 (on Gregory's own aunt Gordiana). Gregory here joins a well-established tradition of condemnation of female garrulousness: it should be noted, however, that his discussion of the 'flux of speech' (see below) is aimed at controlling the garrulousness of men.

as brutally as he had done in dealing with Augustine's question on episcopal living arrangements and monastic community, Gregory explained that a nocturnal emission was not in itself polluting, because it could happen naturally. But if the man had consented to the onset of sexual desire, and had thus provoked the emission, then he could be held culpable.[31] There is no other discussion of bodily *fluxus* and its avoidance in Gregory's work.

'Flux' for Gregory connoted not the flow of semen, but the flux of speech or desire.[32]

For the human mind is like water: when enclosed, it is collected on high . . .but when let loose, it comes to nought . . .The mind is as it were, drawn out in so many streams the moment it lets itself out in a flow of words from the strict enclosure of silence.[33]

Of the decision of sixth-century ascetics to concentrate their attentions on discursive, rather than physiological, signs of moral purity there is no clearer index than this shift in the meaning of *fluxus*. In Gregory's view, it was the words that issued from a man in the daytime, not the bodily fluids ejected at night that would reveal the contents of his heart. The care lavished by Cassian on determining the ascetic's optimal intake of water Gregory devoted to scrutinizing his own rhetorical performance. At the start of the *Moralia*, he informs his readers of his intent not to follow a rigid sequence of exposition, but 'to employ myself at greater length upon the wide field of contemplation and moral instruction'. He is confident that an exegete should not be afraid to digress if edificatory need be, 'to force the streams of discourse towards the adjacent valley, and when he has poured forth enough . . . to fall back into his original channel.'[34] At the end of the work, however, Gregory confesses that having started with the clean intent to edify his hearers, the desire to please them has crept upon him, and he asks for their forgiveness.[35] His speech, once humble, has become contaminated, and he seeks to return it to its pristine state. Such concern with purity of speech was, of course, a lesson Gregory

---

[31] See *Lib.Resp.* ix, in Bede, *Historia Ecclesiastica* I. 27, ed. Plummer, 60–1.

[32] See e.g. *Mor.* VIII. 37. 57, CCSL 143, 377 (*fluxus eloquii*); III. 30. 59, CCSL 143, 151 (*fluxus illiciate cogitationis*); XXX. 21. 40, CCSL 143B, 1659 (*voluptatis fluxus*).

[33] *Mor.* VII. 37. 57–61, CCSL 143, 377–81.

[34] *Mor: Epistula ad Leandrum* 2, CCSL 143, 4.

[35] *Mor.* XXXV. 20. 49, CCSL 143B, 1810–11. See also *Mor.* IX. 25. 37, CCSL 140, 482; both passages are briefly discussed by Meyvaert, 'Gregory the Great and the Theme of Authority' in id. *Benedict, Gregory, Bede*, Ch. 5, 7–8.

had learnt from Cassian: just as he detached the deployment of moral expertise from the issue of cenobitism, so he moved to release the science of plain speech from its dependence on physical asceticism.

The uptake of the body into discourse had specific pastoral consequences: the actual bodies of those in his charge were less important to Gregory than to earlier sixth-century ascetics as an area over which to exercise moral authority. A bishop like Caesarius, or a monastic teacher like the Master, sought directly to change the behaviour of his flock. The concrete details of their daily lives were to bear witness to his pastoral intervention, on the understanding that he could only assess the spiritual welfare of those in his charge through visible, physical signs of their struggle against sin. For Gregory, on the other hand, it seems to have been less important to extract this kind of bodily obedience from his listeners, be they his immediate circle or the people of Rome. To put the contrast in terms of his use of ascetic tradition, Gregory, his immersion in Cassian's texts notwithstanding, found his way back to an augustinian understanding of his pastoral task in terms of ministering to the physical needs of his congregation. He was able to regard their bodies not as potential emblems of ascetic purity, but as frail and suffering matter, debilitated by divine punishment, a condition which could not physically be remedied, but only allayed.

Where Caesarius left his mark at Arles on the churches and on the women in the convent, then, Gregory hesitated before conscripting the bodies of others for ascetic purposes. The *Register* shows that he was involved in all of the same activities as Caesarius, but also that he did not seek to present his authority in terms of a regime of moral surveillance. Gregory's almsgiving,[36] redemption of captives,[37] and his dealings with the holy women in Rome[38] have none of the melo-

[36] See *HEv.* I. 16. 6, PL 76, 1138A for Gregory's use of Isa. 58 to urge a connection between fasting and almsgiving; cf. *Caes.Serm.* 25.1, CCSL 103, 112, and 199. 3, CCSL 104, 804. Gregory's biographers stir up some controversy here. According to *Vita Gregorii* 28, ed. Colgrave, 126, Gregory's successor Sabinian did open the granaries for the multitude during times of famine, but he charged them a price. Gregory appeared to Sabinian three times, berating him 'in far from gentle tones' for his miserly stewardship. When Sabinian would not listen, Gregory kicked him in the head, and he died. Cf. *Liber Pontificalis* 67, where Sabinian's opening of the city granaries is described as an act of charity. John the Deacon is less dramatic in his account of the monthly distributions of corn initiated by Gregory and his followers: John the Deacon, *Vita Gregorii* II. 26, PL 75, 97B.

[37] See e.g. *Epp.* IV. 17; VII. 13; VII. 35, CCSL 140, 235–6; 462–3; 498–9.

[38] See *Epp.* II. 10, III. 17, VI. 42. This evidence is assembled in G. Ferrari, *Early Roman Monasteries: Notes for the History of the Monasteries and Convents at Rome from the V to the X Century* (Rome, 1957), 11–12, 134, 176–8.

dramatic edge of Caesarius' transactions. Although Gregory does seem to have taken a specific interest in fostering conventual life in the city, his letters to Roman abbesses concern their basic material needs, for adequate shelter or for blankets in the cold Roman winter.[39] Neither for captives, nor for holy virgins did Gregory despoil the churches of Rome. As the *Liber Pontificalis* reports, he took care to adorn both St Peter's and St Paul's with gold, silver, and purple-dyed cloth.[40] It was not in this context that he would confront the city clergy.

While Caesarius typically sought to render his message as physically graphic as possible, Gregory's idea of persuasiveness entailed an immediacy of contact with the inner desires of his hearers. 'Hearts, not garments' was his cry.[41] On those rare occasions when he did directly address the people, Gregory declined to comment in any detail on how he wished them to behave. If he addressed sexual desire at all, for example, it was because it connoted attachment to this world. The difference between the married and the continent lay not in sex itself, but in the involvement in property transactions, in worldly business, consequent upon marital sexual activity.[42] In speaking to the Romans, as to his immediate circle, it was not the shaming inventory of pollution but the drastic abandonment of worldly desire on which Gregory dwelt. He was less interested in finding bodily terms for spiritual impurity than in evoking the fundamental distance between heaven and earth:

Look! There is happiness in the heavenly citadel of the elect; they are all enjoying one another's company. And what of us? Tepid in the love of eternal life, we are not aflame with desire, we are without joy. Let us light up our souls, brothers, let our desires be burning for heaven.[43]

Earthly pleasures amount to very little, and so in Gregory's estimation, are not worth extensive rhetorical attention. In the end, perhaps, 'the flesh' need hold no power, because it could be viewed simply as matter. 'For however much gold and silver you heap around yourself, however many clothes you put on your flesh, what is it besides flesh?'[44]

---

[39] *Ep.* VII. 23.

[40] *Lib. Pont.* 66.

[41] *HEz.* I. 9. 34, CCSL 142, 141, citing Joel 2: 13: 'Rend your hearts, and not your garments.'

[42] e.g. *Mor.* I. 14. 20, CCSL 143, 21.

[43] *HEv.* I. 14. 6, PL 76, 1130D.

[44] Ibid. I. 13. 6, PL 76, 1126C.

Gregory's was a Pauline perspective. When pressed by the Corinthians to set out a hierarchy of sexual purity, Paul replied that, in view of the nearness of the end times, this was a badly put question. Gregory took delight in recounting (more than once) the pastoral exploits of the apostle Paul, as described in his letters to the Christian communities of the Eastern Mediterranean. The case of the fractious Corinthians, indeed, was a favourite example: in Gregory's reading of the text, Paul lulled his hearers into a false sense of security with mild words of praise—and then wielded the knife of correction. 'Like a skilled doctor, he saw the wound that needed to be cut, but he saw also a patient who was fearful: he delayed and delayed, and then suddenly he struck.'[45] Where, for Augustine, Paul's letter to the Romans had provided the essential lesson in the inscrutability of divine grace—the impossibility of human knowledge of God's judgement—for Gregory what mattered was Paul's clinical expertise in knowing, not only what to say, but also when to say it, in order to bring about a specific moral effect in his hearers.

Paul was the expert doctor, and only an expert could hope to shoulder the burden of responsibility of authority as Gregory had defined it. He knew what kind of person should be a ruler. Throughout his work, but above all at the start of the *Pastoral Rule*, Gregory warned that the inexpert (*imperiti*) should not seek or be chosen to rule.[46] Cassian, on whose terminology Gregory drew here, had declared the inexpert ineligible for cenobitic life: Gregory welcomed their presence as subjects of pastoral attention, but he could not countenance their tenure of power. This was a warning to those already in office as much as anything else. They should, constantly, 'guard about their ways'.[47] Even the best qualified were, however, bound to err, to fall short of the example set by Paul. The question raised by Gregory's argument was a familiar one: who would watch the watchmen themselves? Once a philosopher became king, to whom could he turn for the frank speech of correction?

---

[45] *HEz.* I. 11. 18, CCSL 142, 177. Cf. *Mor.* XXIV. 16. 41, CCSL 143B, 1219. Also *RP* III. 27, PL 77, 102C.

[46] *RP* I: 'Ne venire imperiti ad magisterium audeant.'

[47] *Mor.* XIX. 12. 20, CCSL 143B, 971.

JOB'S COMFORTERS

In 602, Gregory wrote to the Roman noblewoman Rusticiana at Constantinople, whom he had befriended during his time there.[48] Rusticiana and he both suffer from gout, and this prompts Gregory to offer his advice on the spiritually correct response to bodily affliction.[49] On the one hand he rejoices in the morally purgative effect of her illness, in that it cleans out the noxious humours which, he says, drag his own body down into carnality. On the other, he is worried about Rusticiana, because she is already so frail: she may be in too much pain. His own condition, he then reveals, is so extreme that his body is completely dried up and ready for the grave. He hardly ever has the strength to rise from his bed. He asks her: 'So if gout reduces my body to such dryness, what can I feel about your body, which was too dry already before your sickness?'[50] The letter reaches the limits of spiritual friendship as Gregory hesitates between ascetic stringency for carnal pollution and compassion for bodily weakness.[51]

Rusticiana was the granddaughter of Boethius: Gregory's relationship with her represented for them both, perhaps, a point of contact with the world of the early sixth century, more stable than their own vicissitudinous era. Their correspondence—including, for example, a discussion of her pilgrimage to Jerusalem—evokes the kind of relationships maintained by Eugippius and Proba, Caesarius and his sister Caesaria, looking back in turn to Jerome and Paula, Rufinus and Melania in the fourth century. At the same time, this letter to Rusticiana reveals the differences between Gregory and the ascetic generation of the start of the century. In marked contrast to the moral supervision offered by Caesarius of Arles and the *Rule of the Master*, the kind of authority Gregory wished to exert involved not only an objective assessment of his audience, but a subjective, unconditional identification with their needs.

Such an exercise of power could not leave the preacher himself unchanged. It required, on the contrary, that he imagine constantly what it was like to be someone else.[52] This was a meticulous and exhausting work of compassion, but one whose dynamics fascinated

[48] *Ep.* XI. 26, CCSL 140A, 898–901.
[49] Cf. *RP* III. 12, SC 382, 322–32, on admonishing the sick.
[50] *Ep.* XI. 26, CC 140A, 899.
[51] See also letter to Venantius, *Ep* XI. 8; and Seneca, *Ep.* 67. 4, on how gout teaches endurance of hardships.
[52] Cf. *Mor.* XXXIV. 11. 22, CCSL 143B, 1747. See Straw, *Gregory*, 201–2.

Gregory. He never tired of observing what the experience of power did to the person who held it, the transformations he himself could expect to undergo, even as he undertook the work of transforming others. On occasion, his mind turned more readily to the politics of correction than to the business of correction itself: hence one of the more remarkable passages in his response to Augustine of Canterbury. 'In what ways was sexual intercourse polluting?', Augustine had asked. Not content here with a brisk summary of existing tradition, Gregory frames an analogy between sexual intercourse and the exercise of spiritual authority. 'Lawful intercourse must be accompanied by bodily desire', Gregory acknowledges, before observing:

There are many things that are lawful and legitimate, and yet in the doing of them we are to some extent contaminated. For example, we often correct faults under stress of anger, and thereby disturb our peace of mind . . . So while anger against evil is commendable, it is harmful to a man because in being disturbed by it he is conscious of some guilt.[53]

Gregory approaches the problem of sexual pleasure not by evoking its polluting effect in the community, but with reference to the intimate workings of spiritual authority.

The problem of the ruler in error dogged Gregory, and its appearance in the middle of a discussion of sexual behaviour would have been no surprise to anyone who had heard him preach on Job. A ruler might be possessed of discernment and charity, but he was bound to err, however well-intentioned: in the *Moralia*, Gregory posed the question, classic in kingship literature from the Hellenistic period onwards: should the ruler accept correction of his own conduct?[54] His answer seems unequivocal. Only a truly skilful and loving ruler would possess the humility to respond to admonition of his own conduct, while the purveyor of an empty expertise would be revealed as the hollow and conceited speaker that he was. Gregory saw Job and his friends as providing an extended illustration of the anxiety of these contrasting attitudes. Job, in Gregory's account, fundamentally accepted his testing from God. His friends, although they

[53] See *Lib.Resp.* viii in Bede, *Historia Ecclesiastica* I. 27, ed. Plummer, 58, tr. Sherley-Price, 80–1. For a case of excessively harsh correction, see *Ep.* XII. 5, CCSL 140A, 973, a letter to one Oportunus, whose desolation at Gregory's rebuke elicits the latter's reassurance that he spoke not in anger but out of love.

[54] K. Cooper, 'Discretion and Betrayal: Late Roman Advice on Late Roman Advisors', paper delivered at Leeds International Medieval Congress, July 1994, discusses the ancient context for this characteristic of the wise ruler, observed in kingship literature from the Hellenistic period onwards.

had some knowledge of spiritual matters, lacked true *peritia* as they attempted to offer Job their ready-made admonitions for his unique ordeal. Thus Eliphaz, while his teaching is sound, is inexpert enough to assume that he can tell Job something Job does not already know.[55] Similarly, Baldad blunders on in his diatribe, fearful lest a moment's pause be interpreted as hesitant *imperitia*—Gregory's implication being that a diffident silence would be a far more convincing sign of expert concern for Job.[56] The clumsy arrogance of Sophar is still more ruthlessly exposed, as Gregory has him succumb instantly to the insensitivity he is loud to condemn. Sophar rebukes Job for his domineering outburst—'Shall men hold their peace to thee only?'—and then proceeds to betray his own presumption, in calling on God to show Job the secrets of divine wisdom, the 'manifold law'. Gregory rebukes Sophar's gauche naïvety with Paul's definitive statement of the unfathomable depth of God, commenting: 'Sophar, then, is both an expert through his application to knowledge, and an ignoramus in the inflated effrontery of his words. He lacks solidity, and wants to be a better man than he is.'[57] Such self-styled experts would always refute their own pretensions to prominence, Gregory argued.

Conceding that his emphasis on authority raised the stakes of competition for power, Gregory none the less insisted that the marketplace of claims to expertise was self-regulating. Job's friends believe themselves to be expert in all things, but in the sight of God their vainglorious *imperitia* is unerringly revealed.[58] They prefer to seem holy to those who do not know better, rather than to work for the humility on which enduring sanctity is grounded. In playing to the gallery, such hypocrites become indistinguishable from those whom they desire to impress. Their lack of humility finally bespeaks their ignorance of charity: if unable to accept correction themselves, they will never be able to dispense it appropriately to others. Sophar 'knew what he was saying, but not to whom he was saying it': like all Job's comforters, he was unable to grasp the nature of Job's predicament. As though to demonstrate this further, Gregory uses one of Sophar's shallow truisms—his invocation of the divine 'manifold law'—to release a

---

[55] 'Quantalibet doctrina mens polleat, gravis eius imperitia est velle docere melius', *Mor.* VI. 39. 64, CCSL 143, 333.

[56] Ibid. VIII. 36. 59, 428.

[57] 'Sophar itaque et per scientiae studium peritus et per audaciam tumidae locutionis ignarus, quia ipse gravitatem non habet, meliori optat quod habet, dicens . . .', ibid. X. 6. 7, 538, commenting on Job 11: 3–6.

[58] *Mor.* XXVIII. 2. 11, CCSL 143B, 1401–2, on Job's fourth comforter, Eliu.

soaring aria on the multiplicity of charity, a gregorian resetting of Paul's hymn of love to the Corinthians. Within the domain of his exegesis at least, Gregory could ensure that the banal claims of pretenders to *peritia* were always found wanting.[59]

Within the field of worldly politics, this position may not have been so easy to maintain. In a letter to the egregious Bishop Natalis of Salona, who had thought to justify his dereliction of books for groaning banquet tables with reference to Scripture, Gregory might proclaim his readiness to accept correction from all comers.[60] But this was in itself something of a ploy, calculated to undermine Natalis' complacent hedonism. There were necessary limits to the humility of the ruler. To those whom he trusted—or to those whom he trusted he could shame into compliance—Gregory did not hesitate to berate himself for his own inadequacies, so offering, paradoxically, a demonstration of the authenticity of his claim to genuine expertise. He could not, however, afford to suffer the correction proffered by every latterday comforter of Job, nor could he be certain that such vanity would be disabused. In a key passage in the *Pastoral Rule*, Gregory asked again whether inferiors had the right to correct their rulers, especially when the latter had used excessive force. There were some famous precedents, such as Nathan's correction of the adulterous king David, for the dutiful rebuke of wayward rulers, but this was not where Gregory placed his emphasis. It was never the ruler's part to show humility to those who themselves lacked it. Even at the risk of error himself, it was his task to remove the temptation to self-importance on the part of would-be advisers.[61]

Gregory's discussion here drew support from Augustine, but he went further than Augustine in shielding rulers from possible criticism of their miscalculations. Augustine, we may remember, had ventured in the *Praeceptum* that the ruler's authority could be endangered if his inferiors were given too much licence to protest. In what may well be a direct adaptation of this passage in the *Pastoral Rule*, Gregory comments:

In this it is needful that the care of government should be tempered with such skill in management that the mind of their subjects, when they have been able to think rightly, may in such wise come forward into freedom of speech, as that freedom

[59] *Mor.* X. 6. 8–10, CCSL 143, 541–4.

[60] *Epp.* II. 17, II. 44, CCSL 140, 102–3, 133–6. See Markus, *Gregory*, 157, for a description of the wider conflict at Salona in which Gregory was attempting to intervene.

[61] *RP* II. 8, SC 382, 230–6.

may not break out into arrogance; lest perchance when liberty of speech is allowed them beyond bounds, they lose humility of life.[62]

This echoed but also finely nuanced Augustine's precept: Gregory shifted attention away from the *regendi auctoritas* endangered by too much humility on the part of the ruler, and onto the threatened loss of humility of the inferiors. The effect Gregory thereby achieved was subtly to conceal and so to strengthen the ruler's *auctoritas*. Vulnerable as he may have shown himself to his inner circle, to those whom he perceived to require it Gregory did not hesitate to hold back his sword from blood.

The exercise of power could not but be morally compromising. As any reader of *City of God* knew, the maintenance of earthly peace by itself involved conduct that was not to be distinguished from robbery.[63] It was impossible to speak as a ruler, Gregory added, and not to sin, but to maintain a cloistered silence was fraught with its own dangers:

It should be known that when we withold from speech by an excess of fear . . . we are subject to a mischievous degree of much talking in the heart. Our thoughts become the more hot within, the more the violent keeping of indiscreet silence confines them.[64]

A ruler was never free from the peril of rhetorical flux, but any violence he might do if he spoke was offset by the damage he did if he held held his tongue 'too tightly bound'. If this was a message grimly assimilated by many an early medieval king, according to Gregory it was known already to the rulers of the Old Testament. 'As Solomon says, "There is a time for speaking and a time for silence".'

Gregory was always prepared to speak. The magnetism of Solomon's wisdom lay in its capacity to absorb all and any tension in the community around the king. One man assumed and made light of the burdens of the entire group. The risks involved in offering to play such a role were extraordinary—even if one were to escape the opprobrium of one's enemies and the flattery of associates, the demons of self-loathing and self-aggrandisement were near at hand and certain to

---

[62] Ibid. 234. 'Sed inter haec necesse est ut cura regiminis tanta moderaminis arte temperetur, quatenus subditorum mens cum quaedam recte sentire potuerit, sic in vocis libertatem prodeat, ut tamen libertas in superbiam non erumpat; ne dum fortasse immoderatius linguae eis libertas conceditur, vitae ab his humilitas amittatur', tr. H. R. Bramley (London, 1874), 105–6. Cf. Augustine, above, Ch. 1 n. 57.

[63] Augustine, *Civ.Dei* XIX. 7, CCSL 48, 671.

[64] *Mor.* VII. 37. 57.

attack. Yet these were precisely the risks Gregory sought to calculate and, himself, to run.

While Gregory proclaimed himself condemned as a watchman by the Lord's commission to Ezekiel, the words of Scripture were also a place of refuge. In the *Homilies on Ezekiel*, for example, Gregory pictured himself withdrawing into the shades of the sacred text, away from the heat of this world:

How amazing is the depth of the speech of God! It is a joy to gaze into it, a joy to penetrate its secrets, with grace as a guide. Each time that we look into it, trying to understand, what else are we doing but going into the darkness of the woods, to take ourselves away from the stifling heat of this world into its coolness? There we pick the greenest shoots of ideas when we read, and by interpreting them we chew the cud.[65]

The monastery Gregory had abandoned, but retreat into Scripture was always possible. Something of Gregory's sense of the word of God as a safe haven may not be unfamiliar to a twenty-first-century audience schooled in the literature of exile and displacement, where language serves to offer those driven from their homelands a form of belonging. At the same time, we must recognize that Gregory does not read or write as we do. We may try to keep pace with his capacity to retreat, or to ascend from the literal surface of a text to a realm of allegorical meanings, but he is likely to outrun us. No mere textual hermeneutic, Gregory's allegorizing opened onto an entire cosmology of God-given signs and human efforts to decode them. Scripture was not, in fact, Gregory's only place of refuge: the entirety of creation spoke to Gregory 'like a book' in ways likely to bewilder us.[66] For all that his rhetorical or psychological insights may strike a chord, it must be remembered that Gregory was a visionary in ways we would find alarming, but that were relatively conventional in sixth-century ascetic culture.

The forests of Scripture welcomed the weary preacher, and, in Gregory's vision, they offered shelter to the whole body of the faithful. When he dreamed of community, Gregory turned not to any one Scriptural model, such as the Jerusalem community, but to the whole

[65] *HEz.* I. 5. 1, CCSL 142, 57.   [66] *Ep.* III. 29, CCSL 140, 175.

of Scripture itself.[67] Scripture would speak to everyone as they had need. In the preface to the *Moralia*, Gregory announced this theme: 'Scripture is as it were a kind of river, if I may so liken it, which is both shallow and deep, wherein the lamb may find a footing and the elephant float at large.'[68] The quaintness of this often quoted phrase has perhaps distracted readers from the importance of the theme in Gregory's writings.[69]

Gregory's vision of Scripture as polyphony was not new. In the *Confessions*, in passages Gregory is likely to have known well, Augustine had rehearsed his conversion to a true comprehension of Scripture.[70] As a classically trained rhetor, he had thought scriptural language and subject matter vulgar, until he heard Ambrose preach on the Old Testament. Then he realized:

Its plain language and simple style make it accessible to everyone, and yet it absorbs the attention of the learned. By this means it gathers all men in the wide sweep of its net, and some pass safely through the narrow mesh and come to you [God].[71]

In the *De doctrina christiana* and throughout his work, Augustine developed the techniques of exegesis according to historical, allegorical, and moral senses which were obviously fundamental for Gregory's own work as an exegete.[72]

Both Gregory's debt to augustinian exegesis, and the differences of his own approach, have been well observed. While their interpretative methods may have been similar, Augustine was convinced of the opacity of signs, Gregory of their transparency.[73] This was a luxury Gregory could afford. He inhabited a cultural world already saturated with Scripture, whereas Augustine worked in a context where most of his cultured contemporaries continued to hold Scripture in contempt as he had done himself, and the few who did not do so prided themselves on their ability to unlock its secrets. Augustine's emphasis

---

[67] P. Catry, 'Lire l'écriture selon Grégoire le Grand', *CollCist* 34 (1972), 177–201.

[68] *Ad Leandr.* 4, CCSL 140, 6.

[69] See M. Banniard, '*Iuxta uniuscuiusque qualitatem*: L'écriture médiatrice chez Grégoire', *Grégoire le Grand*, 477–88.

[70] On Gregory's knowledge of the *Confessions*, see P. Courcelle, *Les Confessions de Saint Augustin dans la tradition littéraire* (Paris, 1963), 231.

[71] *Conf.* VI. 5. 8, CCSL 27, 78–9; see also III. 5. 9, CCSL 27, 31.

[72] See J. McClure, 'Gregory the Great: Exegesis and Audience' (Oxford D. Phil. thesis, 1978), esp. Introduction; V. Recchia, 'La memoria di Agostino nella esegesi biblica di Gregorio Magno', *Augustinianum* 25 (1985), 405–34.

[73] See Markus, *Signs and Meanings*, 1–70.

on the unfathomable depths of God's speech was meant to confront both parties with the futility of their assumptions. If no amount of scholarly training would ever suffice to parse the word of God, then, for Augustine—as ever concerned with the risks of élitism—it followed that anyone, not merely a trained exegete, could read with profit and delight. His point in the first three books of the *De doctrina christiana* (composed 397–401) was specifically to disabuse his readers of the notion that interpretation of Scripture required a particular expertise.[74] For Gregory, however, operating in a culture where a widespread familiarity with Scripture could be presumed, there was an issue of expertise. The word of God required proper interpretation, or perhaps more precisely, correct administration. This, in Gregory's terminology, was *praedicatio*, which was in effect the distribution of Scripture according to need. The *praedicatores* were those entrusted with this task, through their word and example.

Scripture, as Gregory read it, itself commanded its own adminis-tration; the word of God gave to preachers a history and a title to power. Where Augustine had deemed the pattern of history in the period after the Incarnation and before Judgement to be indecipher-able, Gregory understood the prophets, the apostles, and now the preachers of his own day as forming part of a continuous outpouring of divine speech.[75] Commenting on Job 36: 27, 'Who taketh away the stars of rain and pours forth showers like whirlpools', Gregory began by identifying the stars as prophets. God then withdrew the teachers of the law 'to his inmost and secret mansions', and 'a more exuberant power of preaching poured forth', namely the apostles. As for the whirlpools:

When he took away the Apostles who were preaching, he watered the world with the doctrine of new grace . . . He disclosed in more abundant profusion by the tongues of subsequent expositors the streams of divine knowledge which had long been concealed.[76]

The genesis of the preachers was a creation story: with the waters in

[74] See *De doctr. chr.* II. 5. 6–6. 7, ed. Green, 60, on Scripture as a cure for all ills, especially pride. God made Scripture obscure to affront human hermeneutical pride. For discussion, see Dawson, 'Sign Theory, Allegorical Reading, and the Motions of the Soul in *De doctrina christiana*', in Arnold and Bright (eds.), *De doctrina christiana*, 123–41, at 131.

[75] Cf. *RM* I. 82–9, SC 105, 348–50. From Paul, Eph. 4: 11, or 1 Cor. 12: 28.

[76] *Mor.* XXVII. 8. 13–14, CCSL 143B, 1339. Cf. XXX. 6. 22–3, CCSL 143B, 1338–9, on the faithful as clods of earth, of different sizes (i. e. merits), bound together in the union of charity.

place, Gregory moved on metaphorically, to the earth. The lord formed the body of the faithful as it were from the dust, and legitimated the hierarchical division of that body:

> Whom do we understand by dust but sinners . . . ? The dust therefore was hardened into clods . . . composed of moisture and earth . . . The Lord daily binds together these clods in the earth, of one dust indeed, but distinguished, as it were, by different size . . . If we observe these clods in the Church according to the diversity of their merits, we are perhaps able to distinguish them more precisely. For there is one order of preachers, and another of hearers; one of rulers, another of subjects.

Scripture gave to everyone according to their need. Its resources were inexhaustible—'by the well instructed it is always found new'—and it was truly universal. Its language constituted the catholic community of believers, soon to be fully realized in the heavenly country.[77]

In his vision of Scripture as a panacea for all ills, distributed by those who had, at least partially, first cured themselves, Gregory drew on, even as he transcended, the tradition of *lectio divina* inspired by Cassian. In the *Institutes* and still more the *Conferences*, Cassian had restrained his Origenist instincts in the discussion of the allegorical meanings of the text. The word of God is presented rather as a talisman against all forms of diabolic temptation. In filling his mind with sacred text, or even with one verse, the ascetic can block out the devil, and prevent his mind from straying (even across the field of Scripture). We have seen how central this model of reading was to the designs of ascetics in Gaul and in Italy in the sixth century. Gregory signals his familiarity with this tradition, but does not hesitate to move beyond it. His deployment of Scripture as the remedy for all ills took him far from Cassian's model of mental occupation. For Gregory, to dwell on allegorical meanings in all their extravagant complexity was to begin to appreciate the different kinds of advice that had to be given to all sorts and conditions of the faithful.

The preacher, in Gregory's view, need not experience the word of God as a blockade on his mind; indeed he need not experience divine speech through reading at all, nor in any material medium.

> When God speaks to us, the heart learns about his word without words and syllables, because his power is known by a kind of inward uplifting. When the mind is full of this power, it is raised up; when empty it is weighed down . . . For God's word is a kind of weight which lifts every mind it fills. It is a light without

[77] *Mor.* XX. 1. 1, CCSL 143A, 1003.

body, which both fills the inner areas, and when they are full draws a boundary around the outside. It is a speech without noise, which opens the ears, and yet does not think to utter a sound.[78]

For Caesarius and the Italian *magistri*, following Cassian, God's words become more and more opaque. Rote memorization hardened them to stone, and this was how to prepare the soul of the reader for presentation to God. For Gregory, the words of God become lighter and lighter until they vaporize. Reading gives way to pure vision, an act of beholding the divine without reference to the page.

For our hearing does not take in at once all the things which are said to it, since it understands sentences by means of words, and words separately as syllables. But our sight immediately perceives the whole object, as soon as it turns towards it. The words of God addressed to us from within are seen rather than heard. . . . God works his way in without the delay of speech, by his sudden light he illumines ignorance.[79]

Although more lyrical, this was no less authoritarian than the more programmatic style of his predecessors. For all that his own speech was enmired in worldly flux, the preacher could bring his hearers the awe-inspiring report of words that were weightless.

Gregory's vision of the power of ethereal discourse was not, moreover, a simple refusal of the ascetic tradition of *lectio divina*. Gregorian speech without noise was not unlike Cassian's 'prayer of fire', the wordless rapture to which the ascetic who had secured his mind from temptation might aspire. And while Gregory did not seek to endorse the regime of *ob-audientia* proposed by the Italian Rules, their vision of heaven, drawn itself from the apocalyptic tradition, may have inspired him, specifically in his thinking about Benedict. Indeed Gregory's *Life* of Benedict in the *Dialogues* could be understood as an attempt to insist, lest anyone be misled by the apparent naturalism of the *Rule,* that its author was a preacher illumined by the lightning of God's speech. Benedict himself, as we have seen, had chosen to exclude most of the apocalyptic material found in abundance in the Master and Eugippius. For Gregory, this threatened to obscure what for him was the essential point: that Benedict, like Paul, was a man who had ascended to the third heaven, and who knew that the end times were near.

---

[78] *Mor.* XXVIII. 1. 2, CCSL 143B, 1396–7. See also *HEv.* I. 1. 4, PL 76, 1080C, on the transience of human speech.

[79] *Mor.* XXVIII. 1. 2, CCSL 143B, 1397.

Gregory's Benedict is, then, a visionary prophet of the last days:[80] his *Rule* Gregory praises for its spiritual discernment and the radiance of its language. These luminous qualities the rest of the narrative has amply suggested. There are three sequences of miracles in the *Life*, each announcing a new quality to Benedict's discernment. The first sequence shows the holy man seeing past the designs of the devil in his monasteries. At Subiaco, he exorcizes a monk who cannot stay at prayer. He sees what the monk's abbot cannot see: the little demon tugging the monk away from the oratory. he strikes the monk with his staff for his blindness of heart, and so cures him.[81] At Montecassino, Benedict performs the reverse miracle. When all the monks building the monastery think there is a fire, Benedict sees that it is a diabolical illusion. Gregory says that the devil has been appearing to Benedict not in secret, nor in his sleep, but 'in open sight', complaining of his persecution.[82]

In the second sequence, Benedict starts to display the gift of prophecy, says Gregory, seeing across time and space.[83] Monks who disobey the strict prohibition on fasting on journeys find that their master has observed all of their misdemeanours (II. 12–13). Totila, king of the Goths, finds his career and death predicted with unerring accuracy by the holy man. This prophecy leads him in turn to predict the future of the city of Rome. While the bishop of Canosa expects Totila to destroy Rome, Benedict knows that the city will fall not at the hands of men, but in 'storms, tempests, and earthquakes, it will collapse in on itself'.[84] 'The truth of this prophecy', Gregory comments, we see all around us in the form of breached walls, shattered houses, and derelict buildings. Gregory thus places present reality within the spotlight of the holy man's prophetic gaze.[85]

In the third sequence of miracles, Gregory promises to discuss Benedict's 'day to day language':[86] in fact the stories that follow come to demonstrate the holy man's powers of vision at their most extra-ordinary. The Goth Zalla, a contemporary of Totila's successor, brings in a prisoner to Benedict: all he has to do is to look up from his

---

[80] This argument is presented at greater length in C. Leyser, 'St Benedict and Gregory the Great: Another Dialogue', in T. Sardella (ed.), *Sicilia e Italia suburbicaria*, 21–43.

[81] *Dial.* II. 4. 1–3, SC 260, 160–2.

[82] Ibid. II. 8. 12–10. 2, SC 260, 168–72.

[83] Ibid. II. 11. 3, SC 260, 174.

[84] Ibid. II. 15. 3, SC 260, 184.

[85] Ibid. II. 15. 3–16. 9, SC 260, 184–90. With his interlocutor Peter, he discusses how much the holy man could know God's judgements, and how much was kept hidden.

[86] Ibid. II. 22. 5, SC 260, 104.

book, and the chains fall off the man. Benedict, Gregory is explicit, has the power of binding and loosing through his eyes.[87] Then come the jewels in the array of Benedict's acts of looking: he sees the soul of his sister Scholastica flying up to heaven, and then, a vision of the whole cosmos.[88] One night at Montecassino, Benedict stood alone in his abbot's tower praying.

He suddenly beheld a flood of light shining down from above more brilliantly than the sun, and with it every trace of darkness cleared away. Another remarkable sight followed. According to his own description, the whole world was gathered up before his eyes in what appeared to be a single ray of light. As he gazed at all this dazzling display, he saw the soul of Germanus, the Bishop of Capua, being carried by angels up to heaven in a ball of fire.

It is at this point, it is tempting to suppose, that Gregory gives full rein in his account of Benedict to the perspective of the Master, whose *Rule* is thronged with angels.

More certain is the epiphany this scene represents in Gregory's scheme of things. Gregory explains that it is Benedict's moral achievements as an ascetic that rocket him, as it were, into a position where he has literally left this world behind, so that it seems small and insignificant to him. It is not accidental that the vision takes place in a tower, and that Benedict's companion Servandus is also an abbot. The tower recalls, inevitably, the tower of the prophet Ezekiel. What Gregory shows here is that the exposed and vulnerable station of the *speculator* is also the platform for extraordinary and radiant *speculatio*. He could find no clearer way of demonstrating that those called to rule were also, necessarily, contemplatives. Immediately after the cosmic vision, there follows the mention of Benedict's *Rule*:

I do not want to hide this from you, that the man of God, amidst so many miracles, by which he shone in the world, also did not in a middling way shine forth through his teaching. For he wrote a rule for monks which is outstanding in its discernment and radiant in its language. Anyone who wants to know more about the holy

---

[87] *Dial.* II. 31, SC 260, 222–6.

[88] Ibid. II. 35. 2–3, SC 260, 236–8; tr. O. Zimmermann, FC 39 (1983), 105. It is anticipated by Benedict's vision of Scholastica's soul ascending into heaven at *Dial.* II. 36, SC 260, 234 (on which see J. H. Wansbrough, 'St Gregory's Intention in the Stories of St Scholastica and St Benedict', *RBen* 75 (1965), 145–51). On Benedict, see P. Courcelle, 'La Vision cosmique de s. Benoît', *REAug* 13 (1967), 97–117; also Boesch Gajano, '"Narratio" e "expositio"'. For angels in the *Rules* of the Master and Benedict, see C. Leyser, 'Angels, Monks, and Demons in the Early Medieval West', paper delivered at XIII International Conference on Patristic Studies, Oxford, 16–21 Aug. 1999.

man and how he lived, should look at the Rule, because the holy man could not have taught other than he lived.[89]

A huge literature attends this passage: here we need only observe that the discernment to which Gregory draws attention is a quality of the angels with whom Benedict keeps company.

Gregory has much to say concerning angels. In a well-known passage in the *Homilies on the Gospels*, he breaks into a lengthy digression on the nine ranks of the angelic hosts, drawing here on the *Celestial Hierarchy* of Pseudo-Dionysius—a source which appears to take him far from the crowded intimacy of the angels in the *Rule of the Master*.[90] But while the Neoplatonic Pseudo-Dionysius stressed the resonance between cosmic and ecclesiastical hierarchies, Gregory's point was, in fact, grounded in the angelology of the western ascetic tradition. His interest lay in the moral character of authority, be it on earth or in heaven. Angels for Gregory were not only the embodiment of the divine contemplation toward which all must strive; crucially, they were also models of virtuous leadership. Here is his description of the seraphim, from the *Homilies on the Gospels*:

And some are set on fire by supernal contemplation, and are filled with eager desire for their Creator alone. They no longer long for anything in this world, they are nourished by love of eternity alone, they thrust aside all earthly things; their hearts transcend every temporal thing; they love, they are on fire, they find rest in this fire; loving speech sets them on fire, and they enkindle others too with their speech: those they touch with their words they instantly set on fire with love of God. What then should I call these people whose hearts, which have been turned into fire, are shining and burning, but Seraphim?[91]

This angelological digression in the middle of a Gospel homily allows Gregory to strike simultaneously two central themes: the interdependence of action and contemplation, and the urgency of the preacher's task in extending inspiration to the community around him. Angels embody an ethical imperative which applied not only to monks, but to all the faithful, and above all those in power.

But what good does it do to speak briefly of these angelic spirits, if we are not zealous to turn them to our profit by appropriate reflection on what we have said?

---

[89] *Dial.* II. 36, SC 260, 242. See A. de Vogüé, 'La Mention de la 'regula monachorum' à la fin de la 'Vie de Benoît (Grégoire, Dial. II, 36): Sa fonction littéraire et spirituelle', *RBS* 5 (1976), 289–98.

[90] See C. Micaelli, 'L'angelologia di Gregorio Magno tra oriente e occidente', *Koinonia* 16 (1992), 35–51.

[91] Gregory, *HEv.* II. 34. 11, PL 76, 1253B; tr. Hurst, 291.

. . . Since we believe that the multitude of humans that is going to ascend to the heavenly city is equal to the multitude of angels that never left, it remains for those humans who are returning to their heavenly homeland to imitate some of these bands of angels, in the process of their return.[92]

LANGUAGE, INSTITUTION, AND CHARISMA

In the mid-seventh century, Lathcen, son of Baith the Victorious and monk of Clonfert-Mulloe, compiled an epitome of Gregory the Great's *Moralia in Job*.[93] Nine manuscripts of this work have survived, and we know Lathcen was read in ninth-century Reichenau and St Gall.[94] In contrast to other excerptors of Gregory in the two generations after his death, who combed the *Moralia* for what Gregory had to say about other verses of Scripture, Lathcen's interest was in the interpretation of the book of Job and nothing else.[95] His epitome was a terse summary of the literal and allegorical meanings of Job as expounded in the *Moralia*—omitting the moral meanings which had so preoccupied Gregory. Much as ascetic readers of Augustine had managed by the sixth century to invoke the authority of his name without bearing the burden of his message, so Lathcen showed that it was possible to summarize all thirty-five books of the *Moralia* 'which Gregory made', while holding at bay their gregorian content.

The very sparseness of Lathcen's treatment—there is no dedicatory preface, the text launches straight into a bald summary of Gregory's preface—makes it difficult to establish the context for the work. A clue may lie in Lathcen's other known composition, the *Lorica*, a breastplate prayer for the protection of 143 parts of the body from attack:[96]

---

[92] Gregory, *HEv.* II. 34. 11, PL 76, 1252C; tr. Hurst, 289.

[93] Lathcen, *Egloga quam scripsit Lathcen filius Baith de Moralibus Iob quas Gregorius fecit*, ed. M. Adriaen, CCSL 145 (1969). On Lathcen, see P. Grosjean, 'Sur quelques exégètes irlandais du VIIᵉ siècle', *Sacris Erudiri* 7 (1955), 67–98, at 92–6.

[94] See Adriaen, CCSL 145, pp. vi–vii, and L. Gougaud, 'Le Témoinage des manuscrits sur l'oeuvre littéraire du moine Lathcen', *Revue Celtique* 30 (1909), 37–46.

[95] On the 7th-cent. excerptors of the *Moralia*, see R. Wasselynck, 'Les Compilations des "Moralia in Job" du VIIe au XIIe siècle', *RTAM* 29 (1962), 5–32, at 5–15; G. Braga, 'Moralia in Iob: Epitomi dei secoli VII–X e loro evoluzione', *Grégoire le Grand*, 561–8.

[96] For editions of the *Lorica*, see M. Herren, *The Hisperica Famina II: Related Poems*, Pontifical Institute of Mediaeval Studies, Studies and Texts 85 (Toronto, 1987), 76–89; and most recently, D. Howlett, 'Five Experiments in Textual Reconstruction and Analysis', *Peritia* 9 (1995), 1–50, at 8–14.

> O God, defend me everywhere
> With your impregnable power and protection.
> Deliver all the limbs of me a mortal
> With your protective shield guarding every member,
> Lest the foul demons hurl their shafts
> Into my sides, as is their wont. . . .
> Then be a most protective breastplate
> For my limbs and for my inwards,
> So that you drive back from me the invisible
> Nails of the shafts that the foul fiends fashion.[97]

Here, perhaps, we see the grounds of Lathcen's attraction to the book of Job, a story of horrific demonic attack eventually vanquished. Here, perhaps, also an explanation for the lapidary character of the epitome: it was itself to serve as a form of *lorica*, to ward off the demons of which it spoke. Lathcen used the *Moralia in Iob* as an apotropaic, according to Gregory a reverence for his writings of the kind he himself had accorded to Scripture.

This may not have been what Gregory had in mind for his exegesis (although we should resist any temptation to assume that Gregory knew nothing of apotropaic spells). None the less, Gregory had come close to soliciting this kind of reception. He had offered his readers a language of authority designed to brook no argument, no matter where applied: it was not unreasonable for them to press his language into immediate, cosmic, service. In pursuing such a language, Gregory himself had gone beyond both institutional and charismatic forms of power—analytical categories that still exercise a certain grip on the modern political imagination.

Viewed in the broad context of western monastic culture, the effect of Gregory's bold deployment of a language of spiritual expertise was to resolve many of the tensions that had beset the ascetic movement from its inception. The temptation to spiritual élitism among ascetics, the envy aroused in those outside the ascetic circle, were no longer dangerous if the boundaries of that circle, traditionally demarcated by the drama of secession to the desert, or by enclosure within cloister walls, were no longer seen to be relevant. This solution to the problem of ascetic élitism lay implicit in the work of John Cassian: Gregory was able to draw it out fully because, instead of becoming embroiled in the issue of cenobitism, he kept his attention fixed upon the Church as imagined by Augustine, the whole body of the faithful in their varying

---

[97] Lathcen, *Lorica*, ll. 29–32, 51–4, tr. Herren, 81–3.

degrees of merit. And he devoted the bulk of his rhetorical energies to developing an enduring discourse of moral authority, of the sort that both Augustine and Cassian had, in their different ways, avoided. Divisions among the faithful, tension between ascetics, clerics, and the laity, the myriad sources of other dissension—all would be bound up by the expertise of the preachers, Gregory insisted.

In the sixth century, Gregory stood apart from other ascetic teachers. Pomerius and Caesarius, the Master, Eugippius, and Benedict, as seen, chose to operate within the institutional structures of the episcopate or the monastery, and most sought to reproduce a single pattern of moral purity in their hearers. This pattern, drawn largely from the writings of Cassian, required the full attention of the audience to the words of the teacher. By contrast, Gregory defined his authority as a moral guide without reference to official ecclesiastical status; he based all of his teaching on the assumption that the experience of his hearers was different from his own and from each other, and therefore required a variety of remedies; and he therefore did not seek to inflict his words on his hearers with the same physical immediacy demanded by Caesarius and the *magistri*. While drawing deeply on Cassian's technique of purification, he did not seek to apply it in an undifferentiated way in any one theatre—be it the body, the monastery, or the diocese—as they had done, but in all theatres simultaneously.

Gregory's determination to devise a language of authority ensured his influence across subsequent centuries (a point not quite captured in discussions of Gregory's 'personality', or even his 'voice').[98] The irony remains, however, that the original purpose of the gregorian language of authority was to respond to the end of time, not to endure through its prolongation. We are left with an interpretative challenge. Even if, parting company with Gregory's Edwardian biographer, we do not regard it as a malady,[99] the eschatological cast of Gregory's mind is likely to bewilder us, because of our knowledge of his long and prosperous heritage. However well meant, our insistence on reading Gregory in light of his future is likely to estrange us still further from him.

[98] See Caspar and Wallace-Hadrill, above, Ch. 6, n. 9.
[99] Above, Ch. 6, n. 10.

BIBLIOGRAPHY

A. PRIMARY SOURCES

* indicates that the attribution of the work is doubtful.

Athanasius, *Vita Antonii*, tr. Evagrius of Antioch, PL 73, 126–70.

Augustine of Hippo, *Confessiones* ed. J. J. O'Donnell, 3 vols. (Oxford, 1992).

—— *Contra Iulianum*, PL 44, 641–874.

—— *De beata vita*, ed. W. M. Green, CCSL 29 (1970).

—— *De correptione et gratia*, PL 34, 915–45.

—— *De civitate Dei*, ed. B. Dombart and A. Kalb, 2 vols., CCSL 47, 48 (1950).

—— *De doctrina christiana*, ed. R. P. H. Green (Oxford, 1995).

—— *De Genesi ad litteram*, ed. J. Zycha, CSEL 28 (1944).

—— *De Genesi contra Manichaeos*, PL 34, 173–219.

—— *De opere monachorum*, PL 42, 201–518.

—— *Enarrationes in Psalmos*, ed. E. Dekkers and J. Fraipont, 3 vols., CCSL 38, 40 (1956).

—— *Epistulae*, PL 33.

—— *Epistulae ex duobus codicibus nuper in lucem prolatae*, ed. J. Divjak, CSEL 88 (1981), tr. R. Eno, *Saint Augustine, Letters VI (1*–29*)*, FC 81 (1989).

—— *Ordo monasterii**, ed. L. Verheijen, *La Règle de S.Augustin*, 2 vols. (Paris, 1967), i. 148–52.

—— *Praeceptum*, ibid., i. 416–37.

—— *Sermones*, PL 38, 39; ed. G. Morin, *Miscellanea Agostiniana* (Rome, 1930); ed. F. Dolbeau, *Augustin d'Hippone, Vingt-six sermons au peuple d'Afrique* (Paris, 1996); G. Madec, *La vie communautaire: traduction annotée des sermons 355–356*, Nouvelle bibliothèque augustinienne 6 (Paris, 1996).

Basil of Caesarea, *Regula a Rufino latine versa*, ed. K. Zelzer, CSEL 86 (1986).

—— *Admonitio ad filium spiritualem**, ed. P. Lehmann, *Sitzungsberichte der Bayerischen Akademie der Wissenschaften*, Ph.-H.Kl., 1955, Heft 7 (Munich, 1955); also PL 103, 683–700.

Benedict of Aniane, *Codex Regularum monasticarum et canonicarum*, PL 103, 394–702.

—— *Concordia Regularum*, PL 103, 702–1380.

Caesarius of Arles, *Regula monachorum*, ed. J. Courreau and A. de Vogüé, *Césaire d'Arles: Oeuvres monastiques*, ii. *Oeuvres pour les moines*, SC 398 (Paris, 1994), 204–26.

—— *Regula virginum*, ed. J. Courreau and A. de Vogüé, *Césaire d'Arles: Oeuvres monastiques*, i. *Oeuvres pour les moniales*, SC 345 (1988), 170–273; tr. M. C. McCarthy, *The Rule for Nuns of St Caesarius of Arles* (Washington, 1960).

Caesarius of Arles, *Sermones*, ed. G. Morin, *Sancti Caesarii episcopi opera omnia*, 2 vols., (Maredsous, 1937), i; repr. in CCSL 103, 104 (1953).

—— *Testamentum*, SC 345, 381–97, tr. W. E. Klingshirn, *Caesarius of Arles: Life, Testament, and Letters*, TTH 19 (Liverpool, 1994).

—— *Vereor*, SC 345, 294–336.

—— *Vita Caesarii*, ed. B. Krusch, MGH SRM 3 (1896), 457–501.

Cassian, *Conlationes*, ed. E. Pichéry, 3 vols., SC 42, 54, 64 (1955–9).

—— *De Incarnatione Domini contra Nestorium*, CSEL 17, 235.

—— *De institutis coenobiorum*, ed. J. C. Guy, SC 109 (1965).

Cassiodorus, *Institutiones divinarum litterarum*, ed. R. A. B. Mynors (Oxford, 1937).

Celestine I, *Cuperemus quidem*, PL 50, 430–6.

Chrodegang of Metz, *Regula canonicorum* 31, ed. J.-B. Pelt, *Études sur la cathédrale de Metz*, i. *La Liturgie* (Metz, 1937).

Concilia Gallia, 314–695, ed. C. Munier and C. de Clercq, CCSL 148, 148A (1963).

Cyprian, *De singularitate clericorum**, ed. G. Hartel, *Cypriani opera omnia*, CSEL 3 (1868), pt. iii, *Opera spuria*.

Decretum Gelasianum de libris recipiendis et non recipiendis, ed. E. von Dobschütz, TU 38, 4 (Leipzig, 1912).

Dionysius the Areopagite, *De coelesti hierarchia*, PG 3, 119–370.

—— *De ecclesiae hierarchia*, PG 3, 369–584.

Ennodius of Pavia, *Epistulae*, CSEL 6.

Eugippius of Lucullanum, *Excerpta ex operibus S. Augustini*, ed. P. Knöll, CSEL 9.i (1885).

—— *Commemoratorium vitae sancti Severini*, ed. P. Régerat, SC 374 (1991).

—— *Regula*, ed. A. de Vogüé and F. Villegas, CSEL 87 (1976).

Evagrius of Pontus, *Sententiae ad monacos*, Latin tr. Rufinus, PG 40, 1277–82.

—— *Sententiae ad virginem*, Latin tr. Rufinus, ed. H. Gressmann, TU 39 (Leipzig, 1913).

—— A. Guillaumont and C. Guillaumont, *Evagre le Pontique: Traité pratique ou le moine*, 2 vols., SC 170–1 (1963).

Eucherius of Lyon, *De laude eremi*, ed. S. Pricoco (Catania, 1965).

Eusebius of Caesarea, *Historia Ecclesiastica*, ed. G. Bardy, 4 vols., SC 31, 41, 55, 73 (1952–60).

Eustratius, *Vita Eutychii*, PG 86, 2273–2390.

Ferrandus, *Vita Fulgentii*, ed. G.-G. Lapeyre (Paris, 1929).

Fulgentius of Ruspe, *Opera*, ed. J. Fraipont, CCSL 91, 91A (1968).

Gennadius of Marseilles (and pseudo-Gennadius), *De viris illustribus*, ed. E. C. Richardson, TU 14 (Berlin, 1896).

Gregory of Tours, *Decem libri historiarum*, ed. W. Arndt and B. Krusch, MGH SRM 1 (1885).

—— *Vita patrum*, ibid., 661–744.

—— *Dialogi*, ed. A. de Vogüé, *Grégoire le Grand: Dialogues*, 3 vols., SC 251, 260, 265 (1978–80).

—— *Expositiones in Canticum Canticorum et In Librum Primum Regum*, ed. P. Verbraken, CCSL 154 (1963); R. Bélanger, *Commentaire sur le Cantique des Cantiques*, SC 314 (1984).

—— *Homiliae in Hiezechihelem Prophetam*, ed. M. Adriaen, CCSL 142 (1971).

—— *Homiliae in Evangelia*, PL 76, 1075–1314; *Gregory the Great: Forty Gospel Homilies*, tr. D. Hurst, Cistercian Studies Series 123 (Kalamazoo, 1990); M. Fiedrowicz, *Gregor der Grosse: Homiliae in Evangelia*, 2 vols., *Fontes Christiani* 28 (Freiburg im Breisgau, 1997).

—— *Libellus Responsionum*, in Bede, *Historia ecclesiastica gentis anglorum*, ed. C. Plummer (Oxford, 1896).

—— *Moralia in Iob*, ed. M. Adriaen, 3 vols., CCSL 143, 143A, 143B (1979–85); ed. R. Gillet, *Grégoire le Grand: Morales sur Job, Livres I–II*, SC 32bis (1975).

—— *Regulae pastoralis liber*, PL 77, 13–126; ed. B. Judic, *Grégoire le Grand: Règle Pastorale*, 2 vols., SC 381–2 (1992).

—— *Registrum epistularum*, ed. P. Ewald and L. Hartmann, 2 vols., MGH Epp. (1891–9); ed. D. Norberg, 2 vols., CCSL 140, 140A (1982).

Isidore of Seville, *De viris illustribus*, PL 83, 1081–1106.

Jerome, *Epistulae*, ed. J. Labourt, PL 22, 7 vols. (Paris, 1949–63).

—— *Opera Homiletica*, ed. G. Morin, CCSL 78 (1958).

—— *Quamlibet sciam**, ed. G. Morin, 'Pages inédites de deux pseudo-jérômes de l'environ l'an 400', *RBen* 40 (1928), 293–302.

—— *De viris illustribus*, PL 23, 631–760.

John the Deacon, *Vita Gregorii Magni*, PL 75, 59–242.

Lathcen, *Egloga quam scripsit Lathcen filius Baith de Moralibus Iob quas Gregorius fecit*, ed. M. Adriaen, CCSL 145 (1969).

—— *Lorica*, ed. M. Herren, *The Hisperica Famina II: Related Poems*, Pontifical Institute of Mediaeval Studies, Studies and Texts 85 (Toronto, 1987), 76–89; D. Howlett, 'Five Experiments in Textual Reconstruction and Analysis', *Peritia* 9 (1995), 1–50, at 8–14.

Leander of Seville, *Regula ad virgines*, PL 72, 871–94.

Leporius, *Libellus emendationis*, CCSL 63, 111–23.

Liber Pontificalis, ed. L. Duchesne, 2 vols. (Paris, 1886–92).

Novatus 'Catholicus', *Sententiae ad monachos*, ed. F. Villegas, *RBen* 86 (1976), 49–65.

Palladius of Hellenopolis, *Dialogus de vita sancti Iohannis Chrysostomi*, ed. A.-M. Malingrey, SC 341, 342 (1988).

Passio Sebastiani, PL 17, 1019–58.

Paterius, *Liber testimoniorum*, PL 79, 683–1136.

Paul the Deacon, *Vita Gregorii*, PL 75, 41–59.

Philo of Alexandria, *De vita contemplativa*, ed. F. Daumas and P. Miquel (Paris, 1963).

Pseudo-Plutarch, *Epitome*, in H. Diels, *Doxographi Graeci* (Berlin, 1879), 264–443.

Pomerius, *De vita contemplativa*, PL 59, 415–520. tr. M. J. Suelzer, *Julianus Pomerius: The Contemplative Life*, ACW 4 (Westminster, Md., 1947).

Porcarius of Lérins, *Monita*, ed. A. Wilmart, *RBen* 26 (1909), 475–80.

Possidius, *Vita Augustini*, ed. M. Pellegrino (Alba, 1955).

Regula Benedicti, ed. A. de Vogüé and J. Neufville, 6 vols., SC 181–6 (1971–2); *RB 1980: The Rule of St Benedict in Latin and English*, ed. T. Fry (Collegeville, Minn., 1981); *La Regola di san Benedetto e le Regole dei Padri*, ed. S. Pricoco (Verona, 1995), 114–275.

Regula Macarii, ed. A. de Vogüé, *Les Règles des saints Pères*, 2 vols., SC 297–8 (1982), i. 372–88.

Regula Magistri, ed. F. Masai and H. Vanderhoven, *Édition diplomatique des manuscrits latins 12205 et 12634 de Paris* (Brussels/Paris, 1953); ed. A. de Vogüé, *La Règle du Maître*, 3 vols., SC 105–7 (1964).

Ruricius of Limoges, *Epistulae*, ed. A. Engelbrecht, CSEL 21 (1891).

Sextus, *Enchiridion*, ed. H. Chadwick, *The Sentences of Sextus*, Texts and Studies NS 5 (Cambridge, 1959).

Visio Pauli, ed. M. R. James, *Apocrypha Anecdota*, Texts and Studies II.3 (Cambridge, 1983).

Vita Gregorii, ed. B. Colgrave, *The Earliest Life of Gregory the Great* (Cambridge, 1985).

Vita Patrum Iurensium, ed. F. Martine, SC 142 (1968).

Pope Zosimus, *Epistulae*, CSEL 35.

B. SECONDARY SOURCES

Alchermes, J., '*Cura pro mortuis* and *cultus martyrum*: Commemoration in Rome from the Second through the Sixth Century' (New York Univ. PhD thesis, 1989).

Allen, P., 'The "Justinianic" Plague', *Byzantion* 49 (1979), 5–20.

Amann, E., art. 'Leporius', *DTC* 9: 434–40.

——'L'Affaire Nestorius vue de Rome', *RSR* 23 (1949), 3–37, 207–44; 24 (1950), 28–52, 235–65.

Amargier, P., *Un Âge d'or du monachisme: Saint Victor de Marseille (990–1090)* (Marseilles, 1990).

André, J. M., *L'Otium dans la vie morale et intellectuelle romaine* (Paris, 1966).

Arnold, A. C. F., *Caesarius von Arelate und die gallische Kirche seiner Zeit* (Leipzig, 1894; repr. 1972).

Arnold, D. W. H., and Bright, P. (eds.), *De doctrina Christiana: a Classic of Western Culture* (Notre Dame, 1995).

Arquillière, H.-X., *L'Augustinisme politique: Essai sur la formation des théories politiques du moyen âge* (Paris, 1934).

Ashworth, H., 'The Influence of the Lombard Invasions on the Gregorian Sacramentary', *Bulletin of the John Rylands Library* 36 (1953–4), 305–27.

Aubin, P., 'Intériorité et extériorité dans les Moralia in Job de saint Grégoire le Grand', *RSR* 62 (1974), 117–66.

Auerbach, E., *Literary Language and its Public in Late Antiquity and the Middle Ages*, tr. R. Mannheim (London, 1967).

Axelson, B., *Ein drittes Werk der Firmicus Maternus? Zur Kritik der philologischen Identifierungsmethode*, Kungl. Humanistika Vetenskapssamfundets i Lund, Årsberättelse, IV (Lund, 1937).

Baasten, M., *Pride according to Gregory the Great: A Study of the 'Moralia'*, (Lewiston, NY, 1986).

Baldovin, J. F., *The Urban Character of Christian Worship: The Origins, Development and Meaning of Stational Liturgy*, Orientalia Christiana Analecta 228 (Rome, 1987).

Bammel, C. P. Hammond, 'The Last Ten Years of Rufinus' Life and the Date of his Move South from Aquileia', *JTS* NS 28 (1977), 372–429.

—— 'Products of Fifth-Century Scriptoria Preserving Conventions used by Rufinus of Aquileia', *JTS* NS 29 (1978), 366–91; 30 (1979), 430–62; 35 (1984), 347–93.

Banniard, M., '*Iuxta uniuscuiusque qualitatem*. L'écriture médiatrice chez Grégoire', *Grégoire le Grand* (below), 477–88.

Beck, H. C. J., *The Pastoral Care of Souls in South-East France during the Sixth Century* (Rome, 1950).

Berschin, W., *Biografie und Epochenstil im Lateinischen Mittelalter*, 3 vols. (Stuttgart, 1986).

Bloomfield, M., *The Seven Deadly Sins: An Introduction to the History of a Religious Concept, with Special Reference to Medieval English Literature* (East Lansing, Mich., 1952).

Boesch Gajano, S., 'Dislivelli culturali e mediazioni ecclesiastiche nei "Dialoghi" di Gregorio Magno', in C. Ginzburg (ed.), *Religioni delle classi popolari*, *Quaderni storici* 41 (1979), 398–415.

—— 'Demoni e miracoli nei Dialoghi di Gregorio Magno', in *Hagiographies, cultures, sociétés* (below), 398–445.

—— '"Narratio" e "expositio" nei Dialoghi di Gregorio Magno', *Bulletino del Istituto Storico Italiano e Archivio Muratoriano* 87 (1979), 1–33.

—— 'La proposta agiografica dei "Dialoghi" di Gregorio Magno', *StudMed* 3rd ser. 21 (1980), 623–64.

Bogaert, P.-M., 'La Préface de Rufin aux Sentences de Sexte et à un oeuvre inconnu', *RBen* 82 (1972), 26–46.

la Bonnardière, A.-M., 'La "Cité terrestre" d'après H.-I. Marrou', in id. (ed.), *Saint Augustin et la Bible* (Paris, 1986), 387–98.

Bonner, G., 'Augustine's visit to Caesarea in 418', in C. W. Dugmore and C. Duggan (eds.), *Studies in Church History* I (London, 1964), 104–13.

Bori P., *Chiesa primitiva: L'immagine della comunità delle origini—Atti, 2,42–47; 4, 32–37—nella storia della chiesa antica* (Brescia, 1974).

Braga, G., 'Moralia in Iob: Epitomi dei secoli VII–X e loro evoluzione', *Grégoire le Grand* (below), 561–8.

Brakke, D., 'The Problematization of Nocturnal Emissions in Early Christian Syria, Egypt, and Gaul', *JECS* 3 (1995), 419–60.

Bremond, B. *et al.* (eds.), *L''exemplum', Typologie des sources du moyen âge occidental* 40 (Turnhout, 1982).

Brown, P. R. L., *Augustine of Hippo: A Biography* (London, 1967).

—— *The Body and Society: Men, Women and Sexual Renunciation in Early Christianity* (New York, 1988).

—— *The Cult of the Saints: Its Rise and Fucntion in Latin Christianity* (Chicago, 1981).

—— *The Making of Late Antiquity* (Cambridge, Mass., 1978).

—— *Power and Persuasion in Late Antiquity: Towards a Christian Empire* (Madison, 1992).

—— *Religion and Society in the Age of St Augustine* (London, 1977).

—— 'Relics and Social Status in the Age of Gregory of Tours' (Reading, 1977), repr. id., *Society and the Holy* (below), 222–50.

—— 'Sexuality and Society in the Fifth Century A.D: Augustine and Julian of Eclanum', in E. Gabba (ed.), *Tria Corda: Scritti in onore di Arnaldo Momigliano* (Como, 1983), 49–70.

—— *Society and the Holy in Late Antiquity* (London, 1982).

Brown, T. S., *Gentlemen and Officers: Imperial Administration and Aristocratic Power in Byzantine Italy, AD 554–800* (Rome, 1984).

Brunert, M.-E., *Das Ideal der Wüstenaskese und seine Rezeption in Gallien bis zum Ende des 6. Jahrhunderts* (Münster, 1994).

Burke, P., *Popular Culture in Early Modern Europe* (London,1978).

Burton Christie, D., *The Word in the Desert: Scripture and the Quest for Holiness in Early Christian Monasticism* (New York, 1993).

Cameron, Alan, 'Paganism and Literature in Late Fourth Century Rome', in *Christianisme et formes littéraires de l'antiquité tardive en occident*, Fondation Hardt pour l'Étude de l'Antiquité Classique, Entretiens XXII (Geneva, 1977), 1–30.

Cameron, Averil, *Christianity and the Rhetoric of Empire: The Development of Christian Discourse* (Berkeley/Los Angeles, 1991).

—— 'Images of Authority: Élites and Icons in sixth-century Byzantium', *Past and Present* 84 (1979), 3–25.

—— 'A Nativity Poem of the Sixth-Century A.D.', *Classical Philology* 74 (1979), 222–32.

Carrias, M., 'Vie monastique et règle à Lérins au temps d'Honorat', *RHEF* 74 (1988), 191–211.

Carruthers, M., *The Craft of Thought: Meditation, Rhetoric, and the Making of*

Images, 400–1200 (Cambridge, 1998).

Caspar, E., *Geschichte des Papsttums*, 2 vols. (Tübingen, 1933).

Catry, P., 'Amour du monde et amour de Dieu chez S. Grégoire le Grand', *StMon* 15 (1973), 253–75.

—— 'L'Amour du prochain chez S. Grégoire le Grand', *StMon* 20 (1978), 287–344.

—— 'Lire l'écriture selon Grégoire le Grand', *CollCist* 34 (1972), 177–201.

Cavadini, J. (ed.), *Gregory the Great: A Symposium* (Notre Dame, 1995).

Chadwick, H., art. 'Florilegium', *Reallexikon für Antike und Christentum* 7 (1966), 1131–60.

—— 'Gregory of Tours and Gregory the Great', *JTS* 50 (1949), 38–49.

—— see also above, A, under Sextus, *Enchiridion*.

Chadwick, O., *John Cassian* (Cambridge, 1950; 2nd edn., 1968).

Chapman, J., *St Benedict and the Sixth Century* (London, 1929).

Chavasse, A., 'Aménagements liturgiques à Rome, au VIIe et VIIIe siècles', *RBen* 99 (1989), 75–102.

Chazelle, C., 'Pictures, Books, and the Illiterate: Pope Gregory I's Letters to Serenus of Marseille', *Word and Image* 6 (1990), 138–55.

Christophe, P., *Cassien et Césaire, prédicateurs de la morale monastique* (Gembloux, 1969).

Clark, E. A., *Ascetic Piety and Women's Faith: Essays in Late Ancient Christianity* (Lewiston, NY, 1986).

—— 'Foucault, the Fathers, and Sex', *Journal of the American Academy of Religion* 56 (1988), 619–41.

—— *Jerome, Chrysostom and Friends: Essays and Translations* (Lewiston, New York, 1982).

—— 'Theory and Practice in Late Ancient Asceticism: Jerome, Chrysostom, and Augustine', *Journal of Feminist Studies in Religion* 5 (1989), 25–46.

—— *The Origenist Controversy: The Cultural Construction of an Early Christian Debate* (Princeton, 1992).

—— *Reading Renunciation: Asceticism and Scripture in Early Christianity* (Princeton, 1999).

Clark, F., *The Pseudo-Gregorian Dialogues*, 2 vols. (Leiden, 1987).

—— 'The Authorship of the Commentary in I Regum: Implications of Adalbert de Vogüé's discovery', *RBen* 108 (1998), 61–79.

Coates-Stephens, R., 'Housing in Early Medieval Rome, 500–1000 AD', *Papers of the British School at Rome* 64, 239–59.

Colish, M., *The Stoic Tradition from Antiquity to the Early Middle Ages*, 2 vols. (Leiden, 1985).

Congar, Y., 'Ordinations *invitus, coactus* de l'Église antique au canon 214', *Revue des Sciences Philosophiques et Théologiques* 50 (1966), 169–97.

Consolino, F., 'Il papa e le regine: potere feminile e politica ecclesiastica nell'epistolario di Gregorio Magno', in *Gregorio Magno* (below), 225–49.

Cooper, K., 'Concord and Martyrdom: Gender, Community, and the Uses of Christian Perfection in Late Antiquity', 2 vols. (Princeton Univ. PhD. thesis, 1993).

——'Discretion and Betrayal: Late Roman Advice on Late Roman Advisors', paper delivered at Leeds International Medieval Congress, July 1994.

——'Insinuations of Womanly Influence: An Aspect of the Christianization of the Roman Aristocracy', *JRS* 82 (1992), 150–64.

—— *The Virgin and the Bride: Idealized Womanhood in Late Antiquity* (Cambridge, Mass., 1996).

——'The Martyr, the *matrona*, and the Bishop: Networks of Allegiance in Early Sixth-Century Rome', *EME* 8 (2000, forthcoming).

——'The Widow as Impresario: The Widow Barbaria in Eugippius' *Vita Severini*', in M. Diesenberger (ed.), *Eugippius und Severinus: Der Autor, der Text, und der Heilige* (Vienna, forthcoming).

Courcelle, P., *Les Confessions de saint Augustin dans la tradition littéraire: antécédents et postériorité* (Paris, 1963).

——'Grégoire le Grand devant les "conversions" de Marius Victorinus, Augustin et Paulin de Nole', *Latomus* 33 (1977), 942–50.

——'Habitare secum selon Perse et saint Grégoire le Grand', *Revue des études anciennes* 69 (1967), 266–79.

—— *Late Latin Writers and their Greek Sources* (Cambridge, Mass., 1969).

——'La Vision cosmique de S. Benoît', *REAug* 13 (1967), 97–117.

Courtois, C., 'L'Évolution du monachisme en Gaule de St Martin à St Columban', *Il monachesimo nell'alto medioevo e la formazione della civiltà occidentale, Settimane di studio del Centro italiano sull'alto medioevo* IV (Spoleto, 1957), 47–72.

Cracco, G., 'Ascesi e ruolo dei viri Dei nell'Italia di Gregorio Magno', in *Hagiographies, cultures, sociétés* (below), 283–97.

——'Chiesa et cristianità rurale nell'Italia di Gregorio Magno', in V. Fumagalli and G. Rossati (eds.), *Medioevo rurale* (Bologna, 1980), 361–79.

——'Gregorio Magno interprete di Benedetto', in *S. Benedetto e otto secoli (XII–XIX) di vita monastica nel Padovano*, Coll. *Miscellanea erudita* 33 (Padua, 1980), 7–36.

——'Uomini di Dio e uomini di chiesa nell'alto medioevo', *Ricerche di storia sociale e religiosa* NS 12 (1977), 163–202.

Cranz, F. E., 'The Development of Augustine's Ideas of Society before the Donatist Controversy', *Harvard Theological Review* 47 (1954), 225–361.

Crouzel, H., 'Jerôme et ses amis toulousains', *BLittEcc* 73 (1972), 125–47.

—— *Origène et la "connaissance mystique"* (Toulouse, 1961).

Dagens, C., 'La Conversion de saint Grégoire le Grand', *REAug* 5 (1969), 149–62.

——'La Fin des temps et l'église selon saint Grégoire le Grand', *RSR* 58 (1970), 273–88.

—— *Saint Grégoire le Grand: culture et expérience chrétiennes* (Paris, 1977).

—— 'Grégoire le Grand et le ministère de la parole: les notions d'ordo praedicatorum et d'officium praedicationis', in *Forma Futuris: Studi in honore di Cardinale Michele Pellegrino* (Turin, 1975), 1054–73.

Dawson, D., 'Sign Theory, Allegorical Reading, and the Motions of the Soul in *De doctrina christiana*', in Arnold and Bright, (ed.), *De doctrina christiana* (above), 123–41.

De Waal, E., *Seeking God: The Way of St Benedict* (London, 1984).

Dictionnaire d'archéologie chrétienne et de liturgie, eds. F. Cabrol, H. Leclercq, and H.-I. Marrou (Paris, 1907–53).

Dictionnaire de spiritualité (Paris, 1937–   ).

Dictionnaire de théologie catholique, ed. A. Vacant, E. Mangenot (Paris, 1903–70).

Doucet, M., 'Pédagogie et théologie dans la Vie de saint Benoît par saint Grégoire le Grand', *CollCist* 38 (1976), 158–73.

Douglas, M., *Natural Symbols: Explorations in Cosmology* (London, 1970).

—— *Purity and Danger: An Analysis of the Concepts of Pollution and Taboo* (London, 1966).

Driver, S., 'The Development of Jerome's Views on the Ascetic Life', *RTAM* 62 (1995), 44–70.

—— 'From Palestinian Ignorance to Egyptian Wisdom: Cassian's Challenge to Jerome's Monastic Teaching', *ABR* 48 (1997) 293–315.

Duchrow, U., 'Zum Prolog von Augustins *De Doctrina christiana*', *Vigiliae Christianae* 17 (1963), 165–72.

Dunn, M., 'Mastering Benedict: Monastic Rules and their Authors in the Early Medieval West', *EHR* 416 (1990), 567–94.

Dunphy, W., 'Eucherius of Lyons in Unexpected (Pelagian?) Company', *Augustinianum* 37 (1997), 483–94.

Duval, Y.-M., 'La Discussion entre l'apocrisiaire Grégoire et le patriarche Eutychios au sujet de la résurrection de la chair: l'arrière plan doctrinal oriental et occidental', in *Grégoire le Grand* (below), 347–66.

Eck, W., 'Der Episkopat im spätantiken Africa: organisatorische Entwicklung, soziale Herkunft und öffentliche Funktionen', *HZ* 236 (1983), 265–95.

Elm, E., 'Die *Vita Augustini* des Possidius: *The Work of a Plain Man and an Untrained Writer?* Wandlungen in der Beurteilung eines hagiographischen Textes', *Augustinianum* 37 (1997), 229–40.

Eno, R.: see above, A, under Augustine of Hippo, *Epistulae*.

Étaix, R., 'Deux nouveaux sermons de saint Césaire d'Arles', *REAug* 11 (1965), 9–13.

—— 'Le *Liber testimoniorum* de Paterius', *RSR* 32 (1958), 66–78.

—— 'Nouveau sermon pascal de saint Césaire d'Arles', *RBen* 75 (1965), 201–11.

—— 'Les Épreuves du juste: nouveau sermon de saint Césaire d'Arles' *REAug* 24 (1978), 272–7.

—— 'Trois notes sur S. Césaire', in *Corona gratiarum*, i. Instrumenta Patristica (Steenbrugge, 1975), 211–27.

Ferrari, G., *Early Roman Monasteries: Notes for the History of the Monasteries and Convents at Rome from the V through the X Century* (Rome, 1957).

Ferreiro, A., '*Frequenter legere*: The Propagation of Literacy, Education, and Divine Wisdom in Caesarius of Arles', *JEH* 43 (1992), 5–15.

—— 'Job in the Sermons of Caesarius of Arles', *Recherches Théologiques* 54 (1987), 13–26.

Fiedrowicz, M., *Das Kirchenverständnis Gregors des Grossen: Eine Untersuchung seiner exegetischen und homiletischen Werke*, Römische Quartalschrift für Christliche Altertumskunde und Kirchengeschichte 50 (Freiburg im Breisgau, 1995).

Fitzgerald, J. T. (ed.), *Friendship, Flattery and Frankness of Speech* (Leiden, 1996).

Fleming, J., 'By Coincidence or Design: Cassian's Disagreement with Augustine Concerning the Ethics of Falsehood', *AugStud* 29 (1998), 19–34.

Folliet, G., 'Aux Origines de l'ascétisme et du cénobitism africain', *StAns* 46 (1961), 25–44.

—— 'Les Trois catégories de chrétiens à partir de Luc (17: 34–36), Matthieu (24: 40–41) et Ezéchiel (14: 14)', *Augustinus magister* (Paris, 1954), 631–44.

—— 'Les Trois catégories de chrétiens, survie d'un thème augustinien', *L'Année théologique augustinienne* 14 (1954), 81–96.

Fontaine, J., 'L'Ascétisme chrétien dans la littérature gallo-romaine d'Hilaire à Cassien', in *La Gallia Romana*, Accademia Nazionale dei Lincei 153 (1973), 87–115.

—— 'Les Relations culturelles entre l'Italie byzantine et l'Espagne visigothique: la présence d'Eugippius dans la bibliothèque de Séville', *Estudios clasicos* 26 (1984), 9–26.

—— 'Valeurs antiques et valeurs chrétiennes dans la spiritualité des grands propriétaires terriens à la fin du IVième siècle occidental', in id. and C. Kannengiesser (eds.), *Epektasis: mélanges J. Daniélou* (Paris, 1972), 571–95.

—— 'Un Sobriquet perfide de Damase: matronarum auriscalpius' in D. Porte and J.-P. Néraudau (eds.), *Hommages à Henri le Bonniec: res sacrae* (Brussels, 1988), 177–92.

Foster, D.,' "Eloquentia nostra" (DDC IV.IV.10): A Study of the Place of Classical Rhetoric in Augustine's *De doctrina christiana* Book Four', *Augustinianum* 36 (1996), 459–94.

Foucault, M., 'Le Combat de chasteté', *Communications* 35 (1982), 15–25; tr. in P. Ariès and A. Bejin (eds.), *Western Sexuality: Practice and Precept in Past and Present Times* (Oxford, 1985), 14–25.

Frank, K. S., 'Angelikos Bios. Begriffsanalytische und begriffschichtliche Untersuchung zum engelgleichen Leben im frühen Mönchtum', *Beiträge zur Geschichte des Mönchtums und das Benediktinsordens* 26 (Munster, 1964).

—— 'John Cassian on John Cassian', *Studia Patristica* 30 (1996), 418–33.

Frederiksen, P., *Augustine on Romans*, Texts and Translations 23, Early Christian Literature Series 6 (Chico, Calif., 1982).

—— 'Paul and Augustine: Conversion Narratives, Orthodox Traditions, and the Retrospective Self', *JTS* NS 37 (1986), 3–34.

Frickel, M., *Deus totus ubique simul: Untersuchungen zur allgemeinen Gottgegenwart im Rahmen des Gotteslehre Gregors des Grossen* (Freiburg, 1956).

Froger, J., 'La Règle du Maître et les sources du monachisme bénédictine', *RAM* 30 (1954), 275–86.

Gaarder, J., *Vita Brevis: A Letter to St Augustine*, tr. A. Born (London, 1997).

Ganz, D., *Corbie in the Carolingian Renaissance* (Sigmaringen, 1990).

—— 'The Ideology of Sharing: Apostolic Community and Ecclesiastical Property in the Early Middle Ages', in W. Davies and P. Fouracre (eds.), *Property and Power in the Early Middle Ages* (Cambridge, 1995), 17–29.

Gautier, N. and J.-Ch. Picard (eds.), *Topographie chrétienne des cités de la Gaule des origines au milieu du VIIIe siècle*, iii. *Provinces Ecclésiastiques de Vienne et d'Arles* (Paris, 1986).

Gehl, P., 'Competens Silentium: Varieties of Monastic Silence in the Medieval West', *Viator* 18 (1987), 125–60.

Genestout, A., 'La Règle du Maître et la Régle de S. Benoît', *RAM* 21 (1940), 51–112.

—— 'Le Plus ancien témoin manuscrit de la Règle du Maître, le Parisinus lat. 12634', *Scriptorium* 1 (1946–7), 129–42.

Glad, C., *Paul and Philodemus: Adaptability in Epicurean and Early Christian Psychagogy* (Leiden, 1985).

Gleason, M., *Making Men: Sophists and Self-Presentation in Ancient Rome* (Princeton, 1995).

Gillet, R., art. 'Grégoire le Grand', *DSp* 6 (1967), 872–910.

—— and de Gaudemaris, A. (eds.), *Grégoire le Grand: Morales sur Job*, Livres I–II, SC 32bis (1975).

—— 'Spiritualité et place du moine dans l'église selon Grégoire le Grand', *in Théologie de la vie monastique* (below), 323–51.

Godding, R., 'Les *Dialogues* de Grégoire le Grand: À propos d'un livre récent', *AB* 106 (1988), 201–29.

—— 'Cento anni di ricerche su Gregorio Magno: A proposito di una bibliografia', in *Gregorio Magno* (below), i. 293–304.

—— *Bibliographia di Gregorio Magno (1890/1989)* (Rome, 1990).

Gordini, G. D., 'Origini e sviluppo del monachesimo a Roma', *Gregorianum* 37 (1956), 220–60.

Gorman, M. M., 'The Oldest Manuscripts of St Augustine's De Genesi ad litteram', *RBen* 90 (1980), 7–49.

—— 'Chapter Headings for St Augustine's De Genesi ad litteram', *REAug* 26 (1980), 88–104.

—— 'The Manuscript Tradition of Eugippius' *Excerpta ex operibus sancti Augustini*', *RBen* 92 (1982), 7–32, 229–65.

—— 'Eugippius and the Origins of the Manuscript Tradition of Saint

Augustine's *De Genesi ad litteram*', *RBen* 93 (1983), 7–30.

Gorman, M. M., 'Marginalia in the Oldest Manuscripts of St. Augustine's *De Genesi ad litteram*', *Scriptorium* 37 (1984), 71–7.

Gougaud, L., 'Le témoinage des manuscrits sur l'oeuvre littéraire du moine Lathcen', *Revue Celtique* 30 (1909), 37–46.

Greenblatt, S., *Renaissance Self-Fashioning: From More to Shakespear* (London, 1982).

Grégoire le Grand, J. Fontaine, R. Gillet, and S. Pellistrandi (eds.), Colloques internationaux du Centre National de la Recherche Scientifique, Centre culturel les Fontaines, 15–19 septembre 1982 (Paris, 1986).

Gregorio Magno e il suo tempo, Studia Ephemeridis 'Augustinianum' 33, 2 vols. (Rome, 1991).

Griffe, E., 'Cassien, a-t-il été prêtre d'Antioche?', *BLE* 55 (1954), 240–4.

Grosjean, P., 'Sur quelques exégètes irlandais du VIIᵉ siècle', *Sacris Erudiri* 7 (1955), 67–98.

Gross, K., '*Plus amari quam timeri*: Eine antike politische Maxime in der Benediktinerregel', *VigChr* 27 (1973), 218–29.

Grossi, V.,'*Correptio–correctio–emendatio* in Agostina d'Ippona: Terminologia penitenziale e monastica', *Augustinianum* 38 (1998), 215–22.

Guillaumont, C. and A., see above, A, under Evagrius of Pontus.

Guillou, A., 'L'Évêque dans la société méditeranéenne des VIe–VIIe siècles: Un modèle', *BCh* 31 (1973), 5–20.

Hagendahl, H., *Latin Fathers and the Classics: A Study on the Apologists, Jerome, and Other Christian Writers* (Göteborg, 1958).

Hagiographie, cultures et sociétés, IVe–XIIe siècles: Actes du colloque organisé à Nanterre et à Paris (2–5 mai 1979), Centre de Recherches sur l'Antiquité Tardive et le Haut Moyen Age, Université de Paris X (Paris, 1981).

Hallinger, K., 'Papst Gregor der Grosse und der Hl. Benedikt', *StAns* 42 (1957), 231–319.

von Harnack, A., *History of Dogma*, 7 vols., tr. N. Buchanan from 3rd German edn. (New York, 1961).

Harries, J. D., 'Bishops, Senators and their Cities in Southern Gaul, 407–476' (Oxford Univ. D.Phil. thesis, 1978).

——*Sidonius Apollinaris and the Fall of Rome* (Oxford, 1994).

Heinzelmann, M., *Bischoffsherrschaft in Gallien: Zur Kontinuität römischer Führungsgeschichten vom 4 bis zum 7 Jahrhundert*, Beihefte der Francia 5 (Munich, 1976).

Heussi, K., *Der Ursprung des Mönchtums* (Tübingen, 1936).

Hodgkin, T., *Italy and her Invaders*, 6 vols. (2nd edn. Oxford, 1896).

Holtz, L., 'Le Contexte grammatical de défi à la grammaire: Grégoire et Cassiodiore', in *Grégoire le Grand* (above), 531–9.

Holze, H., *Erfahrung und Theologie im frühen Mönchtum: Untersuchungen zu einer Theologie des monastischen Leben bei den ägyptischen Mönchsvätern, Johannes*

Cassian und Benedikt von Nursia (Göttingen, 1992).

Homes Dudden, F., *Gregory the Great: His Place in History and Thought*, 2 vols. (London, 1905).

Honselmann, K., 'Bruchstücke von Auszügen aus Werken Cassians: Reste einer verlorenen Schrift des Eucherius von Lyon?', *Theologie und Glaube* 51 (1961), 300–4.

Howarth, H. H., *Saint Gregory the Great* (London, 1912).

Hunter, D. G., 'Augustine's Pessimism? A New Look at Augustine's Teachings on Sex, Marriage, and Celibacy', *AugStud* 25 (1994), 153–77.

—— 'Resistance to the Virginal Ideal in Late Fourth Century Rome', *Theological Studies* 48 (1987), 45–64.

—— 'On the Sin of Adam and Eve: A Little-Known Defense of Marriage and Childbearing by Ambrosiaster', *Harvard Theological Review* 82 (1989), 283–99.

Illmer, D., '*Totum namque in sola experientia usuque consistit*: Eine Studie zur monastischen Erziehung und Sprache', in F. Prinz (ed.), *Mönchtum und Gesellschaft im Frühmittelalter* (Darmstadt, 1976), 430–55.

Jaspert, B., *Die RM–RB Kontroverse*, *RBS*, Suppl. 2 (Hildesheim, 1975; 2nd edn., 1977).

Jenal, G., *Italia Ascetica atque Monastica*, 2 vols. (Stuttgart, 1995).

Jones, A. H. M., 'Church Finance in the Fifth and Sixth Centuries', *JTS* NS 11 (1960), 84–94.

Jones, H. I., 'The Desert and Desire: Virginity, City, and Family in the Roman Martyr Legends of Agnes and Eugenia' (Univ. of Manchester MA thesis, 1998).

de Jong, M., *In Samuel's Image: Child Oblation in the Early Medieval West* (Leiden, 1995).

Judge, E. A., 'The Earliest Use of the Word "monachos" for Monk (P.Coll.Youtie 77)', *Jahrbuch für Antike und Christentum* 20 (1977), 72–89.

Jungmann, J. A., *The Mass of the Roman Rite: Its Origins and Development* (New York, 1955).

Jussen, B., 'Über "Bischofsherrschaften" und die Prozeduren politisch-sozialer Umordnung in Gallien zwischen "Antike" und "Mittelalter" ', *HZ* 260 (1995), 673–718.

—— 'Liturgie und Legitimation, oder Wie die Gallo-Romanen das römische Reich beendeten', in R. Blänkner and B. Jussen (eds.), *Institutionen und Ereignis: Über historische Praktiken und Vorstellungen gesellschaftlichen Ordnens* (Göttingen, 1998), 75–136.

Kaster, R., *Guardians of Language: The Grammarian and Society in Late Antiquity* (Berkeley/Los Angeles, 1988).

Kaufmann, P. T., *Redeeming Politics* (Princeton, 1990).

Kelly, J. N. D., *Jerome: His Life, Writings and Controversies* (London, 1975).

Klingshirn, W. E., 'Charity and Power: Caesarius of Arles and the Ransoming of Captives in Sub-Roman Gaul', *JRS* 75 (1985), 184–203.

Klingshirn, W. E., *Caesarius of Arles: The Making of a Christian Community in Late Antique Gaul* (Cambridge, 1994).
—— *Caesarius of Arles: Life, Testament, Letters*, TTH 19 (Liverpool, 1994).
—— 'Caesarius' Monastery for Women in Arles and the Composition and Function of the *Vita Caesarii*', *RBen* 100 (1990), 441–81.
—— 'Church Politics and Chronology: Dating the Episcopacy of Caesarius of Arles', *REAug* 38 (1992), 80–8.
—— and Vessey, J. M. (eds.) *The Limits of Ancient Christianity: Essays on Late Antique Thought and Culture in Honor of R. A. Markus* (Ann Arbor, 1999).
Knowles, D., 'The Regula Magistri and the Rule of St Benedict', in id., *Great Historical Enterprises* (Oxford, 1963).
König, D., *Amt und Askese: Priester Amt und Mönchtum bei den lateinischen Kirchenvätern in vorbenediktinischer Zeit*, *RBS* Suppl. 12 (S. Otilien, 1985).
Konstan, D., *Friendship in the Classical World* (Cambridge, 1997).
Krautheimer, R., *Rome: Profile of a City, 312–1308* (Princeton, 1980).
Ladner, R., 'L'ordo praedicatorum avant l'ordre des prêcheurs', in P. Mandonnet (ed.), *S. Dominique: l'idée, l'homme et l'oeuvre*, 2 vols. (Paris, 1937), ii. 51–5.
Laistner, M. W., 'The Influence during the Middle Ages of the Treatise "De vita contemplativa" and its Surviving Manuscripts', in id., *The Intellectual Heritage of the Early Middle Ages* (Ithaca, NY, 1957), 49–56.
Lamoureaux, J., 'Episcopal Courts in Late Antiquity', *JECS* 3: 2 (1995), 143–67.
Lawless, G., *Augustine of Hippo and his Monastic Rule* (Oxford, 1987).
Leccisotti, T., Review, *Regula Eugippii* (above, A, under 'Eugippius'), *Benedictina* 24 (1977), 430–1.
Leclercq, H., art. 'Cénobitisme', *DACL* II.2, 3224–31.
Leclercq, J., *L'Amour des lettres et le désir de Dieu: initiation aux auteurs monastiques du moyen âge* (Paris, 1957); tr. K. Misrahi, *The Love of Letters and the Desire for God* (New York, 1963).
—— 'Études sur le vocabulaire monastique du moyen âge', *StAns* 48 (1961).
—— 'Otia monastica: Études sur le vocabulaire de la contemplation au moyen âge', *StAns* 51 (1963).
Ledoyen, H., 'Saint Basile dans la tradition monastique occidentale', *Irénikon* 53 (1980), 30–45.
Le Goff, J., 'Les Exempla chez Grégoire le Grand', *Hagiographies, cultures, et sociétés*, 103–17.
Lehmann, P.: see above, A, under Basil of Caesarea.
Lepelley, C., *Les Cités de l'Afrique romaine au Bas Empire*, 2 vols. (Paris, 1979).
—— 'Saint Augustin et la cité romaine africaine', in *Jean Chrysostome et Augustin*, ed. C. Kannengiesser (Paris, 1975), 13–39.
Leroy, J., 'Les Préfaces des écrits monastiques de Jean Cassien', *RAM* 42 (1966), 157–80.
—— 'Le Cénobitisme chez Cassien', *RAM* 43 (1967) 121–58.

Les Lettres de saint Augustin découvertes par Johannes Divjak: Communications présentées au colloque des 20 et 21 septembre (Paris, 1983).

Leyser, C., 'Angels, Monks, and Demons in the Early Medieval West', paper delivered at XIII International Conference on Patristic Studies, Oxford, 16–21 Aug. 1999.

—— ' "Divine Power Flowed from this Book": Ascetic Language and Episcopal Authority in Gregory of Tours' *Life of the Fathers*", in K. Mitchell and I. Wood (eds.), *The World of Gregory of Tours* (Leiden, forthcoming).

—— 'Expertise and Authority in Pope Gregory the Great: the Social Function of *Peritia*', in Cavadini (ed.), *Gregory the Great* (above), 38–61.

—— *'Lectio divina, oratio pura*: Rhetoric and the techniques of asceticism in the *Conferences* of John Cassian', in G. Barone *et al.* (eds.), *Modelli di santità e modelli di comportamento* (Turin, 1994), 79–105.

—— ' "Let Me Speak, Let Me Speak": Vulnerability and Authority in Gregory the Great's *Homilies on Ezekiel*', in *Gregorio Magno* (above), ii. 169–82.

—— 'Masculinity in Flux: Nocturnal Emission and the Limits of Celibacy in the Early Middle Ages', in D. Hadley (ed.), *Masculinity in Medieval Europe* (Harlow, 1999) 103–20.

—— 'Long-haired Kings and Short-haired Nuns: Writing on the Body in Caesarius of Arles', *Studia Patristica* 24 (1993), 143–50.

—— ' "This Sainted Isle": Panegyric, Nostalgia, and the Invention of "Lerinian Monasticism" ', in Klingshirn and Vessey (eds.), *Limits of Ancient Christianity*, 188–206.

—— 'Semi-Pelagianism', art. A. Fitzgerald (ed.), *Augustine through the Ages: An Encyclopedia* (Grand Rapids, Mich., 1999), 761–6.

—— 'The Temptations of Cult: Roman Martyr Piety in the Age of Gregory the Great', *Early Medieval Europe*, forthcoming.

—— 'St Benedict and Gregory the Great: Another Dialogue' in S. Pricoco, F. Rizzo Nervo, and T. Sardella (eds.), *Sicilia e Italia suburbicaria tra IV e VIII secolo, Atti del Convegno di Studi (Catania, 24–27 ottobre 1989)* (Cosenza, 1991), 21–43.

Little, L. K., 'Pride Goes before Avarice: Social Change and the Vices in Latin Christendom', *AHR* 76 (1971), 16–49.

Llewellyn, P., 'The Roman Church in the Seventh Century: the Legacy of Gregory I', *JEH* 25 (1974), 363–80.

—— *Rome in the Dark Ages* (London, 1970).

—— 'The Roman Church during the Laurentian Schism: Priests and Senators', *Church History* 45 (1976), 417–27.

—— 'The Roman Clergy during the Laurentian Schism: A Preliminary Analysis', *Ancient Society* 8 (1979), 245–75.

Lorenz, R., 'Die Anfänge der abendländischen Mönchtums im 4. Jahrhundert', *ZKG* 77 (1966), 1–61.

Loseby, S., 'Marseille and the Pirenne Thesis, I: Gregory of Tours, the

Merovingian Kings and "Un grand port"', in R. Hodges and W. Bowden (eds.), *The Sixth Century: Production, Distribution and Demand* (Leiden, 1998), 203–29.

Loseby, S., 'Marseille in Late Antiquity and the Early Middle Ages' (Oxford Univ. D.Phil. thesis, 1993).

—— 'Marseille: A Late Antique Success Story', *JRS* 82 (1992), 165–85.

—— 'Arles in Late Antiquity: *Gallula Roma Arelas* and *urbs Genesii*', in N. Christie and S. Loseby (eds.), *Towns in Transition: Urban Evolution in Late Antiquity and the Early Middle Ages* (Aldershot, 1996), 45–70.

Lowe, E. A., *Paleographical Papers*, ed. L. Bieler, 2 vols. (Oxford, 1972).

Lowe, E., 'Asceticism in Context: The Anonymous *Epistolae sangallensis 190*' (Manchester University M.A. thesis, 1998).

Lubac, H. de, *Exégèse médiévale: Les quatre sens de l'écriture* (Paris, 1959–61).

McClure, J., 'Gregory the Great. Exegesis and Audience' (Oxford Univ. D.Phil. thesis, 1979).

MacCormack, S., 'Sin, Citizenship, and the Salvation of Souls: The Impact of Christian Priorities on Late-Roman and Post-Roman Society', *Comparative Studies in Society and History* 39 (1997), 644–73.

McCready, W., *Signs of Sanctity: Miracles in the Thought of Gregory the Great* (Toronto, 1989).

McKitterick, R., *The Frankish Church and the Carolingian Reforms, 789–895* (London, 1977).

Macqueen, D. J., 'St Augustine's Concept of Property Ownership', *Recherches Augustiniennes* 8 (1972), 187–229.

—— 'Contemptus Dei: St Augustine on the Disorder of Pride in Society and its Remedies', *Recherches Augustiniennes* (1973), 227–93.

Machielson, L., 'Fragments patristiques non-identifiées du ms Vat.Pal.577', *Sacris Eruditi* 12 (1961), 488–539.

Madec, G., *Petites études augustiniennes* (Paris, 1994).

—— (ed.), *Augustin prédicateur (395–411), Actes du colloque international de Chantilly (5–7 septembre 1996)* (Paris, 1998).

Mähler, M., 'Evocations bibliques et hagiographiques dans la vie de saint Benoît par S. Grégoire', *RBen* 83 (1973), 398–429.

Malnory, A., *Saint Césaire, évêque d'Arles* (Paris, 1894; repr. Geneva, 1978).

Mandouze, A., *Saint Augustin: L'aventure de la raison et la grace* (Paris, 1968).

Manning, E., 'L'Admonitio S. Basilii ad filium spiritualem et la Règle de saint Benoît', *RAM 42* (1966), 475–9.

Markus, R. A., *From Augustine to Gregory the Great: History and Christianity in Late Antiquity* (London, 1983).

—— 'The Eclipse of a Neoplatonic Theme: Augustine and Gregory the Great on Visions and Prophecies', in H. J. Blumenthal and R. A. Markus (eds.), *Neoplatonism and Early Christian Thought* (London, 1981), 204–11.

—— *The End of Ancient Christianity* (Cambridge, 1990).

——'The End of the Roman Empire: A Note on Eugippius, *Vita Sancti Severini* 20', *Nottingham Medieval Studies* 26 (1982), 1–7.

——'From Caesarius to Boniface: Christianity and Paganism in Gaul', in J. Fontaine and J. Hillgarth (eds.), *The Seventh Century: Change and Continuity* (London, 1992), 250–76.

——art. 'Gregor I', *Theologische Realenzyklopädie* 14, 135–45.

——*Gregory the Great and his World* (Cambridge, 1997).

——'Gregory the Great's Europe', *TRHS*, 5th ser. 31 (1981), 21–36; repr. in id., *From Augustine to Gregory*.

——'Gregory the Great and the Origins of a Papal Missionary Strategy', in *Studies in Church History* 6, ed. G. Cuming (Cambridge, 1970), repr. in id., *From Augustine to Gregory*.

——'Gregory the Great's "Rector" and his Genesis', in *Grégoire le Grand* (above), 137–46.

——The Legacy of Pelagius: Orthodoxy, Heresy and Conciliation', in R. Williams (ed.), *The Making of Orthodoxy* (Cambridge, 1989), 214–34.

——'Papal Primacy: Light from the Early Middle Ages', in id., *From Augustine to Gregory*.

——Review, C. Dagens, *Saint Grégoire le Grand* (above), *JEH* 29 (1978), 203.

——Review, J. Richards, *Consul of God* (below), *History* 65 (1980), 459.

——'The Sacred and the Secular: From Augustine to Gregory the Great', *JTS* NS 36 (1985), 84–96.

——*Saeculum: History and Society in the Theology of St Augustine* (Cambridge, 1970; 2nd edn., 1988).

——'St. Augustine on Signs', in id., ed., *Augustine: A Collection of Critical Essays* (1972), 61–91.

——'Vie monastique et ascétisme chez saint Augustin', in *Atti del Congresso Internazionale su S. Agostino, Roma, 15–20 settembre 1986*, 3 vols. (Rome, 1987), i. 119–25.

——*Signs and Meanings: World and Text in Ancient Christianity* (Liverpool, 1996).

Marrou, H. I., 'Autour de la bibliothèque du pape Agapit', *MEFR* 48 (1931), 124–69.

——*Saint Augustin et l'Augustinianisme* (Paris, 1959).

——'Jean Cassien à Marseille', *Revue du Moyen Age Latin* 1 (1945), 5–26.

——'Le Fondateur de Saint Victor de Marseille: Jean Cassien', *Provence Historique* 16 (1966), 297–308.

——'La Patrie de Jean Cassien', *Orientalia Christiana Periodica* 13 (1947), 588–96.

——'La Technique de l'édition à l'époque patristique', *Vigiliae Christianae* 3 (1949), 209–24.

Marsili, S., 'Giovanni Cassiano ed Evagrio Pontico', *StAns* 5 (1936).

Masai, F., 'Recherches sur les manuscrits et les états de la "Regula monasteriorum" II & III'; 'Les États du ch. Ier du Maître et la fin du Prologue de la Règle bénédictine', *Scriptorium* 21 (1967), 205–26; 22 (1968), 3–19; 23 (1969), 393–433.

Masai, F., 'Recherches sur le texte originel du De humilitate de Cassien (Inst 4.39) et des Règles du Maitre (RM 10) et de Benoît (RB 70)', in J. O'Meara and B. Nauman (eds.), *Latin Script and Letters, AD 400–900, Festschrift L. Bieler* (Leiden, 1976), 236–63.

—— 'L'Édition de Vogüé et les éditions antiques de la Règle du Maître', *Latomus* 26 (1967), 506–17.

Mathisen, R. W., *Ecclesiastical Factionalism in Fifth-Century Gaul* (Washington, 1989).

—— 'For Specialists Only: The Reception of Augustine and his Teachings in Fifth-Century Gaul' in J. T. Lienhard, E. C. Miller, and R. J. Teske (eds.), *Collectanea Augustiniana, Augustine: Presbyter factus sum* (New York, 1993), 27–41.

Matthews, J. M., *Western Aristocracies and Imperial Court, AD 364–425* (Oxford, 1975; 2nd edn., 1990).

Mayr-Harting, H. M. R. E, 'The Venerable Bede, the Rule of St Benedict, and Social Class' (Jarrow Lecture, 1976).

Merdinger, J. E., *Rome and the African Church in the Time of Augustine* (New Haven, 1997).

Meyvaert, P., *Benedict, Gregory, Bede and Others* (London, 1977).

—— 'Diversity within Unity: A Gregorian Theme', *Heythrop Journal* 4 (1963), 141–62; repr. in id., *Benedict, Gregory, Bede*.

—— 'The Date of Gregory the Great's Commentaries on the Canticle of Canticles and on 1 Kings', *Sacris Erudiri* 23 (1979), 191–216.

—— 'The Enigma of Gregory the Great's Dialogues: A Response to Francis Clark', *JEH* 39 (1988), 335–81.

—— 'Problems concerning the "Autograph" Manuscript of St Benedict's Rule', *RBen* 69 (1959), 3–21; repr. in id., *Benedict, Gregory, Bede*.

—— 'Towards a History of the Textual Transmission of the *Regula S. Benedicti*', *Scriptorium* 17 (1963), 83–110; repr. in id., *Benedict, Gregory, Bede*.

—— 'A Letter of Pelagius II Composed by Gregory the Great', in Cavadini (ed.), *Gregory the Great* (above), 94–116.

—— 'Le libellus responsionum à Augustin de Cantobéry: une oeuvre authentique de saint Grégoire le Grand' in *Grégoire le Grand* (above), 543–50.

Micaelli, C., 'Riflessioni su alcuni aspetti dell'angelologia di Gregorio Magno', *Gregorio Magno* (above) ii. 301–14.

—— 'L'angelologia di Gregorio Magno tra oriente e occidente', *Koinonia* 16 (1992), 35–51.

Miquel, P., 'Un Homme d'expérience: Cassien', *CollCist* 30 (1968), 131–46.

Mohrmann, C., *Études sur le latin des chrétiens*, 4 vols. (Rome, 1958–77).

—— 'La Latinité de Saint Benoît: Étude linguistique sur la tradition manuscrit de la règle', *RBen* 62 (1952), 108–39; repr. in ead., *Études*, i. 403–35.

Momigliano, A., 'Cassiodorus and the Italian Culture of his Time', *Proceedings of the British Academy* 49 (1955), 207–45.

Moorhead, J., *Theodoric in Italy* (Oxford, 1992).

Morard, F.-E., 'Monachos, moine: histoire du terme grec jusqu'au 4e siècle', *Freiburger Zeitschrift für Philosophie und Theologie* 20 (1973), 329–425.

Morin, G., (ed.), *Miscellanea Agostiniana*, 2 vols. (Rome, 1930).

—— 'Mes principes et ma méthode pour la future édition de saint Césaire', *RBen* 10 (1893), 62–78.

—— 'Pages inédites de deux pseudo-jérômes': see above, A, under Jerome.

—— (ed.), *Sancti Caesarii episcopi opera omnia*, 2 vols. (Maredsous, 1937).

Moulinier, J.-C., *Saint-Victor de Marseille: les récits de sa passion*, Studi di Antichità Cristiana 49 (Vatican City, 1993).

Mundò, A., 'L'Authenticité de la Regula S. Benedicti', *StAns* 42 (1957), 105–58.

Murray, A., *Reason and Society in the Middle Ages* (Oxford, 1978).

Nagel, S., and Vecchio, S., 'Il bambino, la parola, il silenzio nella cultura medievale', *Quaderni Storici*, NS 19 (1984), 719–63.

Neuhausen, K. A., 'Zu Cassians Traktat *De amicitia* (Coll. 16)', in C. Gnilka and W. Schetter (eds.), *Studien zur Literatur zur Spätantike*, Antiquitas Reihe I, Band 23 (Bonn, 1975), 181–218.

Newhauser, R., 'Towards modus in habendo: Transformations in the Idea of Avarice. The Early Penitentials through the Carolingian Reforms', *Zeitschrift der Savigny-Stiftung für Rechtsgeschichte*, Kanonistische Abteilung 75 (1989), 1–22.

—— *The Treatise on Vices and Virtues in Latin and the Vernacular*, Typologie des Sources du Moyen Age Occidental 68 (Turnhout, 1993).

Norberg, D., *In Registrum Gregorii Magni studia critica* (Uppsala Universiteits Arsskrift, 1937/4; 1939/7).

—— 'Style personnel et style administratif dans le Registrum epistolarum de S.Grégoire le Grand', in *Grégoire le Grand* (above), 489–97.

—— *Critical and Exegetical Notes on the Letters of St Gregory the Great* (Stockholm, 1982).

—— 'Qui a composé les lettres de saint Grégoire le Grand?', *StudMed*, 3rd ser. 21 (1980), 2–17.

—— 'Style personnel et style administratif dans le Registrum epistularum de saint Grégoire le Grand', in *Grégoire le Grand* (above), 489–97.

North, H., *Sophrosyne: Self-Knowledge and Restraint in Classical Antiquity* (Ithaca, NY, 1966).

O'Donnell, J. J., 'The Authority of Augustine', *Augustinian Studies* 22 (1991), 7–35.

—— *Cassiodorus* (Berkeley, 1979).

—— 'The Holiness of Gregory', in Cavadini (ed.), *Gregory the Great*, 62–81.

—— 'Liberius the Patrician', *Traditio* 37 (1981), 31–72.

O'Donnell, J. J., 'The Next Life of Augustine', in W. Klingshirn and M. Vessey (eds.), *The Limits of Ancient Christianity* (above), 215–32.

O'Laughlin, M., 'The Bible, the Demons, and the Desert: Evaluating the *Antirrheticus* of Evagrius Pontus', *StMon* 34 (1992), 201–15.

Olphe Gaillard, M., art. 'Cassien', *DSp* 2 (1937), 214–76.

—— 'Vie contemplative et vie active d'après Cassien', *RAM* 16 (1935), 252–88.

—— 'La Pureté de coeur d'après Cassien', *RAM* 17 (1936), 28–60.

Olsen, G., 'Bede as Historian: The Evidence from his Observations on the First Christian Community at Jerusalem', *JEH* 33 (1982), 519–30.

Orbans, A. P., 'Augustinus und das Mönchtum', *Kairos* 18 (1976), 100–18.

Paranetto, V., 'Connotazione del Pastor nell'opera di Gregorio Magno: teoria e prassi', *Benedictina* 31 (1984), 325–43.

Penco, G., 'Il concetto di monaco e di vita monastica in Occidente nel secolo VI', *StMon* 1 (1959), 7–50.

—— 'La dottrina dei sensi spirituali in Gregorio Magno', *Benedictina* 17 (1970), 161–201.

—— *Storia del monachesimo in Italia dalle origini alla fine del Medioevo* (2nd edn., Milan, 1983).

Pietri, C., 'Aristocratie et société clericale dans l'Italie chrétienne au temps d'Odoacre et de Théodoric', *MEFR* 93 (1981), 417–67.

—— 'Donateurs et pieux établissements d'après le légendier romain (Ve–VIIe s.), in *Hagiographie, cultures et sociétés* (above), 435–53.

—— 'Évergétisme et richesses ecclésiastiques dans l'Italie du IVe à la fin du Ve s.: l'exemple romain', *Ktema* 3 (1984), 317–37.

—— 'Concordia apostolorum et renovatio urbis (Culte des martyrs et propagande pontificale)', *MEFR* 73 (1961), 275–322.

Petersen, J., *The 'Dialogues' of Gregory the Great in their Late Antique Cultural Background* (Toronto, 1984).

—— 'Did Gregory the Great Know Greek?', in W. Sheils (ed.), *Studies in Church History* 13 (1976), 121–34.

Pitz, E., *Papstreskripte im frühen Mittelalter: Diplomatische und rechtsgeschichtliche Studien zum Brief-Corpus Gregors den Großen* (Sigmaringen, 1990).

Plagnieux, J., 'Le Grief de complicité entre erreurs nestorienne et pélagienne: D'Augustin à Cassien par Prosper d'Aquitaine?', *REAug* 2 (1956), 391–402.

Plumpe, J. C., 'Pomeriana', *VC* 1 (1947), 227–39.

Pôque, S., *Le Langage symbolique dans la prédication d'Augustin d'Hippone* (Paris, 1984).

Porcel, O. M., *La Doctrina monastica de San Gregorio Magno y la 'Regula mona-chorum'* (Madrid, 1951).

—— 'San Gregorio Magno y el monacato: Cuestiones controvertidas', *Monastica* 1, Scripta et Documenta 12 (Montserrat, 1960), 1–95.

Pricoco, S., 'Aspetti culturali del primo monachesimo d'Occidente' in A. Giardini (ed.), *Società Romana e Impero Tardoantico*, 4 vols. (Bari, 1986), iv. 189–202.

—— 'Barbari, senso della fine e teologia politica: Su un passo del "De contemptu mundi" di Eucherio di Lione', *Romano Barbarica* 2 (1977), 209–29.

—— 'La Bibbia nel *Praeceptum* di s. Agostino', *Augustinianum* 36 (1996), 495–523.

—— 'Il cristianesimo in Italia tra Damaso e Leone Magno', *Siculorum Gymnasium*, Quaderni XII (Catania, 1983).

—— (ed.), with V. Messana, *Il cristianesimo in Sicilia dalle origini a Gregorio Magno* (Caltanisetta, 1987).

—— *L'isola dei santi: Il cenobio di Lerino e le origini del monachesimo gallico* (Rome, 1978).

—— 'Modelli di santità a Lerino: L'ideale ascetico nel Sermo de vita Honorati di Ilario d'Arles', *Siculorum Gymnasium* 27 (1974), 54–88.

—— 'Il monachesimo in Italia dalle origini alla Regola di San Benedetto', in *La cultura in Italia fra tardo antica e alto medioevo: Atti del convegno tenuto a Roma, 12–16 novembre, 1979, Consiglio nazionale delle ricerche* (Rome, 1981), 621–41.

—— 'Il monachesimo occidentale dalle origine al Maestro: Lineamenti storici e percorsi storiografici', in *Il monachesimo occidentale dalle origini alla Regola Magistri, Studia Ephemeridis Augustinianum* 62 (1998), 7–22.

—— 'Il primo monachesimo in Occidente: Alcune considerazioni su un dibattito attuale', *Studi e ricerche sull'oriente cristiano*, xv (1992), 25–37.

—— '*Tepidum monachorum genus* (Cassian., *conl.* 18.4.2)', in C. Curti and C. Crimi (eds.), *Scritti classici e cristiani offerti a Francesco Corsaro*, 2 vols. (Catania, 1994), ii. 563–73.

—— Review, A. de Vogüé, ed., *Dialogues* (above, A, under Gregory the Great), *Orpheus* NS 2 (1981), 434–42.

—— 'Spiritualità monastica e attività culturale nel cenobio di Vivarium', in S. Leanza (ed.), *Flavio Magno Aurelio Cassiodoro: Atti della settimana di studi, 19–24 settembre 1983, Cosenza Squillace* (Rubbettino, 1985), 357–77.

—— (ed.), *Storia della Sicilia e tradizione agiographica nella tarda antichità: Atti del Convegno di Studi, Catania, 20–22 maggio 1986* (Rubbettino, 1988).

—— see also above, A, under *Regula Benedicti*.

Primmer, A., 'The Function of the *de genera dicendi* in *De doctrina christiana* IV', in Arnold and Bright (eds.), *De doctrina christiana* (above), 68–86.

Prinz, F., *Frühes Mönchtum im Frankenreich. Kultur und Gesellschaft in Gallien, den Rheinländern und Bayern am Beispiel der monastischen Entwicklung* (4. bis 8. Jahrhundert) (Munich, 1965; 2nd edn., 1988).

Quillen, C., 'Consentius as a Reader of Augustine's *Confessions*', *REAug* 37 (1991), 87–109.

Raikas, K. K., '*Episcopalis audientia*: Problematik zwischen Staat und Kirche bei Augustin', *Augustinianum* 37 (1997), 459–81.

Ramsey, B., 'John Cassian: Student of Augustine', *Cistercian Studies Quarterly* 28 (1993), 5–15.

Rapisarda, C. A., 'Lo stile umile nei sermoni di S.Cesario d'Arles', *Orpheus* 17 (1970), 117–59.

Rebillard, E., '*Quasi funambuli*: Cassien et la controverse pélagienne sur la perfection', *REAug* 40 (1994), 197–210.

Recchia, V., *L'esegesi di Gregorio Magno al Cantico dei Cantici* (Turin, 1967).

—— *Gregorio Magno e la società agricola* (Rome, 1978).

—— 'La memoria di Agostino nella esegesi biblica di Gregorio Magno', *Augustinianum* 25 (1985), 405–34.

—— 'Il "praedicator" nel pensiero e nell'azione di Gregorio Magno', *Salesianum* 41 (1979), 333–74.

Resnick, I. M., 'Risus monasticus: Laughter and medieval monastic culture', *RBen* 97 (1987), 90–100.

Richards, J., *Consul of God: The Life and Times of Pope Gregory the Great* (London, 1980).

Riché, P., *Education et culture dans l'Occident barbare, VIe–VIIIe siècles* (Paris, 1962).

Robinson, I. S., 'The Friendship Network of Gregory VII', *History* 63 (1978), 1–22.

Rousseau, P., *Ascetics, Authority and the Church in the Age of Jerome and Cassian* (Oxford, 1978).

—— 'Cassian, Contemplation and the Cenobitic Life', *JEH* 26 (1975), 113–26.

—— *Pachomius: The Making of a Community in Fourth Century Egypt* (Berkeley, 1985).

—— 'In Search of Sidonius the Bishop', *Historia* 25 (1976), 356–77.

—— 'The Spiritual Authority of the "Monk Bishop": Eastern Elements in some Western Hagiography in the Fourth and Fifth Centuries', *JTS* NS 22 (1971), 380–419.

—— 'Cassian: Monastery and World', in M. Fairburn and W. H. Oliver (eds.), *The Certainty of Doubt: Tributes to Peter Munz* (Wellington, New Zealand, 1995), 68–89.

Rousselle, A., 'Gestes et signes de la famille dans L'Empire romain', in A. Burgiuière *et al.* (eds.), *Histoire de la famille*, 2 vols. (Paris, 1986), i. 231–69.

—— 'Parole et inspiration: le travail de la voix dans le monde romain', *History and Philosophy of the Life Sciences*, Section II, Pubblicazioni della Stazione Zoologica di Napoli 5 (1983), 129–57.

—— *Porneia: De la maîtrise du corps à la privation sensorielle, IIe–IVe siècles de l'ère chrétienne* (Paris, 1983); tr. F. Pheasant, *On Desire and the Body in Late Antiquity* (Oxford, 1988).

Rudmann, R., *Mönchtum und kirchlicher Dienst in den Schriften Gregors des Grossen* (S. Otilien, 1956).

Russell, F. H., 'Persuading the Donatists: Augustine's Coercion by Words', in Klingshirn and Vessey (eds.), *The Limits of Ancient Christianity* (above), 115–30.

Sanchis, D., 'Pauvreté monastique et charité fraternelle chez saint Augustin: Le commentaire augustinienne des Actes 4: 32–35 entre 393 et 403', *StMon* 4 (1962), 7–33.

Schanz, M., Hosius, C., and Krüger, G. (eds.), *Geschichte der römischen literatur*, iv (Munich, 1920).

Séguy, J., 'Une sociologie des sociétés imaginées: monachisme et utopie', *AESC* 26 (1971), 328–54.

Seilhac, L. de, 'L'Utilisation par s. Césaire d'Arles de la Règle de s. Augustin', *StAns* 62 (Rome, 1962).

Selb, W., 'Episcopalis audientia von der Zeit Konstantins bis zur Novelle XXXV Valentinians III', *Zeitschrift der Savigny-Stiftung für Rechtsgeschichte*, Romanistische Abteilung 84 (1967), 162–217.

Semmler, J., 'Benedictus II: una regula – una consuetudo', in W. Lourdaux and D. Verhelst (eds.), *Benedictine Culture 750–1050*, Medievalia Lovaniensia Series I/Studia (Louvain, 1983), 1–49.

Shaw, B., 'The Family in Late Antiquity: The Experience of Augustine', *Past and Present* 115 (1983), 3–51.

Smalley, B., *The Study of the Bible in the Middle Ages* (Oxford, 1952, 3rd edn., 1983).

Solignac, A., 'Julien Pomère', art. *DSp* 8 (1974), 1594–1600.

—— 'Les Fragments du "De Natura Animae" de Julien Pomère (fin Ve siècle)', *BLE* 75 (1974), 41–60.

Southern, R. W., *Western Society and the Church in the Middle Ages* (Harmondsworth, 1970).

Spence, S., *Rhetorics of Reason and Desire: Vergil, Augustine and the Troubadours* (Ithaca, NY, 1988).

Stancliffe, C., 'Kings who Opted out', in P. Wormald (ed.), *Ideal and Reality in Frankish and Anglo-Saxon Society: Studies presented to J. M. Wallace-Hadrill* (Oxford, 1983), 154–76.

Stevens, S. T., 'The Circle of Bishop Fulgentius', *Traditio* 38 (1982), 327–40.

Stewart, C., *Cassian the Monk* (New York, 1998).

—— 'From λόγος to *verbum*: John Cassian's Use of Greek in the Development of a Latin Monastic Vocabulary', in E. R. Elder (ed.), *The Joy of Learning and the Love of God: Studies in Honor of Jean Leclercq* (Kalamazoo, Mich., 1995), 5–31.

Stock, B., *Augustine the Reader: Meditation, Self-Knowledge, and the Ethics of Interpretation* (Cambridge, Mass., 1996).

Straw, C., *Gregory the Great: Perfection in Imperfection* (Berkeley, 1988).

—— *Gregory the Great*, Authors of the Middle Ages IV, nos. 12–13 (London, 1996).

—— 'Adversitas et Prosperitas': une illustration du motif structurel de la complementarité', in *Grégoire le Grand* (above), 277–88.

—— 'Gregory's Politics: Theory and Practice', in *Gregorio Magno* (above), i. 47–63.

Théologie de la vie monastique: Études sur la tradition patristique (Paris, 1961).

Tibiletti, C., 'La teologia della grazia in Giuliano Pomerio: alle origini dell'agostinismo provenzale', *Augustinianum* 25 (1985), 489–506.

Tibiletti, C., 'Fausto di Riez nei giudizi della critica', *Augustinianum* 21 (1981), 567–87.

—— 'Polemiche in Africa contro i teologi provenzali', *Augustinianum* 26 (1986), 499–517.

Traube, L., *Textgeschichte der Regula S. Benedicti* (Munich, 1898; 2nd edn., H. Plenkers, 1910).

Van Dam, R., *Leadership and Community in Late Roman Gaul* (Berkeley/Los Angeles, 1985).

—— *Saints and the Miracles in Late Antique Gaul* (Princeton, 1993).

Van der Meer, F., *Augustine the Bishop* (London, 1961).

Van Uytfanghe, M., 'Modèles bibliques dans l'hagiographie', in P. Riché and G. Lobrichon (eds.), *Le Moyen Age et la Bible*, Bible de tous le temps 4 (Paris, 1984), 449–88.

—— 'La controverse biblique et patristique autour du miracle et ses repercussions dans l'Antiquité tardive et le haut Moyen Age latin', *Hagiographie, cultures, sociétés* (above), 205–32, with discussion at 232–3.

—— 'Scepticisme doctrinal au seuil du Moyen Age? Les objections du diacre Pierre dans les *Dialogues* de Grégoire le Grand', in *Grégoire le Grand* (above), 315–24, with discussion at 324–6.

Vannier, M.-A., 'L'Influence de Jean Chrysostome sur l'argumentation scripturaire du *De Incarnatione domini* de Jean Cassien', *RSR* 69 (1995), 453–62.

Verbraken, P., Review, O. Porcel, 'San Gregorio y el monacato' (above), *StMon* 2 (1960), 438–40.

Verheijen, L., *Nouvelle approche de la Règle de St Augustin* (Bellefontaine, 1980).

—— 'La Règle de saint Augustin. L'état actuel des questions (début 1975)', *Augustiniana* 35 (1985), 193–263.

—— 'Spiritualité et vie monastique chez St Augustin: L'utilisation monastique des Actes des Apôtres 4: 31–35', in id., *Nouvelle approche*, 76–105.

—— *Saint Augustine's monasticism in the light of Acts 4: 32–35* (Villanova, 1979).

—— 'Les Lettres nouvelles et la vie monastique autour de saint Augustin', in *Les Lettres de saint Augustin découvertes par Johannes Divjak* (above), 124–7.

—— 'Saint Augustin et les médicins', *L'Année théologique augustinienne* 13 (1953), 327–46.

Vessey, J. M., 'Conference and Confession: Literary Pragmatics in Augustine's *Apologia Contra Hieronymum*', *JECS* 1: 2 (1993), 175–213.

—— 'Ideas of Christian Writing in Late Roman Gaul' (Oxford Univ. D.Phil. thesis, 1988).

—— 'The Demise of the Christian Writer and the Remaking of "Late Antiquity": From H.-I. Marrou's St Augustine (1938) to Peter Brown's Holy Man (1983)', *JECS* 6 (1998), 377–411.

—— '*Opus imperfectum*: Augustine and his Readers, 426–435 AD', *Vigiliae Christianae* 52 (1998), 264–85.

Vitale-Brovarone, A., 'La forma narrativa dei *Dialoghi* di Gregorio Magno:

problemi storico-letterari', *Atti dell'Accademia delle scienze di Torino*, II, *Classe di scienze morali, storiche e filologiche*, 108 (1974), 95–173.

—— 'Forma narrativa dei *Dialoghi* di Gregorio Magno: prospettiva di struttura', *Atti della Accademia delle Scienze di Torino*, II, *Classe di Scienze morali, storiche e filologiche* 109 (1975), 117–85.

Vogel, C., 'Deux Conséquences de l'eschatologie Grégorienne: la multiplication des messes et les moines prêtres', in *Grégoire le Grand* (above), 267–76.

Vogüé, A. de, *Saint Benoît, sa Vie et sa Règle, Études Choisis* (Bellefontaine, 1981) = *Études* below.

—— *Le Maitre, Eugippe et Saint Benoît: Recueil d'articles*, RBS Supplementa 17 (Hildesheim, 1984) = *Recueil* below.

—— 'L'Auteur du Commentaire des Rois attribué à saint Grégoire le Grand: un moine de Cava?', *RBen* 106 (1996), 319–31.

—— 'Benoît, modèle de vie spirituelle d'après le Deuxième Livre des Dialogues de saint Grégoire', *CollCist* 38 (1976), 147–57; repr. in *Études*.

—— 'De Cassien au Maître et à Eugippe: le titre du chapitre de l'humilité', *StMon* 23 (1981), 247–61, repr. in *Recueil*, 417–31.

—— and Courreau, J., (eds.), *Césaire d'Arles: Oeuvres Monastiques*, 2 vols., SC 345, 398 (Paris 1988, 1994); see also above, A, under Caesarius of Arles, *Regula monachorum virginum*.

—— (ed.), *Commentaire sur le Premier Livre des Rois*, i, SC 351 (1989).

—— *La communauté et l'abbé dans la règle de s. Benoît* (Paris/Brussels, 1961), tr. C. Philippi and E. Perkins, *Community and Abbot in the Rule of St Benedict*, 2 vols. (Kalamazoo, Mich., 1979, 1988).

—— 'Les Deux fonctions de la méditation dans les Règles monastiques anciennes', *RHS* 51 (1975), 3–16.

—— 'Discretione praecipuam: À quoi Grégoire pensait il?', *Benedictina* 22 (1975), 325–7; repr. in *Études*.

—— 'Grégoire le Grand lecteur de Grégoire de Tours?', *Analecta Bollandiana* 94 (1976), 225–33.

—— 'Grégoire le Grand et ses "Dialogues" d'après deux ouvrages récents', *RHE* 83 (1988), 281–348.

—— 'La Mention de la 'regula monachorum' à la fin de la Vie de Benoît (Grégoire, Dial. II, 36): Sa fonction littéraire et spirituelle', RBS 5 (1976), 289–98; repr. in *Études*.

—— 'Monachisme et église dans la pensée de Cassien', in *Théologie de la Vie Monastique* (above), 213–40.

—— 'Le Monastère, église du Christ', *StAns* 42 (Rome, 1957), 25–46; repr. in *Recueil*, 709–30.

—— 'Un Morceau célèbre de Cassien parmi des extraits d'Evagre', *StMon* 27 (1985), 7–12.

—— 'Nouveaux aperçus sur une règle monastique du VIe siècle', *Revue d'Ascétique et de Mystique* 41 (1965), 19–54; repr. in *Recueil*, 337–72.

214 *Bibliography*

Vogüé, A. de, 'Quelques observations nouvelles sur la Règle d'Eugippe', *Benedictina* 22 (1975), 31–41; repr. in *Recueil*, 407–16.

—— 'Les Recherches de François Masai sur le Maître et saint Benoît', *StMon* 24 (1982), 7–42, 271–309., repr. in *Recueil*, 259–333.

—— 'La Règle de Césaire d'Arles pour les moines: un resumé de sa Règle pour les moniales', *Revue d'Ascétique et de Mystique* 47 (1971), 396–406.

—— 'La Règle d'Eugippe retrouvée?', *Revue d'Ascétique et de Mystique* 47 (1971), 233–65; repr. in *Recueil*, 373–405.

—— 'La Règle du Maitre et les Dialogues de s. Grégoire', *RHE* 61 (1966), 44–76; repr. in *Recueil*, 42–73.

—— 'La Règle de saint Benoît et la vie contemplative', *CollCist* 27 (1965), 89–107; repr. in *Études*.

—— (ed.), *Les Règles des saints pères*, 2 vols., SC 297–8 (1982).

—— 'Les Règles cénobitiques d'occident', in id., *Autour de saint Benoît* (Bellefontaine, 1975), 15–31, repr. in *Recueil*.

—— 'La Rencontre de Benoît et Scholastique: Essai d'interprétation', *RHS* 48 (1972), 257–73.

—— 'Renoncement et désir: La definition du moine dans le Commentaire de Grégoire le Grand sur le Premier Livre du Rois', *CollCist* 48 (1986), 54–70.

—— 'Les Sources des quatres premiers livres des Institutions de Jean Cassien: Introduction aux recherches sur les anciennes règles monastiques latines', *StMon* 27 (1985), 241–311.

—— 'Saint Benoît en son temps: Règles italiennes et règles provençales au VIe siècle', *RBS* 1 (1972), 169–93; repr. in *Recueil*, 450–514.

—— '*Sub regula vel abbate*: Étude sur la signification théologique des règles monastiques anciennes', *CollCist* 33 (1971), repr. in *Études*.

—— *Les Règles Monastiques Anciennes 400–700*, Typologie des Sources du Moyen Age Occidental 46 (Turnhout, 1985).

—— 'Les Mentions des oeuvres de Cassien chez Benoît et ses contemporains', *StMon* 20 (1978), 275–85, repr. in *Recueil*, 562–72.

—— 'Cassien, le Maître, et Benoît', in J. Gribomont (ęd.), *Commandements du Seigneur et libération évangélique: Études monastiques proposées et discutées à Saint-Anselme, 15–17 février 1976* (Rome: Editrice Anselmiana, 1977), 223–35 (repr. in *Recueil*, 545–57).

—— 'Les Vues de Grégoire le Grand sur la vie religieuse dans son Commentaire des Rois', *StMon* 20 (1978), 17–63.

—— 'Entre Basile et Benoît: l'*Admonitio ad filium spiritualem* du pseudo-Basile', *RBS* 10/11 (1981), 19–34.

—— 'L'Auteur du Commentaire des Rois attribué à saint Grégoire: un moine de Cava', *RBen* 106 (1996), 319–31.

—— 'Le *Glossa Ordinaria* et le Commentaire des Rois attribué a saint Grégoire le Grand', *RBen* 108 (1998), 58–60.

Waldstein, W., 'Zur Stellung der *episcopalis audientia* im spätrömischen Prozess', in D. Medicus and H. H. Seiler, eds., *Festschrift für Max Kaser zum 70. Geburtstag* (Munich, 1976), 533–56.

Wallace-Hadrill, J. M., *The Frankish Church* (Oxford, 1983).

——review of F. Prinz, *Frühes Mönchtum* (above), *EHR* 83 (1968), 370–1.

Wansbrough, J. H., 'St Gregory's Intention in the Stories of St Scholastica and St Benedict', *RBen* 75 (1965), 145–51.

Ward-Perkins, J. B., *From Classical Antiquity to the Middle Ages: Urban Public Building in Northern and Central Italy, AD 300–800* (Oxford, 1984).

Wasselynck, R., 'Les compilations des "Moralia in Job" du VIIe au XIIe siècle', *RTAM* 29 (1962), 5–32.

Wathen, A., *The Meaning of Silence in the Rule of St Benedict* (Washington, 1973).

Weaver, R., *Divine Grace and Human Agency: A Study of the Semi-Pelagian Controversy* (Macon, Ga., 1996).

Weber, H.-O., *Die Stellung des Johnannes Cassianus zur ausserpachomischen Mönchstradition* (Münster, 1961).

White, C., *Christian Friendship in the Fourth Century* (Cambridge, 1992).

Widhalm, G. M., 'Die rhetorischen Elemente in der 'Regula Benedicti', *RB* supplementa 2 (Hildesheim, 1974).

Wilmart, A., 'Le Recueil grégorien de Paterius et les fragments wisigothiques de Paris', *RBen* 39 (1927), 81–104.

——'Le Recueil latin des Apophthegmes', *RBen* 34 (1922), 185–98.

Wills., G., *Saint Augustine* (London, 1999).

Wood, I., 'Avitus of Vienne: Religion and Culture on the Auvergne and the Rhone Valley, 470–530' (Oxford Univ. D.Phil. thesis, 1975).

Wormald, P., 'Bede and Benedict Biscop', in G. Bonner (ed.), *Famulus Christi* (London, 1976), 141–69.

Zelzer, K., 'Zur Stellung des Textes receptus und des interpolierten Textes in der Textgeschichte der Regula s. Benedicti', *RBen* 88 (1978), 205–46.

——'L'Histoire du texte des Règles de Saint Basile et de Saint Benôit à la lumière de la tradition gallo-franque', *RBS* 13 (1984), 75–89.

——'Von Benedikt zu Hildemar: Zu Textgestalt und Textgeschichte der Regula Benedicti auf ihrem Weg zur Alleingeltung', *Frühmittelalterliche Studien* 23 (1989), 112–30.

——'Benedikt von Nursia als Bewahrer und Erneuerer der monastischen Tradition der Suburbicaria', *RBS* 18 (1994), 203–19.

——'Nochmals "À propos de la tradition manuscrite de la Règle bénédictine"', *RBS* 12 (1983), 203–7.

Zinn, G. A., 'Sound, Silence and Word in the Spirituality of Gregory the Great', in *Grégoire le Grand* (above), 367–75.

Zumkeller, A., *Das Mönchtum des heiligen Augustinus* (Würzburg, 1950; 2nd edn., 1968).

——'War Augustins Monasterium in Hippo wirklich ein Kloster? Antwort auf eine neue Hypothese A. P. Orbans', *Augustinianum* 31 (1981), 391–7.

INDEX